THE VOYAGES OF *STAR TREK*

THE VOYAGES OF *STAR TREK*

A Mirror on American Society through Time

K. M. Heath
A. S. Carlisle

ROWMAN & LITTLEFIELD
Lanham • Boulder • New York • London

Published by Rowman & Littlefield
An imprint of The Rowman & Littlefield Publishing Group, Inc.
4501 Forbes Boulevard, Suite 200, Lanham, Maryland 20706
www.rowman.com

6 Tinworth Street, London SE11 5AL, United Kingdom

British Library Cataloguing in Publication Information Available

Library of Congress Cataloging-in-Publication Data

Names: Heath, K. M., 1952– author. | Carlisle, A. S., 1953– author.
Title: The voyages of Star trek : a mirror on American society through time / K. M. Heath, A. S.
    Carlisle.
Description: Lanham : Rowman & Littlefield, [2020] | Includes bibliographical references and index.
    | Summary: "This volume looks at how each Star Trek series reflected the cultural landscape of
    its time-from the original series that ran from 1966 to 1969 to the most recent iteration-and how
    it became a worldwide phenomenon, not only generating numerous spin-offs and multiple fea-
    tures but inspiring countless other pop culture shows, films, books, graphic novels, etc."—
    Provided by publisher.
Identifiers: LCCN 2020011301 (print) | LCCN 2020011302 (ebook) | ISBN 9781538136966 (cloth) |
    ISBN 9781538136973 (epub)
Subjects: LCSH: Star Trek television programs—History and criticism. | Star Trek films—History
    and criticism.
Classification: LCC PN1992.8.S74 H48 2020 (print) | LCC PN1992.8.S74 (ebook) | DDC 791.45/
    75—dc23
LC record available at https://lccn.loc.gov/2020011301
LC ebook record available at https://lccn.loc.gov/2020011302

♾ ™ The paper used in this publication meets the minimum requirements of
American National Standard for Information Sciences Permanence of Paper for
Printed Library Materials, ANSI/NISO Z39.48-1992.

For Eddie,
I am a kite, and you, my kite string.

CONTENTS

PREFACE

Why do we find *Star Trek* so engaging? Is it to escape into other worlds? Why do we attach ourselves to some franchises and not others? Why do some have staying power, while most fade into memory? In this book we explore the phenomenon of *Star Trek* from an anthropological point of view. *Star Trek* has a dedicated fanbase and as such can be studied like any other culture. We argue that *Star Trek* has survived across five decades in the face of rapid culture change because it adapts to the times while staying true to its core mission: humanity's hope for a better future.

The introduction covers the premise of the book: why *Star Trek* has remained popular for more than fifty years and the theories and tools an anthropologist can use to study culture. In addition, we include a brief history of Gene Roddenberry, along with his vision for *Star Trek* and the methods we used to collect and analyze the data. Chapters 1, 3, 4, 5, 6, and 8 explore how the various *Star Trek* TV series mirrored American culture of the time but also foreshadowed events yet to be. Chapters 2 and 7 focus on the two interim periods, when a television series was not in production. These two chapters focus on fandom, animation, and other activities that kept the culture of *Star Trek* alive and well. Chapter 9 probes the successes, failures, and challenges of the *Star Trek* movies. Chapter 10 discusses the fifty-plus years of the *Star Trek* franchise success as well as future *Star Trek* series, shorts, and movies. We also summarize two prime aspects of *Star Trek*: the storytelling and the cinematography. This book does not address "Trekkies" versus "Trekkers," canon, or the Kelvin timeline, but it examines *Star Trek*'s interaction with American culture.

This book is for a wide audience. The study population includes the *Star Trek* television and film productions. Fans of *Star Trek* should find the subject fascinating. However, the book also covers more than fifty years of American history and culture that will appeal even to folks with minimal interest in *Star Trek*. We hope that reflective laypeople will find the correlation between the visual franchise of *Star Trek* and contemporary culture insightful. General readers with interest in film, history, American culture, and pop culture will learn how the human condition shapes the arts and how, in turn, the arts mirror and foreshadow the human condition. Although the book was not written for academics or students, it certainly contains material they will find engaging.

This book began in an undergraduate course in cultural methods in anthropology at Indiana State University. A methods course covers a wide array of material, but actually collecting field data is impossible for a regular classroom college course. To compensate, students were required to watch and record observations of randomly selected episodes of *Star Trek*. The experiment was a success and inspired the book. However, all the data used in this book were collected by the authors only.

We are deeply grateful to John McCullough, Jessica Frease, Marina Hall, and Steve Aldrich, who offered useful critiques on chapters. KMH is deeply indebted to Larry Gant, a best friend since high school, an accomplished academic, and the finest Trekkie I know, for valuable suggestions, constructive insights, and comments. KMH especially owes thanks to Rick Lotspeich for providing significant editorial comments on all chapters; Corey Michael Dalton and Matthew Lowe for lengthy discussions about *Star Trek*, topic presentation, and editorial advice and assistance throughout the project; Brylynn Ellis for proofreading and formatting assistance; Lillian (Lucy) Chew, Indiana State University, for providing final formatting and editorial assistance; and Ryan Rushing for all things *Star Trek*. We appreciate the opportunity to present our *Star Trek* work at three Pop Culture Association meetings. We gained valuable feedback regarding our presentations as well as insight to pop culture from the myriad of other presentations. Finally, this book would not have been possible without the vital assistance and guidance from the editorial board at Rowman & Littlefield. We wish to thank Niki Guinan, copyeditor, for her careful attention to details. We are very grateful.

Ann would like to thank her husband, Eric, and her son, James, for their unflagging love, patience, and support during both the research and writing phases of this project.

INTRODUCTION

"When you work with fossils . . . when you look at that bigger picture, yes, you realize that either you change and adapt, or . . . you go extinct."—Louise Leakey[1]

Star Trek has survived unprecedented culture change over the last fifty years: from a flower-painted Volkswagen van to glamping in a Mercedes-Benz luxury RV to self-driving electric cars; from windmills on a farm to windmill farms powering cities; from the rise of Evangelicals to the rise of America's religious "Nones." Fans became Trekkies and rocked at Woodstock, hip-hopped with Jay-Z, and were awestruck by Lady Gaga. They lived in split-level homes, moved into McMansions, and became advocates for tiny houses. With their televisions turned on, Trekkies watched the end of the Vietnam War, witnessed live the terrorist attack on the Twin Towers, and beheld Bran ascend to the Iron Throne.[2] Families clustered around their home television sets to witness President Nixon resign in disgrace, while entire communities packed public venues to watch multiple big screens as Barack Obama was sworn in as the forty-fourth president of the United States. How can any media creation sustain itself through such rapid culture change?

CULTURE CHANGE AND TELEVISION

Television became a household staple in the United States after World War II and had a profound effect on American culture as it brought the world into the living rooms of viewers. During the 1970s, cable and satellite TV expanded the viewing experience. Looking back over the history of television, it becomes apparent that different types of programming vary in their longevity. Nonscripted shows have survived the test of time. News shows hold the record for duration. *Meet the Press* has been on the air for more than seventy years, while such talk shows as *The Tonight Show* have held strong for more than sixty years. Soap operas and sports are next in staying power, with a fifty-year run, while educational, children's, and reality shows are holding at thirty years. However, prime-time scripted series usually sprint to the finish line. Only two primetime scripted series in the United States have been on the air for at least thirty years: *The Simpsons*, an animated comedy, has had a continuous run since 1989, and *Star Trek*, with six series (seven, with the animated version), has been periodically distributed from 1966 to 2020. Only *Star Trek* has a duration greater than fifty years on television in the United States, with a fan base culture that carries it through space and time. The parallel success in Britain is *Doctor Who*, which first aired in 1963.[3] Like *Star Trek*, *Doctor Who* is a time-space adventure, and both are without destination.[4]

Since the dawn of humanity, culture change has been slow, very slow, and usually not recognized until pointed out by archaeologists or historians. Today, culture change is rapid and accelerates exponentially. In a short fifty years, a single lifetime, we have seen the emergence of globalization driven by technology, particularly digital technology. We have traveled through space and time on our televisions, computers, tablets, and smartphones. Scripted series developed in response to this new technology. Shows need to be entertaining to attract advertisers and their commercials, which in turn generate financial rewards; viewers buy products, encouraging additional advertising and network income. After all, television is a corporate enterprise driven by profits.

However, entertainment alone was not enough. To succeed, shows had to tug at the heartstrings of the viewers in a personal way by mirroring some aspect of contemporary culture. Three early long-running scripted series did just that: *Gunsmoke* (1955–1975), *The Jack Benny Program* (1950–1965), and *The Adventures of Ozzie and Harriet* (1952–1966). Before their television debut, all three had a long run on radio, with a dedicated following of listeners. In *Gunsmoke*, Matt Dillon was the Marshall of Dodge City, Kansas, during the 1870s, when the American West was being settled. *Gunsmoke* depicted the perceived greatness of the American frontier, which fit well with America's post–World War II experience. *The Jack Benny Program* was a comedy. The only regular minority character was Rochester, an African American who was the valet and chauffeur to Jack Benny, in keeping with predominantly White culture. *The Adventures of Ozzie and Harriet* may be considered the first sitcom and represented the image of America's perfect family.[5] All three of these television series were dominated by White, male Christians with obedient, timid, or sinful women. Ethnic diversity was seldom observed, but on the rare occasion it was, the overall presentation was in a demeaning or inferior light. They were sexist, racist, and out of touch with the changing times of the 1960s. They showed their age, and as they became obsolete and irrelevant, new generations of viewers did not tune in. Television series that mirrored earlier culture but did not adapt to culture change eventually became fossils and ended up in the archives of scripted series.

But that was not the fate of *Star Trek*; it adapted to culture change and is one of the few media products that has enduring relevance to next-generation viewers. Each new *Star Trek* series mirrored the contemporary culture, some more successfully than others. *Star Trek* normalized controversial issues by making them part of the everyday activities of the series, such as multiethnic crew members and women in commanding roles. *Star Trek* also addressed issues of the time through specific episodes. Many carried subtle messages, while others were blatantly obvious. Some *Star Trek* episodes were educational reminders of our past, some foreshadowed American culture that had not yet come to be, and some just posed "what if" questions. Yet they all contained messages (subliminal, subtle, or overt) that would trigger the viewer to reflect on his or her own culture.

RODDENBERRY: THE CREATOR OF *STAR TREK*

Star Trek's fifty-plus years of success are arguably due to its ability to adapt to change, and that is thanks to Gene Roddenberry's vision of the show, which the writers of the various series largely followed after his death in 1991. He developed a framework of core principles that all *Star Trek* series share while allowing the show to grow, change, and develop with the times. Numerous books, articles, and interviews have been published about Gene Roddenberry. The following briefly highlights his life and vision for *Star Trek*.

Gene Roddenberry (1987) Creator of Star Trek. *Photofest*

Roddenberry, born in 1921 and raised in Los Angeles, California, became a combat pilot in World War II. After the war, he had a short stint as a commercial pilot with Pan American World Airways but resigned after several crashes. He returned to Los Angeles in 1949 and followed in his father's footsteps as a police officer. At the same time, he began writing scripts for television. He resigned as a police officer in 1956 to fully focus on his career as a writer.

Roddenberry began successfully writing scripts for television and pitching new series for the networks. Several series and scripts involved adventurous travels on land and sea and in the air and would include multiethnic characters. Over a period of eight years, Roddenberry would meet and work with several actors who later would play key roles in *Star Trek*: Leonard Nimoy (Spock), DeForest Kelley (Dr. McCoy; a.k.a., Bones), Nichelle Nichols (Uhura), and Majel Bennett (Nurse Chapel, Lwaxana Troi, the voice of the computer, and others), who later became his second wife. Eventually, he turned his adventurous travels with multi-ethnic characters into a science fiction series called *Star Trek* and registered it with the Writers Guild of America in 1964. Then he began to pitch it to producers. After several failures, *Star Trek* premiered September 6, 1966, in Canada on CTV and September 8, 1966, in the United States on NBC.

There are four core visions in Roddenberry's *Star Trek*. First, the show would be a "wagon train to the stars," which was Roddenberry's pitch to NBC.[6] He had worked on westerns and was fascinated by shows like *Gunsmoke*; *The Wild, Wild West*; *Have Gun Will Travel*; and, of course, *Wagon Train*. All were very popular shows in the 1950s and 1960s. His analogy to *Wagon Train* was fitting. As the American West was a new frontier, space was the final frontier. *Wagon Train* told stories of people who would trek to the West, while the voyages of the *Enterprise* told stories of people who would explore space. Both, in effect, would *boldly go where no man has gone before*. These travels are fun, exciting, challenging, dangerous and rewarding. In outer space, exploration can, in effect, go on forever.[7]

Second, *Star Trek* would be based on science. Roddenberry was a humanist and viewed the future of humanity as moving beyond religion. Finding solutions to complex problems in the unknown would rely on science, facts, evidence, and critical thinking.

Third, *Star Trek* would be modeled on *Gulliver's Travels*. Similar to Jonathan Swift and Shakespeare, Roddenberry addressed contemporary social, political, and philosophical issues through the arts. Subjects that may fuel fiery responses in real time are more acceptable when embedded in fiction. *Star Trek* writers integrated controversial contemporary topics into science fiction, on other planets, with other species, and in a different time.

Finally, *Star Trek* would portray the future of human existence on Earth as without war, disease, poverty, hunger, money, or religion. This portrayal has been wrongly interpreted as a utopia, but that was not his intent. Instead, he saw a perfect world as a goal, a destination for the future that people would try to reach. This was the hope that *Star Trek* offered.

The writers had little latitude to deviate from Roddenberry's core visions, which became permanently etched into the foundation of *Star Trek*. These visions were likewise deeply etched into the psyche of *Star*

Trek fans. However, similar to the Prime Directive of noninterference with other cultures, principles sometimes fail, but the goal is not lost. After Roddenberry's death, writers took creative license to expand beyond the core visions. Moreover, these core visions are differentially ranked in *Enterprise*, which is pre-Federation, and *Discovery*, which is post-Federation but still pre–*Star Trek*. The writers never abandoned or replaced any of the core visions, but like our Constitution, they have received amendments to adapt to a changing culture.[8]

METHODS AND INTERPRETATION

Between 1966 and 2005, 5 *Star Trek* TV series, representing 28 seasons and 702 episodes, were broadcast to the homes of faithful fans: *Star Trek*, the original series (*TOS*); *The Next Generation* (*TNG*); *Deep Space Nine* (*DS9*); *Voyager* (*VOY*); and *Enterprise* (*ENT*). In addition to the five classic series, NBC produced two seasons (twenty-two episodes) of *Star Trek: The Animated Series* (*TAS*) between 1973 and 1974. As of January 1, 2020, CBS All Access has produced and aired two seasons (twenty-nine episodes) of *Star Trek: Discovery* (*DSC*) and ten *Star Trek: Short Treks* (*ST*). In addition, *Star Trek: Picard* premiered on CBS All Access on January 23, 2020, followed by *Star Trek: Lower Decks*, an animated series, which began streaming August 6, 2020. In 1979, *Star Trek* expanded from the small to the big screen in theaters, and to date, Paramount Pictures has produced thirteen *Star Trek* movies. Since 1966, not a year has gone by without a *Star Trek* event: television originals as well as reruns, movies, books, conventions, merchandise, and fan-produced films.

How does one go about analyzing fifty-plus years of *Star Trek*? First, we compare and contrast the storytelling (i.e., script) of a particular *Star Trek* series or movie with a window of the associated American culture within that time frame. We are particularly interested in cultural aspects of race and ethnicity, women's rights, such contemporary issues as LGBTQ rights, the rise of computer and digital technology, and group interaction. Then we invoke cultural analysis to probe how well a *Star Trek* series, episode, or movie adapts, mirrors, and foreshadows contemporary American culture. Some episodes may obviously address contemporary issues, while others are metaphorical. This is the descriptive narrative between *Star Trek* and culture.

Second, what people say and what they do are frequently different. An individual's perception may be at odds with what is actually happening. Here we analyze the cinematography of *Star Trek*, what the viewer actually sees. If *Star Trek* itself is viewed as a culture, then it should be quantitatively analyzed as anthropologists study other cultures. For this portion of the analysis, we randomly selected 15 percent of each of the thirty seasons of the six television series (not including *TAS*), for a total of 110 episodes. In addition, we viewed 100 percent of the thirteen movies. We used snapshot techniques to measure behavior at regular intervals. Each selected commercial-free episode was watched on a computer. We first recorded the title and premier airdate of each episode or release date of each movie. Then, at about five-minute intervals for episodes and about ten-minute intervals for movies, we recorded behavior for all individuals observed within a five-second time frame. During our five-second snapshot window, we recorded the names of all characters observed, such as Kirk, Sisko, Michael, and so on. If the name was unknown, we would list them as military, civilian, or simply unknown.

After watching the episode, we recorded the age, sex, and race of each actor. The vision of *Star Trek* is that age, sex, and race will have equity in humanity's future. As we know, to date, that goal has not been reached. Actual age is an uncontroversial quantitative measure, and here we recorded the age of the actor at the time the episode first aired. Sex is the biological classification of the actor as female or male. Humans belong to one race, the human race. Unfortunately, cultures identify race based on physical features, including skin color, and governments also record these arbitrary differences as such. Therefore, to make comparisons between American culture and *Star Trek*, we recorded actors as White, Black, or Asian.

We also recorded features of the character, including species and group identity (human or alien and "in" or "not in" the Federation/Starfleet) as well as rank and occupation, if known. Humans are a prosocial, multiethnic species with a diversity of cultures. We have an amazing capacity for cooperation and forming groups, lineages, clans, and tribes. We also have a dark side: creating "others." In anthropology and psychology, this is frequently referred to as "in-group love" and "out-group hate." *Star Trek* offers a unique opportunity to address "othering" on Earth by viewing "othering" in outer space.

The character's military ranking is based, in part, on the US Navy and Coast Guard (high command, captain, lieutenant, ensign, and NCO). We also included the category "other military" and "civilian." Occupation status included the following: leader, chief, high support, midsupport, low support, and service worker. Occupation was roughly based on broad categories at a university or company. Leaders have authority over others, but in most circumstances, no one has authority over leaders. Chiefs and managers have authority over others but also have people with authority over them. High support have no authority over others but perform a crucial necessary function equivalent to someone with a postgraduate degree or some advanced training, such as scientist, counselor, advisor, ambassador, engineer, advanced technician, or navigator. Midsupport would be equivalent to such occupations as nurse, teacher, historian, or botanist. Low support has specialized training or extensive experience, including soldier, guard, cadet, secretary, reporter, or construction worker. Service workers would include such occupations as barkeep, cook, and maintenance. This data collection resulted in 6,862 snapshots from the episodes and 1,087 snapshots from the movies that were entered into a database and analyzed. The results of these snapshots are presented near the end of each respective chapter analyzing *Star Trek* series and movies. The snapshot data is summarized in the final chapter.

Why collect data? What value does data have on understanding how *Star Trek* adapted, mirrored, and foreshowed American culture? Data provides a framework that guides us toward evidence-based analyses and conclusions. The adventure is not diminished by evidence but rather enriched by it. Gene Roddenberry insisted *Star Trek* be grounded in science, evidence, and facts; here we honor his vision.[9]

I

MIRROR, MIRROR

Star Trek: The Original Series, 1966–1969

"Something parallel. A parallel universe coexisting with ours on another dimensional plane. Everything's duplicated."—James T. Kirk[1]

A counterculture was emerging in the United States when Bob Dylan wrote "The Times They Are a-Changin'."[2] The baby boomers were reading *Dune* and *Lord of the Rings*, listening to the Beatles, rediscovering Khalil Gibran, practicing yoga, delving into Eastern philosophies, and smoking weed. They were marching in the streets, protesting outdated ideas, and promoting a myriad of seemingly disconnected agendas. Between 1966 and 1969, with the backdrop of this emerging counterculture, *Star Trek* (*TOS*) burst onto the small screen with a new, futuristic worldview.

The image of *TOS* clearly reflects this counterculture. The Prime Directive of noninterference with other cultures and Starfleet as an exploratory rather than a military operation suited the anti–Vietnam War movement. The clique of seven (Kirk, Spock, McCoy, Uhura, Sulu, Chekov, and Scotty) on the *Enterprise* represented core issues of the civil rights and women's liberation movements: In the future race, sex, and gender will not be criteria for societal worth, occupational choice, or employment advancement. Kirk, Spock, and McCoy (Bones) are a not-so-holy trinity. Kirk represents the rebel from Iowa in charge, while Spock (who struggles to keep his emotional, earthly, maternal side subdued) counterbalances Kirk's risk-taking behavior by relying on logic acquired from his Vulcan father. McCoy is a southerner with latent racist issues, which habitually flare up during contentious encounters with Spock. The remaining four, Uhura (an African woman), Sulu (of Asian descent), Chekov (proud of his Russian heritage), and Montgomery Scott (born in Scotland), each signify the collapse of discriminatory "-isms."

However, a counterculture can only exist against the backdrop of a mainstream culture—a dominant, albeit frequently forgotten, presence in America. In 1966, Frank Sinatra won the Grammy for album of the year; the Oscar for best picture went to *The Sound of Music*; and the top moneymakers at the box-office were *The Bible: In the Beginning* and *The Good, The Bad, and the Ugly*.[3] The mass media was reflecting the male-dominated, Christian individualism in an America that could do no wrong.

For many Americans, *TOS* was a cowboy western set in outer space.[4] The *Enterprise*, or another ship in the Federation fleet, frequently engages in defensive combat. An enemy is out there, and they must be checked, kept at bay. Intervention is necessary. "The City on the Edge of Forever" (April 6, 1967) not only is about a peace movement set in the World War II era, reflective of the anti–Vietnam War movement of the 1960s, but it also implies that, if the peace movement succeeds, great destruction and evil will follow. *TOS* belonged to both worlds.

President Lyndon Johnson decided to escalate US involvement in Vietnam in 1965. The war waged on, and in January 1968, the North Vietnamese and the communist Viet Cong launched the Tet Offensive. Both sides suffered heavy human and economic losses, which resulted in dwindling support for the war in the United States and Johnson's decision not to seek reelection.[5] Shortly after the Tet Offensive began, *TOS* aired "A Private Little War" (February 2, 1968), a not very subtle allegory for the Vietnam War. What is particularly remarkable about "A Private Little War" is that Captain Kirk flagrantly ignores the Prime Directive of non-interference by intentionally interfering with the Neural culture to equalize the balance of power. The insinuation was not lost on viewers. "A Private Little War" was not the first or last episode that directly addressed war. "The Doomsday Machine" (October 20, 1967) has the capacity to destroy entire planets—a reminder of the destructive capacity of nuclear weapons—while "The Savage Curtain" (March 7, 1969) explores the role of good and evil in wartime. Many *TOS* episodes could be interpreted very differently based on one's worldview, which is part of the powerful ongoing relevance of *TOS*.

Two other movements in the 1960s were concurrent with the antiwar movement: the civil rights movement and the women's liberation movement. Blacks had their own battles to address before they could focus on the antiwar movement. In the 1950s and 1960s, Blacks fought for equal rights as part of the civil rights movement. Although President Johnson signed the Civil Rights Act in 1964, their battle for justice was not over.[6] Women also realized that, like their sisters one hundred years earlier, in order to be taken seriously, they also needed to gain equal rights.[7] *TOS* is seen by many as the champion of hope: In the future, humanity and equal rights for all will prevail. Does *TOS* stand up to this image?

RACE, *STAR TREK*, AND THE 1960S

The United States is mostly White—then more than now. Other races and ethnicities are minorities; some fare better than others in the public, private, and media domains. Then again, definitions of race and ethnicity are not fixed and are largely characterized by arbitrary criteria from self-reported census information. Hispanics were never considered a separate ethnic group until recently; therefore, census data is not available. Native Americans were not considered citizens by the federal government until 1924, and perceptions of Asians in America waxed and waned depending on international relations.[8] Racism prevailed in all sectors of society, including the US military. In 1948, President Truman signed Executive Order 9981, abolishing racial discrimination in the armed services.[9] However, military desegregation based on race and ethnicity was not fully achieved in all branches of the military until the passage of the Civil Rights Act in 1964. Thus, the clique of seven officers on the bridge of the *Enterprise* provided hope to viewers that a society free from racial and ethnic discrimination was possible.

The most divisive racial and ethnic tension in the United States was that between Whites and Blacks and was manifested in miscegenation laws. A case in point: the story of the Lovings. Mildred was Black, Richard was White, and they were in love. To avoid the Racial Integrity Act in force in Virginia and because Mildred was pregnant, she and Richard Loving were married in Washington, DC, in 1958. On their return to Virginia, three armed officers broke into the home of the newly-weds and arrested them for being married. They were subsequently convicted. At the time of their arrest, twenty-four states had laws against interracial marriage. In 1963, the ACLU intervened on their behalf, and finally, in 1967, the Supreme Court found that laws prohibiting interracial marriage were unconstitutional. [10]

Against the backdrop of this raw, contentious, social decision of the Supreme Court, "Plato's Stepchildren" (November 22, 1968) brought the first network interracial kiss into the living rooms of Americans. In this episode, McCoy heals Parmen, the leader of a planet whose inhabitants have psionic powers. Deeply grateful, Parmen invites McCoy to stay on their planet. When McCoy declines, Parmen attempts to make him acquiesce by using his psychic abilities to humiliate Kirk, Spock, Uhura, and Nurse Chapel by inducing them to perform against their will for the inhabitants' entertainment. Spock and Chapel are forced to kiss, as are Kirk and Uhura.

NBC executives expected hostilities over the kiss, especially among its network affiliates in the Deep South, where racism and discrimination still ran rampant. In fact, the infamous kiss was scheduled for censorship, to be replaced with a simple embrace for the viewing audience in the South. The final shot was designed to not include a kiss. However, William Shatner deliberately ruined the final take by looking up at the camera and crossing his eyes. They were forced to use the actual kiss, although the shot was filmed and edited in a way that the viewing audience never actually saw Kirk's and Uhura's lips touch. [11] Although hailed as the first interracial kiss broadcasted on a network, it is important to note that the kiss is not romantic but rather is forced upon them by Parmen. The characters are shown as embarrassed and unable to prevent the kiss. "Plato's Stepchildren" must have made for interesting conversation around the Thanksgiving dinner table the following Thursday.

Racial tensions in America were also manifest during the long, hot summer of 1967. [12] Riots erupted throughout the United States but were particularly notable in Newark and Detroit, leading to the Kerner Commission, which investigated the status of Black Americans living in urban areas. The violence was rooted in the political, social, and economic factors of poverty but was also tied to Black militancy, police abuse, decaying inner cities, and segregated housing. The riots left areas of cities seriously damaged or destroyed, and the monetary impact of looting and destruction was estimated in the millions.[13] When Dr. Martin Luther King Jr. was assassinated on April 4, 1968, more rioting occurred in hundreds of cities but notably in Baltimore, Chicago, and Washington, DC.[14] Blatant racism was destroying the fabric of society. During this time, Congress passed the third civil rights act, also known as the Fair Housing Act, which made discrimination based on race, color, disability, religion, sex, familial status, or national origin illegal. President Johnson signed the act into law on April 11, 1968.[15]

The following year, in "Let That Be Your Last Battlefield" (January 10, 1969), the crew finds themselves caught in the middle of a conflict between two men, who continue their struggle aboard the *Enterprise*. Both men are from the Planet Cheron: Lokai has been accused of leading a revolt against the ruling class, and Bele, an officer, has been pursuing him for what amounts to 50,000 years Earth time. While Lokai is Black on the left side of his face and White on the right, Bele is the opposite. They hurl racial insults at one another—"you half-Black, you half-White"—and call the *Enterprise* crew "mono-colored trash, do-gooders, and bleeding hearts." They fail to enlist sympathy from the crew for their respective causes because the crewmembers do not comprehend the significant difference of being White on one side and Black on the other, as shown by a brief exchange between Chekov and Sulu:

CHEKOV: There was persecution on Earth once. I remember reading about it in my history class.

SULU: Yes, but it happened way back in the twentieth century. There's no such primitive thinking today.

Eventually Lokai and Bele manage to transport themselves back to Cheron, the only two sapient beings on a dead planet left in ruins after hate annihilated the entire populace in a mutual holocaust. Lokai and Bele do not care and continue their hate-filled flight and pursuit, and the *Enterprise* leaves them to it. While "Let That Be Your Last Battlefield" may have been glaringly obvious in its message, it continues to be one of the most memorable episodes in *TOS*.

During the Vietnam War, the military continued to integrate service members, but racial inequalities persisted into the 1960s, particularly for Blacks. In Vietnam, Blacks were promoted to warrant officers (a non-commissioned officer with a rank above a sergeant but below a lieutenant) but seldom attained leadership roles.[16] Outside the armed services, minorities held leadership positions as civil rights leaders, such as Dr. Martin Luther King Jr. and Malcolm X, but they were intraracial positions.

Although minorities owned small service-oriented businesses, such as beauty salons, they were not well represented in management and executive positions. Success in business was dependent on networking, which overwhelmingly occurred at Whites-only country clubs and in executive associations largely closed to minorities.[17] Asians, however, were becoming successful and earning near-equal pay with Whites as early as the 1960s. They were viewed by Whites as the model minority. Although Asians fared better than Blacks, they had their own glass ceiling.[18]

WOMEN, *STAR TREK*, AND THE 1960S

Post–World War II America experienced a population explosion, known as the baby boom, between 1946 and 1964. By the time *TOS* aired, 40 percent of the US population was under twenty years old, and the largest cohort was coming of age in 1964. But by 1970, birth rates in the United States had dropped to a record low.[19] That population crash happened for several reasons but was made possible in part by the FDA approval of oral contraception (the pill) in 1960. Helen Gurley Brown published *Sex and the Single Girl* in 1962, selling more than two million copies in the first three weeks. Her advice for women was twofold: become financially independent and sex outside of marriage is your prerogative. By 1965, more than six million American women were on the pill, despite the fact it was still illegal to sell it to unmarried women in twenty-six states.[20] America was experiencing a sexual revolution, a fact not lost on *TOS*.

Today, while watching *TOS*, we see women scantily dressed in miniskirt uniforms as being exploited by lothario men, particularly by the sexual antics of Captain Kirk. But in context of cultural relativism, *TOS* was at the forefront of the sexual liberation for women—sex without marriage and careers outside the home.

The first two episodes of *TOS*, "The Man Trap" (September 8, 1966) and "Charlie X" (September 15, 1966), should have tipped off the viewing audience that women in Starfleet were not just objects to be admired. In fact, women in *TOS* frequently initiate flirtation. In the first episode,

Uhura becomes bored at her station and flirts with Acting Captain Spock, while in the second episode she again flirts with Spock for her own amusement and the amusement of other crewmembers. Likewise, Uhura flirts with parallel-universe Sulu in "Mirror, Mirror" (October 6, 1967), then backhands him and threatens him with her knife, all to create a distraction. It is important that Uhura knows she can not only initiate sexual advances but also can reject those unwanted by her. Uhura uses her sexuality in two different ways, and these two incidents mirrored the newly felt sexual independence of 1960s counterculture women.

On the downside, women are also depicted as tricksters, shrews, property, and Barbie dolls (with attendant emphasis on physical beauty). In "This Side of Paradise" (March 2, 1967), Leila uses the euphoria-inducing spores of a flowering plant to break down Spock's emotional barriers. In "Mudd's Women" (October 13, 1966), the unappealing con artist sells obedient, beautiful mail-order brides who believe they can only retain their beauty by using a Venus pill until they realize their own self-worth and can remain beautiful on their own. *Enterprise* anthropologist Carolyn

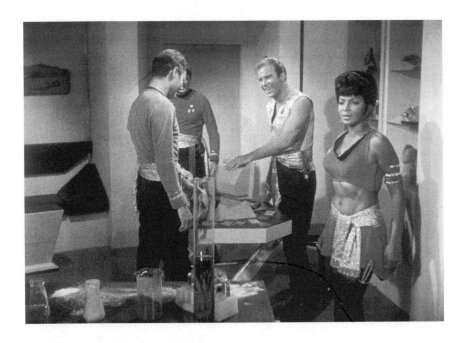

Bones, Scotty, Kirk, and Uhura in the Mirrored Universe. *Paramount Television/ Photofest © Paramount Television*

Palamas, in "Who Mourns for Adonais" (September 22, 1967), is useful to the landing party and becomes famously titillating in the dress Apollo bestows on her. Although she wants to be a goddess and rule beside Apollo, Carolyn gives up her dream for the sake of her comrades, but she weeps when Apollo discorporates and spreads himself to the winds. In "What Are Little Girls Made Of?" (October 20, 1966), Roger Korby builds the lovely android Andrea simply to obey his orders. In "I, Mudd" (November 3, 1967), Mudd's wife, Stella, is such a despicable nag that, when they separate, he creates an android version of her and programs her to shut up when told so he can always have the last word.

However, *TOS* women are often stereotypically portrayed as searching for marital bliss and fulfilling the role of the dutiful caregiver. For example, *Enterprise* nurse Christine Chapel gives up a promising career in bioresearch to join Starfleet and travel the universe in the hope of finding her missing fiancé, Dr. Roger Korby. Although she eventually finds him in "What Are Little Girls Made Of?" she discovers his essence is in the physical body of an android, and she then loses all romantic interest in him. Prior to finding her long-lost fiancé, she falls in unrequited love with Spock and is brazen enough to tell him so in "The Naked Time" (September 9, 1966). Despite her quest to find a man, as a nurse on the *Enterprise*, she is emotionally supportive of other women, is unfailingly loyal to Dr. McCoy, and makes significant nursing-care contributions. However, in "Space Seed" (February 16, 1967), Lieutenant Marla McGivers, more dilettante than ship historian, chooses exile as wife to ruthless superhuman Khan rather than continue her career in Starfleet. In all eight episodes in which Yeoman Janice Rand appears, she is presented as nothing more than Kirk's personal assistant who behaves like a servant, without the audience ever seeing an intelligent professional.

Traditional gender roles in the United States in the 1950s and early 1960s ascribed men as breadwinners and women as mothers and housewives. But by the late 1960s, women were more likely to work outside the home and were forgoing parenthood.[21] *TOS* appealed to both cultures: career-seeking women who could take charge of their own sexuality via the pill as well as the obedient women content with their station.

Women were also joining the military for positions other than nursing. Even though women were trained for and had technical and professional skills, such as engine repair, equipment maintenance, and intelligence, most of those jobs were closed to women; instead they were retrained to do what the military considered to be women's work. Under combat conditions in Vietnam, women were expected to wear heels and skirts to project a feminine image. Civil rights and gender equality issues did not influence the armed forces until 1967, when Congress finally voted to allow women the right to be promoted to the higher ranks of general and admiral.[22] Moreover, there was not a single woman CEO in any Fortune 500 company in the 1960s. There was not a single woman who owned a seat on the New York Stock Exchange until 1967, when Muriel Siebert joined 1,365 male members, 175 years after the exchange was founded. Between 1965 and 1969, two women served in the US Senate; in the same period, eleven women sat as US representatives, approximately 3 percent of the entire House.[23]

TOS mirrored the US counterculture of the 1960s with the sexual liberation of women while at the same time upholding the conventional conservative, stereotypical image of women. *TOS* also foreshadowed women in the United States who would seek careers in the military, who would aspire for rank, who would pursue professional occupations, and who would make their own choices. The crew of the *Enterprise* valued and respected Uhura as an equal, and the viewing audience witnessed that every week.

AGE, *STAR TREK*, AND THE 1960S

In 1964, most college students in the United States were still too young to vote but were old enough to be drafted. University campuses became the perfect stage for liberal counterculture movements. Columbia University and UC Berkeley were famous hotbeds for youth rebellion and social unrest. It was Jack Weinberg, age twenty-four and key tactician of the free speech movement at Berkeley, who is credited with coining the phrase "Don't trust anybody over thirty." While that was just Weinberg's partial comment to a reporter telling him to back off, the expression became a catchphrase for the counterculture because it clearly bothered and annoyed mainstream adults.[24]

In 1967, CBS canceled its popular and long-running series *Gunsmoke*. The network's reasoning for cancellation was that most of the *Gunsmoke* viewers were over fifty years old instead of the eighteen- to thirty-four-year-old demographic that was the new target audience. In the mid- to late 1960s, NBC aimed its programming, including *TOS*, toward urban, upper-income households between eighteen and forty-nine years old. NBC stated it would continue airing *Bonanza* and *The Dean Martin Show* because both appealed to all age groups. At the same time, CBS was airing *My Three Sons*, and ABC ran *Bewitched*, both of which had comparable shares of the young adult viewing population. *TOS* was considered a success within the targeted demographic audience.[25]

Hippies were, in part, identified by their music, and nearly all the musicians of that generation, including the Beatles and Dylan, were under thirty years old; many were under twenty-five. A large portion of their listening audience was still in their teens. Cher was only nineteen years old when she and Sonny, then age thirty, released "I Got You Babe" in 1965.[26] Culturally, their age difference was generations apart. After their divorce, Cher continued as an icon of the antiestablishment, while Sonny pursued a career as the mayor of Palm Springs and later as a Republican congressman. That thirty-years-old cut-off point was real. When *The Sound of Music* won the Oscar for best picture in 1966, the lead actors were Julie Andrews and Christopher Plummer, thirty-one and thirty-seven years old, respectively. Clint Eastwood in *The Good, the Bad and the Ugly* was thirty-six years old and in 1986 became the mayor of Carmel-by-the-Sea and later an outspoken Republican. The establishment was over thirty, and the anti-establishment was younger.[27]

Kirk's age is finally established in "The Deadly Years" (December 8, 1967) at thirty-four, while Spock was born in 2230, making him thirty-seven years old. The youngest character is Chekov, who is twenty-two years old during "The Deadly Years," while McCoy is the oldest at age forty. In this episode, Kirk, Spock, McCoy, Scotty, Chekov, and Lieutenant Galway beam down to Gamma Hydra to resupply an experimental station of six individuals all under thirty years of age. Upon arriving, they find four dead and two surviving—all related to rapid aging. Aboard ship once again, everyone in the landing party except Chekov begins to show signs of rapid aging. It is finally determined that Chekov was unaffected because of the adrenaline he released over his shock at finding the dead colonists. But the others physically and mentally decline at the rate of thirty years per day. Just in the nick of time, Dr. McCoy develops a serum that restores the landing crew to their actual age.

In keeping with the motto to not trust anyone over thirty years old, *TOS* brought us "Miri" (October 27, 1966). The *Enterprise* responds to an automatic distress call from a planet similar to Earth. While on the surface, they encounter a terrified adolescent girl named Miri, who informs them that she and the other children have to hide from the grups (grownups) who go insane and then die. They find a lab with documentation about the disease that activates at puberty, at which time insanity sets in, followed by death. They could all die within seven days. Kirk convinces the children of the dire situation, and McCoy conjures up a cure in the primitive lab. The landing party and children are treated, and Kirk requests that the Federation send teachers and advisors to help the children. McCoy suggests they also send truant officers.

GROUP IDENTITY, *STAR TREK*, AND THE 1960S

After winning World War II, the image America had of herself was one of pride, success, prosperity, and a unified front of nationalism; the result was the baby boom. But in a short ten to fifteen years, many Americans realized this prosperity was not distributed fairly. The dominant group was prospering; however, others were not, and they began to form countergroups and to develop their own identities and interests. The coming-of-age baby boomers were gathering around the likes of Timothy Leary with a philosophy of "Turn on, tune in, drop out." Some of these hippies participated in other groups, but many did not. The antiestablishment movement, the antiwar movement, the civil rights movement, the women's liberation movement, the Stonewall uprising, and even the early environmental movement each had their own concerns. In a world where time is limited, many self-identified with one or two of these groups, but activists were limited to one group. In the 1960s, America was a patchwork of in-groups loosely aligned against the establishment but with very little common interest. After all, President Richard Nixon, the champion of the establishment, won the presidency in 1968.

TOS aired during the rise and subsequent political defeat of the antiestablishment movements in the United States. While Americans saw their country fractured into groups with little in common, they could watch *TOS* and see a unified Earth that had formed an alliance with different species with different demographics, foods, domestic lives, governments, religions, philosophies, and aesthetics, all united for the greater good: the Federation of Planets with Earth as its capital. There is good and evil out there, and Earth and her alliances represent the good. Viewers could also relate to Spock, who is the only main character conflicted between two groups. He represents the dilemma that many Americans face: how to fit in and fit into what?

In *TOS*, the Romulans were everyone's enemy. In the "Balance of Terror" (December 15, 1966), the *Enterprise* is undertaking a cat-and-mouse, pursue-and-hide course of action against the Romulans when Uhura picks up a signal from the enemy ship. Humans have their very first look at Romulans, who appear eerily similar to Vulcans. The physical similarities trigger long-held prejudices in Lieutenant Stiles against Romulans, which is transferred to Spock—a feeling that was understood by many Americans. Spock eventually saves the life of Stiles, who apologizes for his bigotry, while Kirk defeats the Romulans and saves the remaining Earth outposts.

Likewise, Klingons have a long history of antagonistic relationships with everyone, as well as occasionally with each other. They are the ultimate warriors with a proclivity toward violence, combat, and honor; their military is not only respected but also feared. The Klingon Empire became a major power in the Beta Quadrant through conquest and incorporation of various other systems. The High Council, consisting of twenty-four members of the great houses, rules their government. The council frequently feuds among themselves and often makes temporary alliances, challenging the leadership of the Klingon Empire.

In "Errand of Mercy" (March 23, 1967), the Klingons attempt to take over the planet Organia. The *Enterprise* rushes to their aid but are apparently too late. Kirk and Spock beam down to the planet and are taken prisoners by the Klingons. Eventually the Organians disarm both sides, and it is revealed that they are powerful energy beings with no need of physical bodies. Kirk asserts that he and the Federation are not in favor of war and just want to maintain peace in the quadrant. Klingon Commander Kor admits that the powers of the Organians are too great, and because of this, there would be no war, but Kor also says of war, "It would have been glorious."[28] Again, the Federation is on the side of good, while the alien Klingons are a threat to the peaceful coexistence of the universe. In-group/out-group identity is powerful in *TOS*. The notion of a united Earth with total and complete internal peace and the sense of human oneness must have been a comfort to viewers living in a fractured and chaotic society.

SNAPSHOTS: A PICTURE IS WORTH
A THOUSAND WORDS

TOS is perceived to be a series at the forefront of the counterculture of the 1960s, a futuristic universe where discrimination based on race, sex, and age no longer exists. But what is actually reflected in the snapshots? What do viewers actually see? What are the subliminal cues? We collected 753 snapshots from 12 episodes of *TOS*.[29]

Minority Representation

An astounding 89 percent of individuals viewed in *TOS* between 1966 and 1969 are White. The clique of seven represents 525 snapshots, which is not surprising, as these are the main characters of the series. Of these, 80 percent represent the trinity of Kirk (191), Spock (126), and McCoy (101); all three actors are White, and the characters were perceived as White (despite Spock being of mixed species). The remaining four clique members represent Earth's racial and ethnic diversity as well as national pride without borders. However, we only captured a total of 107 snapshots of them: 51 of Scotty, 21 of Uhura, 21 of Sulu, and 14 of Chekov.

The minorities in *TOS* represent only 11 percent of all snapshots, and of these, none are captains; nonetheless, they fare far better than minorities in contemporary American society of the times. In *TOS*, minorities are overwhelmingly identified as lieutenants (36 Blacks and 21 Asians), a rank carrying authority over others, and these are in high-support positions. Minorities had advanced in rank and occupation but never broke the glass ceiling.

TOS mirrored American culture of the 1960s in terms of race. Minorities are seldom seen and are rarely the focus of an episode. Whites dominate the screen and make the final decisions. Minorities are kept under the glass ceiling in terms of rank and occupation. However, *TOS* foreshadowed the integration of race in service, public, and private domains. The bridge is interracial, and the working environment is interracial. Each individual, with his or her unique skills, is a necessary and valuable member of the crew of the *Enterprise*. *TOS* appealed to both the conventional and counterculture of America in the 1960s.

Female Representation

Women represent about 50 percent of people on Earth, yet only 13 percent of the snapshots in *TOS* capture women. Of the 193 snapshots representing captains, none are women. This fact is made painfully obvious in "Turn about Intruder" (June 3, 1969), when Janice Lester, still resentful of never achieving a captaincy, steals Kirk's body and acts as captain, with disastrous results. However, 10 percent of the women captured are lieutenants with authority over others, and all of these are Uhura. Nurse Chapel is also a Starfleet officer but has no authority over others. Keep in mind, *Star Trek*'s pilot episode, "The Cage" (1964), was partially rejected because Number One, second only to the captain, is a woman. The glass ceiling was real for women in the United States as well as on *TOS*.

Age

The actors in *TOS* fit the age group of the establishment. In our captured snapshots, the average age of male actors is pushing forty, while women average thirty-three years old. The antiestablishment culture was young, and *TOS* was pitched to this new, hip culture with mod fashions and themes. After all, Kirk is the youngest Starfleet member to achieve the rank of captain. But the series also appealed to an older crowd. Most of the actors in *TOS* are over thirty years old, and so are the characters. The series shows the pitfalls of old age as well as youth. It may have been designed for the younger generation, but it appealed to the established mainstream culture of America, as well.

In-Group versus Out-Group

A total of nine different species were captured in the snapshots: Humans, Vulcans, Neuralites, Cheronites, Sarpeidons, Polluxions, Changlings, Vaalians, and an unidentified species. A total of 92 percent of observed individuals are "in" the Federation; of that, 75 percent are Humans, and 17 percent are Spock, representing a dual ethnicity of Vulcan-Human. The remaining 8 percent of species are "outsiders" with questionable characters at best and at worst out right dangerous and a threat to the Federation, to Starfleet, and to Earth. In the captured snapshots, only Humans and Spock have military rank in Starfleet. Similar to occupational status, Humans, along with Spock, were viewed 352 times as leaders or chiefs, and all are "in" the Federation. However, only thirty-seven aliens were observed, whose status includes nine leaders, three midsupport, and twenty-three low-support positions; all were observed within their own species' cultures. For many in the 1960s, whether they were defending the establishment or fighting to change it, *TOS* offered hope that, in the near future, Humans on Earth would unite into one in-group, "Earthlings," and that the out-group would be other species on planets in galaxies far removed from Earth.

CANCELLATION

From 1966 to 1969, a radically new liberal culture was butting heads against a long-standing conservative culture. Between the late 1960s extremes of Sinatra and Woodstock, *TOS* traveled through space and into our living rooms, offering hope in a time of chaos. If the image of *TOS* fit the counterculture and the snapshots of *TOS* fit the mainstream culture, then why was the series canceled on television? *TOS* was never a failure; it was just not a success.

TOS was given poor time slots and received negative critical reviews. Season 1 placed *TOS* on Thursday evening opposite *Bewitched*, which was the number 1 series on TV. *TOS* was moved to Friday for the second season, opposite *Gomer Pyle, U.S.M.C.* But the ratings did not increase, and the critics still considered *TOS* a marginal show. Rumored that the show would be canceled after the second season, fans sent an estimated 100,000 letters to the network in support of *TOS*, and it was guaranteed a third season, purportedly in a Monday evening time slot. However, it remained on Friday, this time against *Judd for the Defense*. The third time was not the charm; ratings fell again, poor reviews continued, and advertising revenues dropped. *TOS* was canceled but went immediately into syndication, where, within a few short years, it became a cult classic.[30]

2

INTERLUDE I

Star Trek Fandom: 1969–1987

"This then is the essence of the *Star Trek* phenomenon: the fans have claimed the show as their own. They are its caretakers. They are the keepers of the dream."—David Gerrold[1]

After *TOS* was canceled, syndication became particularly important to *Star Trek*. Episodes were often run daily and in order of production. These reruns created a niche for fans to experience and reexperience the series, ensuring the show would not fade into obscurity. There were avid "Trekkie" fans from the very first episode of *TOS*. Victoria McNally, a professional writer on pop culture, noted that the fans were not all the "stereotype of the pedantic, socially [mal]adjusted nerd living in his mom's basement"; they were professionals, scientists, astronauts, and women.[2] Trekkies published fanzine magazines, clubzines, and general newsletters about *TOS*. They analyzed episodes, discussed individual characters, and wrote fiction and nonfiction about *TOS*. They organized *Star Trek* conventions. Fandom was a means for devotees to organize, interact, and develop their own cultural entity through a shared interest in the mythos of *Star Trek*. Fans had carried *Star Trek* through time and space. A subculture emerged and was not missed by the entertainment industry.

THE PRINTED WORD: MOVING *STAR TREK* THROUGH TIME

From the very beginning, women were an integral part of *Star Trek*. Several story editors and scriptwriters for *TOS* were women, but the most well known is Dorothy Catherine (D. C.) Fontana, who attracted women to *Star Trek*. As early as 1967, women were writing *Star Trek* zines, poems, books, and compendiums. Devra Langsam and Sherna Comerford edited *Spockanalia*, the first *Star Trek* fanzine, in 1967. It included original work by fans as well as letters from Roddenberry, Fontana, and cast members of *TOS*. Juanita Coulson published *ST-Phile*, a collection of nonfiction writing and artwork from 1968. Dana (Friese) Anderson and Elyse Pines edited and published *Vulcanalia* and distributed a *TOS* newsletter between 1967 and 1969. The first *Star Trek* slash fiction was an R-rated fanzine published in 1974 by Diane Merchant about a romance between Kirk and Spock, although neither were directly identified. This progressive slant established it as a landmark piece for the gay community and created a subculture within a subculture with their own fanzines.[3]

In addition to fandom fanzines, Paramount licensed the right to publish novels and comics based on *Star Trek*. Bantam books published a series of novels based on *TOS* from 1967 to 1978, while Ballantine published novels based on *Star Trek: The Animated Series* (*TAS*) between 1974 and 1978. To date, hundreds of *Star Trek* novels have been published. Yet most popular for fans and collectors, by far, were the comics. Gold Key Comics produced sixty-one *Star Trek* comics between 1967 and 1979. These first *Star Trek* comic books were based on *TOS*, with new adventures of the *Enterprise* crew. The artists were not familiar with the franchise and frequently deviated from the show's style, so they were declared noncanon. *Star Trek* comics and graphic novels have been in production from 1967 to the present, with only a few breaks due to licensing agreements. Comic strips in newspapers and magazines also became popular in the United States and Britain. Paramount Pictures authorized a *Star Trek* comic strip to run in the *Los Angeles Times Syndicate* newspaper, which premiered the same week as the release of *Star Trek: The Motion Picture* (December 7, 1979). As time marched by, the printed word and the fans kept *Star Trek* alive and well.[4]

CONVENTIONS: MOVING *STAR TREK* THROUGH SPACE

Star Trek entered homes across America beginning in 1966. Families and friends would gather around the television and occasionally host *Star Trek* parties. The series ended in 1969, but *TOS* went into syndication that year. Nonetheless, it was limited to television, which at that time was limited to private homes. *Star Trek* clubs sprang up in several countries, which had Starfleet chapters divided into hierarchies, with the larger and older clubs named for *Star Trek* starships. Club leaders were given titles like admiral or captain. Chapters were even formed for the Klingon Assault Group. Of course, these early clubs were pre-internet, and most tended to be small; members had to physically get together for meetings and role-playing.[5]

However, *Star Trek* fans began spreading their wings and going to science fiction conventions like WorldCon, the flagship convention for the prestigious literary World Science Fiction Society. The convention was comprised of mostly older, White, male professionals, whereas *Star Trek* fans were younger and included women and minorities, who frequently dressed in costumes and behaved toward *Star Trek* as they would a rock star. The professionals sneered at their devotion and viewed *Star Trek* as science fiction for nonreaders. Fans felt unwelcomed at WorldCon and began organizing their own conventions.[6]

Although earlier gatherings of *TOS* fans had occurred, the first *Star Trek* convention after the cancellation of the TV series was held in New York City at the Hilton Hotel in January 1972. The organizing committee, including Jacqueline Lichtenberg, expected a few hundred people, but more than three thousand fans, many in costume, attended, representing Americans from all walks of life. The convention was called *Star Trek* Lives! The cost for attendance was $2.50, which would be approximately $15.50 in 2019. Those lucky attendees had the opportunity to meet Gene Roddenberry, Isaac Asimov, Majel Barrett, Hal Clement, and D. C. Fontana. NASA loaned a large replica of the real *Enterprise* spacecraft, and a dealer's room offered a slew of merchandise for sale. In addition, Paramount set up a screening room to show thirteen episodes of *TOS*, including the original pilot episode, "The Cage" (pilot pitched to NBC in 1965 but rejected, copyright 1964). The event received nationwide attention in newspapers and *Variety* magazine. The marketing possibilities were not lost on Paramount. An annual event was born: Trekkies had become a force.[7]

Star Trek Lives! fan-based conventions were held annually in New York City between 1972 and 1976. More than seven thousand tickets were sold for the 1973 convention, whose official guest cast members included James Doohan (Scotty) and George Takei (Sulu). When Leonard Nimoy (Spock) caught wind of the event, he stopped by and was mobbed by Trekkies. By this time, similar conventions were taking place on the West Coast. They then spread to other areas of the country. The biggest conventions began paying *Star Trek* guests for making an appearance, and the fee was large for the time. Many of these meetings had more than 10,000 attendees. The 1976 convention at the Oakland Municipal Auditorium in the Bay Area featured William Shatner, Leonard Nimoy, George Takei, and James Doohan along with NASA scientists, astronauts, and other special guests, including LSD guru Timothy Leary, merging the pop culture of *Star Trek* with science and technology. This was in response to NASA inviting the cast of *TOS*, along with Gene Roddenberry, to the debut of the space shuttle *Enterprise*.[8] *Star Trek* conventions were spreading outside the United States, as well. The first *Star Trek* convention in Britain was held in 1974, and in 1978, TrekCon I was held in Australia. Trekkies were on the move globally.

STAR TREK: THE ANIMATED SERIES

Fandom not only kept *Star Trek* alive through printed material and conventions but also gave birth to a *Star Trek* culture that was growing through time and space. Although Roddenberry and Paramount were not on good terms after the cancellation of *TOS*, Paramount finally caved and allowed Filmation, in collaboration with Roddenberry, to proceed with an animated series.

Star Trek: The Animated Series (*TAS*) was originally developed for children and was broadcast on Saturday mornings between September 8, 1973, and October 12, 1974. There were only two seasons, sixteen and six episodes, respectively, and each episode was twenty-four minutes in length. *TAS* animation left much to be desired, but several of the story lines were written by well-known literary figures and writers from *TOS*. Much to adult fans' delight, lead characters were voiced by original actors from *TOS*: William Shatner, Leonard Nimoy, DeForest Kelley, George Takei, Nichelle Nichols, and James Doohan (who also lent his voice to dozens of other characters). Walter Koenig was the only original *Star Trek* actor who was not included in *TAS*, although he did pen the episode "The Infinite Vulcan" (October 20, 1973).[9]

Mr. Spock, *Star Trek the Animated Series* (1973–1975). *NBC/Photofest* © *NBC*

Many of the *TAS* story lines carried messages for young audiences. In "Yesteryear" (September 15, 1973), Spock passes through the time portal to save the life of his childhood self. We experience Vulcan and his home village; meet his parents, Sarek and Amanda; and see him travel on a rite of passage with his beloved pet sehlat, I-Chaya. While traveling in the desert, his pet is mortally wounded, and young Spock must decide to end its life or prolong its suffering. He chooses to put I-Chaya out of its misery, a profound episode for children with pets.

Particularly noteworthy are *TAS* story lines that focus on secondary characters. A standout episode is "The Lorelei Signal" (September 29, 1973), where beautiful women on a planet are draining the energy of the men on the *Enterprise*. Uhura takes over as captain and, along with Nurse Christine Chapel and other female crew members, rescues the men to save the day. Other story lines are sequels to *TOS* episodes and include such key themes as the Prime Directive as well as returning characters, such as the Tribbles and Harry Mudd. The recreation room was established on *TOS*, but the rec room in *TAS* added a new technology that is a precursor to the holodeck, which spills over to subsequent TV series. And let's not forget that *TAS* first revealed Kirk's middle name, Tiberius.

TAS was well received by critics and was awarded an Emmy for outstanding entertainment in a children's series in 1975 for the episode "How Sharper than a Serpent's Tooth" (October 5, 1974). D. C. Fontana, a frequent writer for *TOS*, considered *TAS* to be the final year of the five-year mission of the *Enterprise*. Later, Roddenberry decanonized *TAS* because he was perturbed over the last episode representing Robert April as the first captain of the *Enterprise* rather than Christopher Pike. But with the passage of time, references from *TAS* appeared in future *Star Trek* series, and many fans consider it canon.[10]

PROFITS ON THE HORIZON

After *TAS* aired, fandom increased dramatically. Conventions were popping up not just in large coastal cities but also in towns all across America as well as in other countries. A major goal of these conventions was to provide a place to buy, sell, and trade *Star Trek* merchandise, collectibles, and memorabilia. Paramount viewed *Star Trek* as a passing fancy and had very little interest in the franchise or the merchandise. Paramount was interested in making movies, and they were generous in their licensing of *Star Trek* products between 1967 and 1979. In 1974, Mego Toys approached Paramount for a license to produce *Star Trek* products. They were in the right place at the right time. They paid just $5,000 for a license that earned them $50 million in profits.[11]

By 1978, Paramount realized that the *Star Trek* franchise was a force rich in profit potential. They overhauled their licensing agreements and cancelled most earlier deals. Gold Key Comics' license was canceled and given to Marvel Comics. *Star Trek* novels had to be approved and published under Pocket Books Publishers, and any convention using the name *Star Trek* required a licensing agreement. Even though many of the products are considered noncanon, Paramount reaped $4 billion in profits by 2002.[12] Paramount took control of the purse.

STAR TREK MOVIES

As the turmoil of the 1960s and the Vietnam War were ending, media entertainment began shifting from happyville movies to science fiction movies with a focus on space, technology, and environmental and social issues on Earth. Stanley Kubrick's surreal and futuristic epic movie *2001: A Space Odyssey* (April 3, 1968) broke ground for all subsequent sci-fi films. Every viewer will always remember HAL-9000's line, "I'm sorry, Dave. I'm afraid I can't do that."[13] Several years went by before a set of other sci-fi movies were released that focus on earthly dystopian themes: *Silent Running* (March 10, 1972), about deforestation; *Soylent Green* (April 19, 1973), addressing overpopulation; *Westworld* (November 21, 1973), in which creepy technology goes awry; and *Logan's Run* (June 23, 1976), exploring the theme of dystopia versus utopia. Then came the all-time blockbusters: *Close Encounters of the Third Kind* (November 16, 1977) and *Star Wars: Episode IV—A New Hope* (May 25, 1977).[14] None of these movies were produced or distributed by the great and powerful Paramount.

Wanting a piece of the pie, Paramount squelched Roddenberry's desire to have a second television series, *Star Trek: Phase II*, in favor of a movie. It was the era of *Star Wars*, which was wildly successful at the box office, not only in the United States but also around the world. For the deeply devoted fans of *Star Trek*, Roddenberry wanted something to rival not only *Star Wars: A New Hope* but also the story and special effects of *2001: A Space Odyssey*. For once, Paramount and Roddenberry were of like mind, even if for different reasons. Trekkies were going to get their first big-screen movie.

Paramount released four *Star Trek* movies between 1979 and 1986. The first one, *Star Trek: The Motion Picture* (*TMP*; December 6, 1979), stands alone. Paramount followed this up with a loose-knit trilogy of films, each released two years apart: *The Wrath of Khan* (*WOK*; June 4, 1982), *The Search for Spock* (*SFS*; June 1, 1984), and *The Voyage Home* (*TVH*; November 11, 1986). All four movies are genuinely *Star Trek* with the original cast from *TOS*. The fans stayed loyal and faithful to *Star Trek*, but they were hungry for more. What Trekkies wanted and what *Star Trek* needed was a series, a once-a-week, hour-long episode, not a two-hour movie-theater experience every other year. They would not have to wait much longer.[15] A short ten months after the release of *TVH*,

Star Trek: The Next Generation (*TNG*) premiered and returned *Star Trek* to the living rooms of viewers.

3

ENCOUNTER AT FARPOINT

The Next Generation: 1987–1994

"I'm not a family man, Riker, and yet, Starfleet has given me a ship with children aboard. . . . And I don't feel comfortable with children. But since a captain needs an image of geniality, you're to see that's what I project."—Jean-Luc Picard[1]

The year was 1987, twenty-two years after *Star Trek* the original series (*TOS*) first premiered; culturally both America and *The Next Generation* (*TNG*) could have been in another galaxy. American culture, or at least an "image" of the culture, was one of peace and prosperity and focused on the family, an antithesis to the polarized culture of the 1960s. In Berlin, Germany, President Ronald Reagan challenged Mikhail Gorbachev of the Soviet Union to "tear down this wall."[2] *Platoon* won the Oscar for best picture of the year with its portrayal of America's sleazy involvement in the Vietnam War, while Nancy Reagan declared war on drugs with the slogan "Just Say No."[3] Evangelical Christians continued driving their message into the public realm. Meanwhile, rock-and-roll protests and psychedelic themes were replaced, via MTV, with Michael Jackson's *Thriller* and other theatrical performances, refashioning pop music. Personal computers and video games became affordable for everyday home use. America's turbulent past was just that—in the past.

Reflecting the times, *TNG* lured viewers into a wholesome *Star Trek* series. The *Enterprise* has become a ship housing not only career graduates from Starfleet academy but also their families. Even the main characters have an air of wholesomeness. Unlike Captain Kirk, Captain Jean-Luc Picard is a thoughtful, reserved gentleman, while Number One, Commander William Riker, fulfills the role of a kinder, gentler Romeo. Chief Engineer Geordi La Forge is a cool, level-headed technological nerd with a visor compensating for his blindness. Officer Deanna Troi is an empath and the ship's counselor, while Dr. Beverly Crusher is a working single mother. Officer Worf, head of security, is a crusty Klingon on the outside but with a teddy bear heart, and Data is an awkward android whose quest is to identify with humanity.

In the two-part premier episode, "Encounter at Farpoint" (September 28, 1987), we meet Q, the omnipotent entity who puts the officers of the *Enterprise* on trial for past crimes against humanity. Picard argues that Humans have learned from their mistakes and are no longer a product of the past. Q tells the captain he will be watching and judging their actions, warning before he vanishes that it will not be his last visit. Meanwhile, on Farpoint Station, Starfleet members find that their material desires are miraculously met, only to find out later these purchases were not real. Finally, the crew of the *Enterprise* release a captive life-form from the planet, who then joyously reunites with its mate, another happy ending with a focus on the family, albeit an alien family.

TNG also foreshadowed the imposing capitalistic culture in America as well as the rapidly growing role of technology in society and the home. We meet the Ferengi, a species whose culture revolves around business transactions, profits, and greed. The audience is introduced to the holodeck, a virtual reality simulation device that is usually a source of entertainment and learning but that can become dangerous when malfunctioning or reprogrammed for malicious purposes. The Borg make their dramatic debut in "Q Who" (May 8, 1989), hinting at the dangers of advanced technology, which could lead to the demise of humanity.

TNG was multigenerational, showed the complexities of women's roles and the advances and challenges of Blacks in America, and metaphorically addressed LGBTQ topics. A thread running through all seven seasons is peacekeeping, treaty formation, and unification among species and their territories. Similar to *TOS*, *TNG* mapped onto the contemporary cultural "image" of the United States while mirroring and foreshadowing realistic events as well as confronting America's societal dark side. From the premier episode, *TNG* was a huge hit with audiences and critics and was nominated for dozens of awards, winning seventeen Emmys and the prestigious Peabody Award for "The Big Goodbye" (January 9, 1988).[4]

MULTIGENERATIONAL

The characters of *TNG* are multigenerational and so were the viewers. Those who served in the Vietnam War (1964–1975) were thirty-two to forty-three years old then, while the over-thirty crowd of the 1960s were more than fifty-five years old. The last of the baby boomers, born in 1964, were graduating from college, and the first millennials were entering kindergarten. In 1987, the top selling album was *Bad* by Michael Jackson, then twenty-nine years old, and in 1990, the Grammy Awards went to Bette Midler and Bonnie Raitt, forty-five and forty-one years old, respectively. [5]

The movies show an even wider spread of multigenerational content. In 1990, the Oscar Award for best picture went to *Driving Miss Daisy*, a story about a growing friendship over twenty-five years between an old southern Jewish woman and her middle-aged Black chauffeur. Jessica Tandy, then in her eighties, and Morgan Freeman, at fifty-three years old, portrayed the main characters. However, the top box office hits that year were *Home Alone* and *Ghost*. The former is about a large upper-middle-class White family who go on Christmas vacation and accidently leave their youngest son home alone. The majority of the movie is centered on Kevin, played by Macaulay Culkin, who was only ten years old in 1990. *Ghost*, however, is a tragic romance between Sam and Molly, a young, upwardly mobile couple who rehabilitate an apartment in Manhattan. Sam (Patrick Swayze, thirty-eight) is suddenly murdered, but his ghost remains behind to protect Molly (Demi Moore, twenty-eight) from a sinister plot with the help of Oda Mae (Whoopi Goldberg, thirty-five), a con artist turned honest psychic.[6]

The American population no longer categorized people as older than or younger than thirty years. The youth of the 1960s had matured, formed families, gained employment, and fit solidly into the middle of US demographics, bookended by children and the elderly. *TNG* mirrored this pattern. Trekkies and now their children could relate to characters in *TNG*. Patrick Stewart, who played Captain Jean-Luc Picard, was fifty years old in 1990, representing the under-thirty cohort of the 1960s. During the premier episode, "Encounter at Farpoint" (September 28, 1987), viewers are introduced to Wesley Crusher, the fourteen-year-old son of Beverly, who is only in her late thirties. Wesley is portrayed as a precocious prodigy child. His father had died several years before, and Picard takes on the role of a surrogate father, which sometimes conflicts with his role as Wesley's captain on the *Enterprise*. Conversely, the last scene in "Farpoint" has Data walking through the *Enterprise* corridor with the aging Dr. McCoy from the original *Star Trek*. The past meets the present meets the future—the audience was hooked.

LGBTQ AND GENDER IDENTITY

In the 1980s, anti-LGBTQ prejudice and violence was on the rise because of fears about the HIV/AIDS outbreak.[7] In response, activists in the LGBTQ community formed the Queer Nation organization in May 1990, and the public was becoming more aware of their issues for two reasons.[8] First, more people were coming out about their sexual orientation—family members, neighbors, and classmates. Second, the LGBTQ community was becoming more vocal and more politically active. In 1993, President Bill Clinton signed the "Don't Ask, Don't Tell" policy, directing military personal not to tell and not to ask about sexual orientation. This was the first step in protecting LGBTQ in the military, as long as they stayed in the closet.[9]

LGBTQ issues were no longer taboo topics for the public, as long as they were whispered, and this was also true for the entertainment world. *An Early Frost* (1985), a made-for-TV movie about a son with AIDS coming out to his parents, became successful, but mainstream entertainment was pretty much mum on the subject. *Seinfeld* (1989–1998) had several episodes about homosexuality, but these episodes were set in comic relief. Interestingly, a most unexpected TV series, *The Golden Girls*, aired an episode, "Scared Straight" (1988), about Blanche's brother coming out as gay.[10] Nonetheless, in this time period, in mainstream television and movies, LGBTQ characters are minor, secondary characters, and even then, their sexual orientation is only implied or suggested. Comic books were more open on the subject. In the *Hellblazer* series, John Constantine was a sorcerer, a con artist, and bisexual. Although not about homosexuality, the *Sandman* series does have gay characters and deals with some LGBTQ themes. However, both of these comics targeted a specific subculture and were not widely known by the population at large.[11]

TNG subtly hinted at tolerance for sexual identity via Starfleet dress code. Men and women had the option of wearing a skant (miniskirt) or a romper (one-piece pantsuit). Men wearing a skant were usually secondary characters in background scenes and were seen in only ten episodes during the first three seasons. Nonetheless, this was the first time in a mainstream science fiction pop culture TV series that men wearing dresses were treated as a cultural norm.

TNG openly addressed gender identification in "The Host" (May 13, 1991) when they introduced the Trill species to the *Star Trek* family. Oden, a Trill diplomat, boards the *Enterprise* to negotiate peace between two species. Unbeknownst to the crew, Trills can volunteer as hosts to symbionts, who are androgynous beings and virtually immortal. While on the *Enterprise*, Oden and Beverly strike up a romance. However, Oden receives fatal injuries in a surprise attack, and in order to save the symbiont implanted in him, Beverly must transfer it to a temporary host. As there are no other Trills onboard, First Officer Commander Riker volunteers as host. He continues Oden's romantic interests in Beverly as well as finalizing the peace negotiations. Later, the symbiont is removed from Riker and transferred to a female Trill host who wishes to continue the romance with Beverly, but she rejects her advances and states, "Perhaps, someday, our ability to love won't be so limited."[12]

Later, *TNG* devoted an entire episode to gender identity and conversion therapy. In "Outcast" (March 16, 1992), the *Enterprise* aids the J'naii, an androgynous species, to recover a shuttlecraft. Commander Riker is assigned to work with Soron, a J'naii, and soon a romantic relationship develops. However, the cultural norm on Soron's planet is to be gender-neutral, as they believe they have evolved beyond gender identity and sexual interests. After returning to her home planet, Soron undergoes therapy to correct her misguided sexual interests in Riker. When they next meet, Soron tells Riker that she has received therapy and is happy to be normal again.

Of 178 *TNG* episodes, only 10 include men in skants, and most are background crewmembers who would be missed if one blinked. Only two full episodes are devoted to romantic relationships involving androgynous species. Subtle, yes, but given the culture of "Don't Ask, Don't

Tell," these baby steps by *TNG* were poking holes in culture's stereotypes.

WOMEN, *STAR TREK*, AND THE 1980S

Unlike the LGBTQ battle for equality, women in America were viewed as capable of having it all—a career, a family, and an active social life. From 1980 to 1990, the wage gap between men and women closed rapidly. In a mere ten years, women's wages went from 60 percent to 72 percent that of men. But women were far from being equal with men. In 1991, Anita Hill and several other women accused Clarence Thomas, nominee for the Supreme Court, of sexual harassment. Their accusations were dismissed, and Thomas was appointed to the court for life. This was a wake-up call for women that the battles for liberation and equal treatment were far from won, and they began running for offices and to the polls; 1992 was designated the "Year of the Woman."[13]

In reality, the American cultural "image" of women had changed very little. Such box office hits as *Die Hard*, a story of a macho cop played by Bruce Willis, are stark contrasts to movies like *Pretty Woman*, in which Julia Roberts plays a strikingly beautiful prostitute who begins a relationship with a wealthy man. Nonetheless, American women were entering into professional positions formerly held predominantly by males. Women were obtaining law and medical degrees, but the glass ceiling was still largely in place when it came to leadership. In 1991, President George H. W. Bush signed the National Defense Authorization Act, suspending discrimination against women in the military, although some restrictions still existed.[14]

In many aspects, *TNG* mirrored the hypocritical image of women in America while illustrating the diversity and complexities of women's roles in societies. The audience saw women as mothers, caretakers, and professionals. Women were viewed as tough, outspoken, and successful, with minds of their own. Tasha Yar is chief of security during the first season. As seen in "Code of Honor" (October 12, 1987), Tasha Yar holds her own against the humanoid species of the planet Ligon II. She is smart and savvy when dealing with the leader, Lutan; demonstrates her martial arts expertise against Hagon; and excels in combat with Lutan's wife,

Yareena. Tasha Yar is never viewed as weak or second to men but rather as a strong, self-assured woman in charge.

The image of Dr. Beverly Crusher in *TNG* is not as clear-cut as that of Tasha Yar. Beverly is the chief medical officer on the *Enterprise*. Although her role is primarily one of nurturer, she stands out as a leader in "Suspicions" (May 10, 1993). Beverly arranges for five interspecies scientists to meet on the *Enterprise* to discuss a metaphasic shield designed by Reyga, a Ferengi. During the test flight aboard an *Enterprise* shuttlecraft, Jo'Bril, a Takaran scientist, dies under suspicious circumstances. Beverly terminates the meeting, but Reyga insists his shield works properly. A few hours later, he is found dead. Beverly pursues the cause of his death, even after being ordered to drop it. She is convinced that Reyga's shield had been sabotaged and takes the shuttlecraft out for another test flight. While in flight, Jo'Bril emerges from his hiding place and informs Beverly that his species can simulate death. They engage in hand-to-hand combat; during the struggle, she wrestles the phaser from him, kills him, and returns to the *Enterprise* with evidence that Jo'Bril had committed murder and sabotage.

In "Sub-Rosa" (January 31, 1994), Beverly returns to her home on Earth colony Caldos to attend her grandmother Felisa's funeral. After the funeral, she stays in her grandmother's house to organize affairs. While reading her grandmother's diary, she learns Granny had a good-looking thirty-four-year-old lover named Ronan. After reading erotic passages, she begins to have the same feelings. She learns Ronan is a spirit from Scotland and has been in a romantic relationship with all of her maternal line for more than six hundred years. Beverly becomes mesmerized with Ronan and intends to remain with him, but urged on by Picard, she fires her phaser at the spirit and vaporizes him. She breaks out in tears for killing her erotic lover.

Beverly's image on *TNG* is complicated. She can be strong and intelligent in her work but weak when it comes to romance. She is a single, professional, working mother, but when she becomes head of Starfleet Medical in San Francisco, she leaves her only child, Wesley, behind on the *Enterprise* in the care of Picard. A woman could relate to the many roles Beverly has to juggle to be called successful.

Aboard the *Enterprise*, Beverly's best friend is Commander Deanna Troi, ship's counselor. Deanna's father is a Human and her mother is a Betazoid. From her maternal line, she acquired the gift of empathy. She is highly sensitive and aware of others' feelings and emotions. She has an on-and-off relationship with Riker, and they eventually marry. Although Deanna is frequently caught up in romantic interludes, two episodes stand out where her emotions are very personal. In "The Child" (November 21, 1988), Deanna becomes impregnated with an alien entity, but it is, in fact, her genetic clone. The fetus grows at an accelerated rate, and in a short time, she gives birth to a son she names Ian, after her father. Meanwhile, the *Enterprise* is in danger from an unknown radiation. Ian realizes he is the cause and allows his body to die as he reverts to white light. Deanna's juxtaposed sadness, at his death, and joy, that she had him in her life, can only be understood by someone who has loved and lost a child.

Similarly, Deanna shows intense personal emotions when she loses her empathic abilities in "The Loss" (December 31, 1990). As with people who are in the beginning stages of Alzheimer's or have recently lost a limb, she becomes very irritated. She sees her disability as limiting and notices people are treating her differently. She gets angry at Beverly when she cannot pinpoint the problem and does not know if it is temporary or permanent. Deanna feels trapped and incomplete without her empathic ability and plans to resign from her duties. After talking to Guinan, the bartender, she realizes she can still fulfill her duties as a counselor with only her Human abilities and training. The cause is determined to be contact with two-dimensional beings, and as they move away from the ship, she recovers her empathic abilities and sense of happiness.

Lwaxana Troi is the Betazoid ambassador to the Federation. Her flirtatious and outgoing demeanor, especially when aboard the *Enterprise*, frequently embarrasses her only living child, Deanna. She has had many lovers and husbands and views Picard as a potential mate. In "Manhunt" (June 9, 1989), Lwaxana boards the *Enterprise* on a mission to transport diplomats to a conference. She is at her peak of sexuality and tries once again to romance Picard, who will have none of it. To escape her unwanted advances, he hides in the holodeck. She then turns her attentions to Riker. He seeks out Picard in the holodeck, and Lwaxana follows. In the moment, she is smitten with an avatar, Dixon, who returns her advances. However, Lwaxana sets her sexual escapades aside when, through telepathy, she identifies two ambassadors carrying explosives and saves the conference. This episode provides a representation of turning the table; women have been sexually harassed for thousands of years.

Lwaxana's wit, intuition, and intellect, as well as her sexuality, save the day once again in "Ménage à Troi" (May 28, 1990). While on shore leave on Betazed, Daimon Tog, a Ferengi, becomes infatuated with Lwaxana but also realizes that he could exploit her telepathic gifts to enhance his financial status. After being rejected by Lwaxana, he kidnaps her, along with Deanna and Riker, and beams them back to his ship. Lwaxana uses her sexuality and volunteers herself to Tog in exchange for the release of her daughter and Riker. Picard contacts the Ferengi ship and participates in a charade initiated by Lwaxana that he is a scorned lover and will destroy the Ferengi ship unless Lwaxana is returned to him. Tog complies, and the *Enterprise* returns to Betazed.

Contrary to the flamboyant Lwaxana, Guinan is the *Enterprise* crew whisperer. She is the quintessential bartender and manager of the Ten Forward Lounge. Her El-Aurian species has extreme longevity, and she is more than five hundred years old. Throughout her life, she has lived on historic Earth as well as other planets. Due to her age and travels, she has firsthand experience and extensive knowledge about the past. But her strength is as a listener. When Wesley experiences his first doomed teenage romance ("The Dauphin," February 20, 1989), he is consoled by many aboard the *Enterprise* but to no avail. He finally goes to Ten Forward and pours his heart out to Guinan, a listener, which is sometimes all that is needed.

Moreover, Guinan knows when people need counseling and is very capable of manipulating the situation to benefit a friend. In "Suspicions" (May 10, 1993), Guinan is aware that Beverly could use a confidant, so she poses as a patient with a tennis elbow. She listens to Beverly on multiple visits and, as a friend, supports her to continue her investigations. Guinan is able to subtly guide others to decide for themselves the paths they should take. In many ways, she is a better counselor than Deanna.

The women in *TNG* gave hope to female viewers. Guinan makes a positive impact on many people aboard the *Enterprise* without authority, prestige, or rank, while Beverly shows the difficulties associated with wanting it all, and Tasha Yar is equal to men in every way. Deanna's character exaggerates the empathic woman but, through her, exposes the complex emotions of women, men, and other sentient beings. However, her mother, Lwaxana, is the poster girl for the older woman: She is energetic, has a very active sex life, and is an ambassador. In contemporary American culture, women were moving forward at a crawl, but in *TNG*, women are well ahead of the game.

NORMALIZING BLACK SUCCESS: GEORDI LA FORGE

Compared to twenty years earlier, the United States portrayed an image that Black equality had been achieved. *The Cosby Show* and *A Different World* had top Nielsen ratings: The former presents an upper-middle-class Black family consisting of a doctor, a lawyer, and five children, while the later follows college students at an elite Black university.[15] Considering that Blacks only represented 12 percent of the US population, both shows must have been watched by many White households. Blacks in America were making headway in individual accomplishments. Colin Powell became chairman of the Joint Chief of Staff, and John Lewis, beaten during the civil rights movement of the 1960s, was elected congressman from Georgia in 1987. The *Harvard Law Review* elected its first Black president in 1990, Barack Obama. Black poverty fell from 35 percent in 1970 to 30 percent in 1990. Moreover, 29 percent of Blacks were in professional, technical, and management positions, such as professors, physicians, engineers, and attorneys.[16]

TNG has the equivalent image of a successful Black male in Geordi La Forge. He began his career as helmsman on the *Enterprise* and was later promoted to the rank of chief engineer. He is a tech-savvy scientist whose only handicap is not the color of his skin but rather his blindness, which is corrected by a mechanical visor. His ability to solve engineering problems is superlative, and on numerous occasions that ability helps save the *Enterprise*.

In "Booby Trap" (October 30, 1989), the *Enterprise* is losing power reserves after being captured in a Menthar booby trap, and La Forge must find the cause and resolve the issue, or the life support systems will be destroyed. He is baffled and needs another genius to talk through the problem, so he creates a hologram of Dr. Leah Brahms, who designed and built most of the warp engines for Starfleet. Brahms argues that, although perilous, the controls must be turned over to the computer, but La Forge opts to reduce power and manually maneuver the ship out of the trap. The *Enterprise* is freed.

La Forge has another opportunity to work with the actual rather than the virtual Brahms when she visits the *Enterprise* at Starbase 313 to study modifications he made to the ship's engines ("Galaxy's Child," March 11, 1991). She is not at all pleased and insults La Forge for not following protocol when he made extensive alterations to the engines she designed. Brahms continues to criticize him, but on further inspection, she is impressed by his refinements, admits he has indeed improved on her design, and encourages him to write a scientific paper and share his work. From the Federation and Starfleet point of view, La Forge is hailed as the developer of the tachyon detection grid capable of identifying cloaked Romulan ships. Like Scotty before him, La Forge repeatedly proves himself invaluable as a bridge officer and chief engineer on the *Enterprise*. He mirrors the intellectual, professional Black American in the United States during the late 1980s and early 1990s.

CULTURAL IDENTITY: WORF

However, Black Americans' success was causing another crisis, that of cultural identity. Americans were refusing to classify their race or ethnicity on forms, interracial marriage was on the rise, and neighborhoods and schools were becoming racially integrated. How does one fit in and still retain one's cultural identity? Black children, living in impoverished neighborhoods and aspiring to success, were frequently shunned by their own communities. Successful Blacks working in professions dominated by Whites are aware of the constant looks they receive because they stick out in the crowd.[17]

Race and cultural identity became an issue in transracial adoptions when Black social workers began investigating the effects on the families, particularly the children. The argument was that Black children raised in White households would not only lose their Black heritage but would also not be prepared to deal with racism. *TNG* brilliantly captures these emerging social issues in the character of Worf. The viewers not only saw a Klingon who was raised by Humans but also a Black male who was raised by White parents.[18]

Lieutenant Worf, son of Mogh of the Klingon house of Martok (an important social and political Klingon house) and of the Human family Rozhenko, is chief of security aboard the *Enterprise* after the death of

Tasha Yar. The Romulans attacked the Klingon colony at Khitomer, and Worf's Klingon parents were killed in the raid. Sergey Rozhenko, a Federation starship officer, rescued young Worf and took him to his home planet, where he and his wife raised him. Worf's parents eventually moved to Earth. His upbringing had a profound effect on his adult life, which is both overtly and quietly depicted in Worf's character.

Worf wanted to be part of his birth heritage, and at fifteen years old, he visited the Klingon home planet of Qo'noS and declared his intention to perform the rituals necessary to become a Klingon warrior. He felt at home on Qo'noS, although the Klingons considered him polluted because he was raised by and working with Humans. Later Worf became the first Klingon to join Starfleet and was allowed to wear a Klingon sash over his uniform. Nonetheless, Klingons frequently teased and mocked Worf for being in Starfleet and spending most of his time among Humans.

During an officer-exchange program with the Klingons on the *Enterprise*, Worf meets his biological brother and learns that his dead father, Mogh, was accused of collaborating with the Romulans in the Khitomer massacre. Upon returning to Qo'noS, Worf and Captain Picard discover the true traitor, but revealing that individual would surely result in a Klingon civil war. Rather than risk that outcome, Worf opts to keep quiet and accept discommendation, a Klingon legal penalty that includes shunning the individual, his house, and his descendants for seven generations; the loss of social status; and being stripped of one's honor throughout the entire universe ("Sins of the Fathers," March 19, 1990).

After all of Worf's efforts to reconnect with his Klingon heritage, he is an outcast. He has accepted his fate, until he realizes he has a son, Alexander, conceived during a short fling with the half-Human, half-Klingon ambassador K'Ehleyr. Alexander's mother disliked the Klingon lifestyle, embraced her Human half, and raised her son accordingly. Worf is reluctant to acknowledge his son, knowing that he will inherit the dishonor of the Klingon discommendation. However, after Alexander's mother is killed, Worf accepts custody of Alexander but sends him to live on Earth with his Human grandparents ("Reunion," November 5, 1990). After caring for their grandson for a short time, the Rozhenkos return Alexander to Worf on the *Enterprise* because they feel he needs a father ("New Ground," January 6, 1992). Worf accepts his son and his role as a single parent.

About a year later, while the *Enterprise* is in dry dock, Worf's parents come to visit. Worf does not want to see them because they cannot understand his dishonor due to the discommendation. Worf finally agrees to meet his parents in Ten Forward but is called away. The Rozhenkos meet Guinan, who tells them that Worf believes they do not understand. When he comes to Ten Forward and stares out the window into space, he is not looking toward the Klingon Empire but toward their home ("Family," October 1, 1990). Later, in his quarters, Worf tells his parents he was glad they came, but he must bear his discommendation alone. They tell him that is not true, and even if it sounds Human, they love him and are always there for him, no matter what. Worf is clearly in two worlds and not wholly in either.

OF BORDERS AND BOUNDARIES

During the 1960s, in-groups were clearly defined with boundaries in the United States. The counterculture was at odds with the establishment, and subgroups within these divisions were not necessarily supportive of each other. But that was then. The image of American culture in the *TNG* era was one of forgive and forget, with an emphasis on the latter. Now, apparently, we had achieved our goals, made peace with each other, and moved on or were perhaps just exhausted from years of turmoil. Nonetheless, Americans seemed content, and society was flourishing. Groups were crossing borders and boundaries and peacefully negotiating independence. Windows of opportunity were emerging, both real and virtual.

In 1986, President Ronald Reagan met with Mikhail Gorbachev, the general secretary of the Communist Party of the Soviet Union in Reykjavik, Iceland, to discuss nuclear disarmament. No treaty was signed, but the trust built up between these two leaders led to a domino effect around the world, breaking down hard boundaries. The Cold War was lifting. In November 1989, East Berliners began crossing the wall into West Berlin, and within a few months, the twenty-eight-year-old wall was nearly demolished. In less than a year, Germany's reunification was complete. A year later, the Soviet Union was dissolved, and fifteen independent republics emerged on the border of a newly freed Eastern Europe. On November 1, 1993, the Maastricht Treaty established the European Union. Peace and cooperation, even between countries with long-term hostilities toward each other, seemed possible.[19]

This was not lost on *TNG*, as a recurring theme in the series is peacekeeping and forming treaties. In "Sarek" (May 14, 1990), Ambassador Sarek from Vulcan boards the *Enterprise* to complete a peace treaty with the Legarans. After arrival, Picard learns that Sarek has a degenerative mind disease that makes him hyperemotional and clearly unable to run negotiations. Picard mind melds with Sarek to give him control over his emotions, thereby allowing him to complete the treaty with the Legarans.

Picard again is placed in a sticky situation in order to protect peace in "The Wounded" (January 28, 1991), when a rogue Federation captain, Maxwell, at the helm of the *Phoenix*, attacks a Cardassian science station. Picard is prepared to fire on the *Phoenix* when O'Brien, an old colleague of Maxwell, convinces him to surrender. Upon analysis of the situation, Picard is convinced that the science station is in fact a military base. He warns the Cardassians, "We'll be watching."[20] The Federation has little confidence in the Cardassians holding up their end of the treaty and suspects them of harboring bioweapons ("Chain of Command, Parts 1 and 2," December 14 and 21, 1992, respectively). Picard, Worf, and Beverly are sent on a covert mission to find the facts. While away, Jellico commands the *Enterprise* and deals directly with the Cardassians, but they inform him they have captured Picard. War is imminent when Riker deploys a minefield that threatens the Cardassians into disarming, retreating, and returning Picard. In 2367, the Federation and the Cardassians sign a truce, and in 2370, a peace treaty is signed, formalizing a demilitarized zone, defining new borders, and clarifying claims to planets.

Hoping beyond hope to make peace with one's archenemy is reflected in *TNG* "Unification, Parts 1 and 2" (November 4 and 11, 1991, respectively). Spock is now the Vulcan ambassador to the Federation but is suspected of defecting to Romulus. Picard and Data find him on the planet with a following of Romulans, including some government officials, who are in support of reuniting with the Vulcans. Similar to the meeting between Gorbachev and Reagan, peace is not directly achieved, but trust and hope is now on the horizon.

AND THE OUT-GROUP IS

So, who or what was the out-group? America and much of the world was living in a fantasy that human tribalism, us versus them, had been defeated, and treaties with the enemies were the wave of the future, and this is mirrored by *TNG*. However, *TNG* also foreshadowed the future out-group that was just beginning to enter the everyday world of American culture: digital technology. In the United States and Japan, computer and console games expanded rapidly from 1986 to 1994, not only because of major advances and sophistication in hardware and software, but also because home units were becoming commonplace. Early releases of games, such as *The Legend of Zelda*, were largely through Nintendo. The number of games increased from around ten top-rated games in 1986 to hundreds in 1994. The public was becoming increasingly concerned about the impact of gaming on the players, particularly children. In 1993, the US Senate held a hearing on video game violence. In response to the hearings, in 1994 the video game industry assigned age and content ratings to video games, but the system was voluntary. Technological entertainments were beginning to concern the public and the government.[21]

TNG addresses these issues in several episodes. After a vacation to the planet Risa, Riker returns to the *Enterprise* with a game and shares it with his friends. Soon, the crew is hooked on this computer game that is psychologically addictive and allows the Ktarians to control the crew in hope of controlling Starfleet. Data is the only one unaffected, but he is shut down to prevent him from interfering with the game. Wesley and a friend visit the *Enterprise* from Starfleet Academy. Wesley repairs Data, who breaks the control of the games by flashing a light pattern that halts the connection between the game and the player ("The Game," October 28, 1991). The crew of the *Enterprise* is returned to reality.

The holodeck is the ultimate entertainment dream of the future, where one can battle with the Avengers, travel with Marco Polo, and visit Spock on Vulcan. On the *Enterprise*, the holodeck is a wonderous escape from being confined on a ship in space. But it, too, has pitfalls. In "Hollow Pursuits" (April 30, 1990), Barclay, an insecure and nervous crewman, spends most of his time in the holodeck with virtual reality members of the *Enterprise* that he designed. He begins avoiding reality until La Forge requires his assistance to solve a crucial issue on the *Enterprise*. Because of his success in the real world, he deletes most of his holodeck programs.

We all love amusement parks, and we all assume the rides are well maintained. The holodeck is fun until one is trapped in a malfunctioning program. Such an event occurs in "The Big Goodbye" (January 11, 1988), a 1940s detective program, when Dr. Whalen, the ship's historian, is actually shot. Similarly, in "A Fistful of Datas" (November 9, 1992), a western program takes on Data's appearance and threatens Worf, Deanna, and Alexander. However, by far the most unnerving episodes involve Sherlock Holmes's character Moriarty, whose hologram strives to become real, leave the holodeck, and take over the *Enterprise* ("Elementary, Dear Data," and "Ship in a Bottle," December 5, 1988, and January 25, 1993, respectively).

Unlike games and futuristic holodecks, robots were everywhere in the 1980s and 1990s. Robots were in the movies, from *Transformers* to *RoboCop* to *Terminator 2* and, of course, *Star Wars'* R2-D2 and C-3PO. Robots were popular as toys, such as Radio Shack's Armatron, as well as the functional vacuum cleaner Tomy Dustbot.[22] Robots were replacing manufacturing workers, and there were robotic body parts and even robotic surgery. Then there was Data.

Data and his brother Lore are identical androids in appearance, with positronic brains. They are both physically and intellectually superior to Humans. Their "parents," Drs. Noonian and Juliana Soong, gave Lore an emotion chip, which made him unstable, cruel, vengeful, and malicious. Because of that failure, Data was designed without an emotion chip in hopes that he would discover his humanity on his own ("Inheritance," November 22, 1993). Data eventually joins Starfleet and lands a position on the *Enterprise*. He always seeks to become more human, and the officers of the *Enterprise* treat him as an equal. However, in the "Measure of a Man" (February 13, 1989), Commander Maddox, a Starfleet cyberneticist, boards the *Enterprise* to take Data back to the lab to study him. Data refuses, which prompts a trial to determine if Data is a machine and property of Starfleet or a sentient being with rights to self-determination. Picard, acting as the defendant's attorney, offers Data's personal belongings into evidence and asks Data why he has them. He replies that they remind him of his friendships and, when pressed, confesses he had had an intimate relationship with Tasha Yar. In the end, the judge rules Data has a right to choose for himself.

Entertainment and robots were not the only real-world technological advancements in the *TNG* era. Manufacturing jobs peaked in the United

States in 1979, with 19 million people employed on assembly lines. In the early 1980s, mechanization and automation began replacing human labor. Job loss was real, and for many Americans, the machine was coming after their livelihoods.[23]

Techno-innovation was traveling at warp speed. Public and private researchers were developing the smallest and the largest technology the world had ever known: nanoprobes and the Star Wars Initiative. Nanoprobes are microscopic mechanical devices that have a myriad of uses, from medical to space science to artificial intelligence.[24] However, in *Star Trek*, nanoprobes are used to take over and alter a victim. The Strategic Defense Initiative (SDI) was proposed by President Ronald Reagan as space-based defense battle stations and was popularly referred to as the Star Wars Initiative. They would detect and destroy incoming missiles in space before they reached the United States.[25] The audience was primed to meet the greatest threat ever known to the universe: the Borg.

The Borg is a collective of humanoid drones who have been implanted with nanoprobes and altered with cybernetic implants to prepare them to be assimilated into the hive, a collective mind. The purpose of the Borg is to absorb technology and knowledge of all cultures in a quest for perfection. When encountered, the drones announce, "Resistance is futile." The drones have the ability to swiftly adapt to an opponent's weapons, making the hive virtually indestructible. They are divided into groups by function and rejuvenate in cubicles. The Borg originates in the Delta Quadrant, and its premiere space vessel is an enormous cube, hundreds of times the size of the *Enterprise.*

In "Q Who" (May 8, 1989), the *Enterprise* is moved into the J-25 system by Q, who abruptly vanishes. Picard begins exploring the area when he encounters the cube, meets a drone, and visits the hive. Q frequently appears and disappears, allowing the crew of the *Enterprise* to learn the true nature and serious threat of the Borg.

The Borg begins invading Federation space in earnest in "The Best of Both Worlds, Parts 1 and 2" (June 18, 1990, and September 24, 1990, respectively). Even knowing for more than a year that the Borg was coming, the Federation is unprepared. When the *Enterprise* comes into contact with a Borg cube, the Collective demands that Picard personally surrender. He refuses. The cube traps the *Enterprise* in a tractor beam; the drones begin to transport to the bridge and kidnap Picard. He is taken to the cube and told he has been chosen to be the liaison between the Borg and Humans to precipitate assimilation. He again refuses, saying Humans would rather die than become part of the Collective. Picard is assimilated, and his knowledge and experience is added to the hive collective consciousness. Picard is eventually rescued from the Borg cube, returned to the *Enterprise*, and has his implants removed. However, forty starships and all of their personnel are lost in the process, and he is forever left with the memory of being Borg-Locutus. The Borg is the ultimate out-group, high-tech gaming is potentially dangerous, and Data is an android-wannabe-Human who is an outsider to everyone except his small group of friends.

Captain Jean-Luc Picard captured by The Borg in "The Best of Both Worlds, Part 2" (September 22, 1990). *Paramount/Photofest © Paramount*

SNAPSHOTS: A PICTURE IS WORTH A THOUSAND WORDS

TNG has an image of being wholesome and family oriented and more progressive than *TOS*. *TNG* holds up to this image and appears to have adapted to contemporary American culture in terms of storytelling. But what does the viewer actually see on-screen? We collected snapshots of

TNG from 27 episodes, resulting in 1,386 snapshots, and the results are presented here.[26]

Minority Representation

A total of 23 percent of the snapshots capture Black characters, nearly twice the proportion of the Black population in the United States. This is a giant leap forward from the 8 percent visibility of Black characters in *TOS*. In addition, 25 percent of Blacks in *TNG* are ranked lieutenant commanders, together with ten snapshots representing Vice Admiral Haden. This mirrored the promotion of four-star general Colin Powell to chairman of the Joint Chiefs of Staff in 1989. His advancement broke the glass ceiling for Blacks in the military, and this was reflected on the screen.

TNG portrays Blacks in a very favorable light when it comes to occupation. Thirty-three percent of snapshots capture Blacks as leaders or chiefs, compared to only 6 percent in *TOS*. Successful Blacks are visible in *TNG*, mirroring American culture. In 1989, Reginald Lewis was the CEO of a billion-dollar business; in 1990, Sharon Pratt Kelly was elected mayor of Washington, DC; and in 1993, Toni Morrison won the Nobel Prize in Literature. Particularly impressive was when Mae Carol Jemison, an engineer and physician, joined NASA as an astronaut and was aboard the space shuttle *Endeavor* in 1992. As a child, she was profoundly influenced by *Star Trek*, and after her tenure at NASA, she appeared in the *TNG* episode "Second Chances" (May 24, 1993).[27]

Although 23 percent of the snapshots comprise Black characters, they are dominated by Chief Engineer Geordi La Forge; Chief Security Officer Worf; and Guinan, the bartender of Ten Forward. Their visibility, together with La Forge's intellect, Worf's determination, and Guinan's wisdom, is important to the story line of *TNG* and important for the audience to experience. Unfortunately, Asian representation in *TNG* is minimal.

Female Representation

Of the snapshots captured, only 26 percent (357) are women, but that is a significant improvement from the 13 percent visibility in *TOS*. Ranking within Starfleet captures only three female captains and no female admirals. On a positive note, 20 percent of women are ranked as lieutenants in the Federation, and 23 percent have occupations as chiefs within their professions, both representing positions of authority over others. In *TOS*, only 10 percent of the snapshots capture women with rank who have authority over others, and no women were observed in an occupation with authority over others.

TNG aired from 1987 to 1994, the era of the woman. But most advancements for women in contemporary American culture occurred near the end of the *TNG* era. Leadership roles, as well as prestigious and high-paying jobs, were still limited. In 1990, only three women chief executive officers (CEOs) were in the Fortune 500 Club; in 1993, Janet Reno became the first female attorney general of the United States; and in 1995, Eileen Collins became the first female to pilot a shuttlecraft.[28] *TNG* portrays women as more professional than *TOS* and certainly in better light than was actually happening in contemporary American culture.

Age

The perception that *TNG* is a multigenerational series is supported by the snapshots. The average age of men is forty-one years old, with a wide range of ages, from thirteen to seventy-two years. For women, the average age is thirty-six years old, with a narrower range of ages, from twenty-three to fifty-nine years. The mean ages are only two and three years older for men and women, respectively, than in *TOS*, but the age range is much larger in *TNG*, specifically regarding the presence of children and older females.

In-Group versus Out-Group

The snapshots capture eighteen different species, of which only five species are hostile to the Federation (Borg, Romulans, Ktarians, Talarians, and Ligonians), and their visibility over the 178 episodes of *TNG* is minimal. The remaining species are either in the Federation, treaty-bound to the Federation, or neutral to the Federation and are visible in many episodes. There are not only more species in *TNG* than in *TOS*, but they also have military rank within Starfleet. Non-Humans represent 2 percent of captains and 37 percent of lieutenants, unlike *TOS*, in which military rank is limited only to Humans and Spock. Similarly, occupations of authority, leaders and chiefs, are limited to Humans and Spock in *TOS*, whereas in *TNG*, 39 percent of leaders and chiefs are non-Humans. *TNG* had moved beyond *TOS* to be more diverse and inclusive, which mirrored the contemporary culture of America during *TNG* era.

SUMMARY

TNG was well adapted to the contemporary culture of the viewing audience. It is multigenerational and wholesome while at the same time addressing advances and challenges faced by gender and race in the United States. *TNG* mirrored the global peace negotiations and countries gaining self-determination in the *TNG* era and also foreshadowed the looming technological promises and pitfalls of the near future. *TNG* is not *TOS* and for that reason attracted new fans while holding onto *TOS* Trekkies. In effect, *TNG* preserved the *Star Trek* franchise for future generations.

4

Q-LESS

Deep Space Nine: 1993–1999

"You spend your entire life plotting and scheming to acquire more and more possessions, until your living areas are bursting with useless junk. Then you die. Your relatives sell everything and start the cycle all over again."—Odo[1]

Deep Space Nine (*DS9*), which aired between January 3, 1993, and June 2, 1999, overlapped in real time with *TNG* for just one year. Whereas *TNG* aired primarily when the United States was entering a period of peace and prosperity, *DS9* was firmly ensconced in the "Good Decade" of the 1990s. Culturally, this time frame in America is quite homogeneous, spanning the Bill Clinton era (1993–2001).[2]

In the early 1990s, digital technology was in its infancy, but by the end of the decade, America had a coming-out party. Technology was affordable and became ubiquitous in many households, although we were still waiting on smartphones and the phenomenon of social media. We read actual paper books, newspapers, and magazines. Harry Potter was introduced to young and old alike. Cable television became available to most of America and channeled something for everyone—religion, cartoons, food, news, sports, movies. Gen-Xers embraced Kurt Cobain as their martyred messiah and voice of their generation, while hip-hop broke through to become commercial and mainstream.[3]

The economy grew, income rose, and poverty fell, as did violent crime. America prospered. Women and minorities were appointed to the president's cabinet and to government posts. The war in Bosnia ended, and peace was brokered in Northern Ireland. The Soviet Union collapsed, and apartheid in South Africa had ended. Communist countries were in transition, and peace and democracy were spreading around the world. Americans were blinded by good fortune. They put the tumultuous past behind them and were completely unprepared for what was coming on September 11, 2001.[4]

It was against the cultural background of the "Good Decade" that *DS9* premiered on the small screen. *DS9* deviated from *TOS* and *TNG* in several ways. Gene Roddenberry had passed away several years earlier and was not involved; instead, the creators were Rick Berman and Michael Piller. It was also the first of the *Star Trek* series to air as part of the new UPN network. *DS9* was the only *Star Trek* series to run consecutively with other *Star Trek* series, overlapping *TNG* from 1993 to 1994 and *Voyager* (*VOY*) from 1995 to 1999. The series is less episodic and instead has several story arcs.

Unlike its predecessors or successors, *DS9* is set on a space station at the edge of Federation space, without a starship in residence until season 3. The space station is situated near a wormhole connecting the Alpha and Gamma Quadrants and between territories of the Bajorans and the Cardassians, who are devout enemies. The station is not owned by the Federation but rather by the Bajorans and jointly operated by the Bajorans and Starfleet. The station is a self-contained community; therefore, *DS9* has a large cast of recurring characters, some in Starfleet but most not. The Federation crew are assigned to this new frontier for several reasons: to assist in determining if the Bajorans qualify for admission into the Federation, to mediate conflict between the various residents and species who live at and visit the station, to maintain peace between the Bajorans and Cardassians, and to protect the region from incursions by the antagonistic Dominion Empire of the Gamma Quadrant. Rather than moving through space seeking new worlds and civilizations, previously unknown species arrive at the space station.

DEEP SPACE NINE AND CONTEMPORARY CULTURE

America's future looked very rosy in the 1990s. However, the seeds of discontent were germinating. *DS9* continued in the *Star Trek* tradition by tackling such contemporary American issues as greed, belief systems, gender identities, tolerance for ethnic and cultural diversity, and inter- and intragroup conflict. Did *DS9* adapt to the "Good Decade" by reflecting the positive aspects of American culture as well as mirroring its dark underbelly? Did *DS9* foreshadow a culture of the near future?

Love of Money

Though the 1980s were known as the decade of greed, the 1990s were no less money grubbing. Financial regulators allowed risky maneuvers by the big banks, which increased their profitability. Stock options and other compensation schemes for corporate bigwigs became a favored method of making oneself rich. The failure of the Financial Accounting Standards Board (FASB) to enforce accounting standards meant investors had no idea how the corporate bosses were ripping them off. Ethics flew out the window; the long and short of greed in the 1990s is the high muckety-mucks and their accounting conspirators made millions by deceiving shareholders. *Star Trek* did not miss the opportunity to mirror the ugly side of American greed.[5]

The Ferengi are ubercapitalists; earning a profit is their sole goal of life. They are motivated by greed, and their life centers around the 285 Rules of Acquisition—the personal code of ethics and the basis for all commerce and financial dealings. In fact, the tenth rule states that "greed is eternal" ("Profit Motives," February 20, 1995). Although Earth had abandoned its currency-mediated markets of the twenty-first century, the Ferengi are enamored with America's ancient economic system of commerce and business and consider Wall Street a sacred site.

Quark, owner of the local bar, is an ardent devotee of the Rules of Acquisition and the epitome of Ferengi greed. He is as shady as they come: He lies, cheats, cons, blackmails, takes bribes, smuggles, and engages in all kinds of illegal activities in his quest to acquire riches ("Q-Less," February 7, 1993; "The Nagus," March 21, 1993). However, over the years, Quark assists the Starfleet crew, develops a mutual respect and trust for members of the Federation and fellow aliens, and can be empathetic even in the absence of profit. In "The Circle" (October 3, 1993), Quark informs Benjamin Sisko (Starfleet commander of *DS9*) of an illegal arms deal that could threaten *DS9* as well as the peacekeeping efforts in the region (see also "Profit and Loss," March 20, 1994; "Starship

Down," November 6, 1995; "Behind the Lines," October 20, 1997). The Ferengi play a major role in the story lines of *DS9* and in mirroring and foreshadowing the financial corruption and greed of the United States during the 1990s and beyond.

Religion and Politics

Roddenberry, a confirmed secular humanist, opposed introducing religion into the franchise; nevertheless, *Star Trek* frequently explored the meaning and limits of belief systems even when Roddenberry was involved conceptually.[6] Both *TOS* and *TNG* delve into belief systems, from Greek gods to Vulcan mysticism to the Klingon faith based on honor and the many belief systems encountered in the cultures of other species. The Federation stance, based on the Prime Directive, is that belief systems should be treated as simple cultural differences and should be respected. However, *DS9* maintains a religious theme throughout its run based on the Bajoran belief system, which centers around the prophets, noncorporeal aliens who live in the wormhole (also known as the Celestial Temple).

The Bajorans pray to the prophets as though they were gods. The Bajorans believe Commander Benjamin Sisko is the emissary of the prophets because he was the first being to traverse the wormhole and have actual contact with their prophets ("Emissary, Parts 1 and 2," January 3, 1993). Sisko reluctantly accepts the title, although initially he does not believe it.

Bajoran religious beliefs about the prophets are universal among their people. The 112 religious leaders (equivalent to priests) are known as Vedeks and constitute the Assembly, whose elected leader is the Kai. Similar to the United States, some of the more conservative Vedeks disregard scientific facts, while more liberal Vedeks are open to religion and science being complementary. The extremist sects believe Bajorans are superior to all other races and species. The Bajorans are governed jointly by the secular Bajoran Republic and the Vedek Assembly, whose influence can be formidable. In short, the Bajorans are governed by a kind of theocratic democracy.

In the episode "In the Hands of the Prophets" (June 20, 1993), an influential Bajoran orthodox religious leader, Vedek Winn Adami, objects to Keiko O'Brien teaching schoolchildren the science behind the wormhole; calls it blasphemy; and threatens Keiko, who stands her ground. Sisko's son, Jake, tells his father he thinks the argument over teaching science and religion is stupid, but Sisko reminds Jake that it is important to be tolerant of others' beliefs. Sisko tries to find a middle ground between Keiko and the demands of the orthodox Bajorans but is unsuccessful. Adami encourages one of her disciples to bomb the school. The school is bombed and the culprit caught, but she refuses to implicate Winn in the crime. Shortly after, Vedek Winn is elected Kai of the Assembly.

Toward the end of the series, *DS9* introduces the Pah-wraiths: prophets who engage in evil acts, are exiled from the Celestial Temple, and are imprisoned in the Fire Caves on Bajor. Pah-wraiths have cult followers themselves, most notably the Cardassian Gul Dukat, and, for a short time, Kai Winn. The Pah-wraiths are an important addition to the story line, as they represent how false prophets can corrupt religion. The Pah-wraiths also set up the plot to depict the Manichaean fight between good and evil and emphasize the difference between true believers and those whose faith is based in ambition, such as Gul Dukat and Kai Winn ("The Reckoning," April 29, 1998).

As is the case on *DS9*, politics and religion are often intertwined in the United States, despite the constitutional First Amendment separating church and state. In 1969, the evangelical religious right, led by Jerry Falwell and Pat Robertson, was considered on the fringe, with a small following, and was ambivalent about entering politics. However, twenty years later, after several televangelists went down in flames because of scandals and widespread distrust, the Christian Coalition was founded by Pat Robertson and Ralph Reed, a Republican activist.[7] The outlook of the Christian Coalition and companion groups, such as Focus on the Family, was deeply fundamentalist and political. Their goal was to influence American law and public policy. The groups became synonymous with the Republican Party, as did their stance against such issues as abortion, homosexuality, science, feminism, and desegregation.[8]

The 1990s saw a decline in membership of mainstream Protestantism, with a corresponding growth of evangelicals, who became the foot soldiers of the Christian Coalition. As with Kai Winn, the teaching of evolution in schools came under attack by the evangelical right, with demands that science curricula should include "creation science." Roddenberry would not have approved of the religious thread in *DS9*, but he would have approved using religion to map onto this particular American contemporary issue.

Gender Identity

TNG originally introduced the Trill, but in *DS9*, they become a major presence. The planet Trill has an indigenous species known as symbionts, which are small, sentient, and genderless life-forms that swim in underground pools. Also indigenous to the planet are the Trill species, who resemble Humans. Symbionts can be surgically implanted into a male or female Trill who has volunteered, trained for, and passed a series of tests for joining suitability. The host and the symbiont become completely dependent on one another for survival. Because a symbiont can live for hundreds of years, it has more than one host in its lifetime. Each host carries all the memories and some of the personalities of the former hosts of his or her symbiont, and the Trill host always takes the name of his or her symbiont as a surname.

In *DS9*, the joined Trill, Jadzia, a female, is the eighth host of the Dax symbiont. Some of the Dax hosts were male, and some were female. Torias, a male Trill, was the fifth Dax host. In "Rejoined" (October 30, 1995), Jadzia Dax retains memories of the previous seven hosts of the symbiont Dax. Lenara (a female Trill hosting a symbiont named Kahn) arrives on *DS9* to conduct scientific experiments regarding the wormhole. In previous joinings, Torias (male) Dax had been married to Nilani (female) Kahn. The symbionts Dax and Kahn recognize one another as Torias and Nilani and realize they still have feelings for one another. However, there is a strict Trill taboo against reassociation, reviving a romantic relationship from the past, which the Trill consider unnatural. To violate the taboo means exile from Trill society. When the Trill host dies, so does the symbiont because there is not a new Trill host available. For the Trill, nothing is more important than protecting the life of the symbiont.

Despite the taboo, Dax and Kahn have trouble separating their pasts from the present. They begin spending time together, exchanging furtive looks, holding hands, and spending a night reminiscing about the past. Kahn tells Dax she has missed him so much. Jadzia Dax tells Lenara Kahn she is willing to pay the price for reassociation and wants her to stay on *DS9* to do research. Lenara Kahn is not willing and returns to

Trill, but before she departs, they share a romantic, open-mouthed kiss. That kiss, on-screen, between two women and unabashedly sensual, created an uproar similar to the Kirk-Uhura kiss in *TOS*. The story is about love, but what is staring the audience in the face is *lesbian* love, not palatable to all *Star Trek* viewers.

As noted in chapter 3, the Clinton administration established the "Don't Ask, Don't Tell" policy in 1993 regarding military service of gays, bisexuals, and lesbians. LGBTQ people could serve in the military as long as they stayed in the closet; closeted service members were protected from harassment and discrimination. Some argued that having people with openly LGBTQ identities in the military would undermine standards of morale and unit cohesiveness, which are needed to make the military successful. However, there is a long history of gays in the US military (going back to the Revolution) who served with honor and distinction.

By the mid-1990s, attitudes about homosexuality were becoming more tolerant, and several states had legalized same-sex marriage. Unfortunately, soon after "Rejoined" was released, Congress passed the Defense of Marriage Act (DOMA) in 1996, which was signed into law by President Clinton without fanfare. DOMA was a federal law recognizing legal marriage as only between one man and one woman. The act did not override state marriage laws. A state was not required to recognize a same-sex marriage from another state, so a same-sex couple's marriage might be legal in California, but Indiana, for example, did not have to accept the marriage as lawful.[9]

"Rejoined" was timely; the episode both mirrored and foreshadowed contemporary American culture regarding LGBTQ issues. Jadzia Dax is a major character in *DS9*. Jadzia is a heterosexual woman, while her symbiont, Dax, is pansexual. Observing Jadzia's romances with men and eventual marriage to Worf, one would never know there is an androgynous entity coexisting in her body, until Sisko reminds the audience when he calls Jadzia "old man."

Minorities

The economic recession of the early 1990s hit minorities particularly hard because they were predominantly employed in manufacturing and lived in the inner cities. In 1993, the overall poverty rate was 15 percent, but for Blacks, the poverty rate was 33 percent, and for Hispanics, about 30 percent. The poverty rate for Asians was 15 percent. Nearly 5 percent of US poor lived in high-poverty inner-city neighborhoods, and Los Angeles led the pack when riots broke out there in 1992. The immediate cause of the riots was the brutal beating of Rodney King by officers of the Los Angeles Police Department, but this social tinderbox had evolved from the poor economic status of the city's minorities. To address poverty and homelessness, Los Angeles mayor Richard Riordan considered policies that would put the city's homeless in a fenced campground to keep them off the streets (similar to a center in downtown San Diego). [10]

The challenges of urban poverty and despair are poignantly revealed in "Past Tense, Parts 1 and 2" (January 2 and 9, 1995, respectively), which were broadcast only three years after the Los Angeles riots. In this classic episode, Sisko, Bashir, and Jadzia Dax are inadvertently transported to and stranded on Earth in 2024. All three are found unconscious on the streets without identification. Jadzia, who appears to be a young White woman, is rescued by a wealthy media mogul who believes she has been mugged. He takes her to his upper-crust living quarters and introduces her to San Francisco society. However, Sisko and Bashir, because they are homeless men of color without money and do not exist according to fingerprinting and retinal scans, end up being housed in Sanctuary District A. Every major city in the United States in 2024 has a sanctuary district, a severely overcrowded, filthy area where America's homeless, the poverty stricken, the mentally ill, and all other downtrodden citizens are housed. They are sealed off from the general population and forgotten and abandoned by the US government. Sisko and Bashir are appalled by this and do not understand Americans' apparent apathy toward classism, racism, economic injustice, and violence, although the wretchedness of poverty clearly stretches across all color, age, and gender boundaries. This brief summary of "Past Tense" is entirely inadequate for the nuanced story *DS9* gives us regarding America's inability to address homelessness in the United States. "Past Tense" is an in-your-face story line regarding homelessness in America, and it is as timely now as it was then.

After 1995, the economy recovered, and the living conditions of the poor were improving. By the turn of the century, poverty rates had fallen to 11 percent, high-poverty neighborhoods fell to 3 percent, and minorities were moving to the suburbs. In 1997, people of Asian, Pacific Island, and Native American descent owned about one million businesses in the

United States, an increase of 61 percent from 1992. Black poverty fell to 19 percent, and the number of Black-owned businesses grew by 50 percent between 1992 and 1997.[11] Despite these advances, the context of historical discrimination against nonWhite communities in the United States was not resolved. The stereotype of the Black male as lazy and irresponsible was still embedded in American culture, not only among Whites, but also among Hispanics and Asians.[12]

Unlike Kirk and Picard, Sisko is a commander and not a captain until the third season of *DS9*. He is not just a Starfleet officer but also an attentive, single father who has to balance his professional and parental duties. Sisko's relationship with his son Jake reflects authentic portrayals of a loving, caring Black father and son in a functional and well-adapted relationship. Episodes "The Emissary, Parts 1 and 2" (January 3, 1993), "The Visitor" (October 9, 1995), and "Paradise Lost" (January 8, 1996) demonstrate a number of thoughtful interactions between father and son. These relationships move the characters through a complex pattern of familial discipline, solution-focused problem solving, and future aspirations, which were not missed by most viewers. Sisko is the first Black *Star Trek* protagonist in a lead role, and viewers watched Jake grow up from a boy to an accomplished young man.

This portrayal was in direct opposition to the general perception that Black fathers in the United States in the 1990s were absent from the home and did not take an interest in supporting their children, either emotionally or financially. However, research indicates that the majority of Black fathers, believed to be absent from their children's lives, were simply nonresident. In fact, nonresident Black fathers were more likely to visit and care for their children in a nonfinancial manner than were fathers of other races.[13] Sisko and his son, Jake, presented on a beloved television show, had a strong, positive impact on the image of Black men in American culture.[14]

Captain Benjamin Sisko and his son Jake on *Deep Space Nine* **(1993–1999).** *CBS/ Photofest © CBS*

Group Identity

With the fall of the Soviet Union and the subsequent end of the Cold War in 1991, a large number of nation-states were destabilized and experiencing interstate and intrastate conflicts. In several of these locations, the United States was directly involved in peacekeeping missions, usually under the flag of the United Nations. In 1991–1992, the United States provided a small number of troops to assist the United Nations in the conflict in Croatia and Bosnia-Herzegovina and air assistance to NATO. By 1992, the United States was involved in a humanitarian mission in Somalia, but by 1993, Somalia's humanitarian crisis had turned into a civil war. The United Nations formed a coalition for peacekeeping and nation building in Somalia, and the United States contributed three thousand soldiers. However, the mission failed, and the United States withdrew in 1994, followed by the UN withdrawal in 1995. Yet, in the same year, when the United States withdrew from Somalia, they sent 21,000 soldiers into Haiti to restore order after the overthrow of President Jean Bertrand Aristide. In the meantime, Bosnia's civil war was escalating, and the United States provided 16,500 troops to the UN mission to stabilize that country.[15]

Concurrently, in 1994, Rwanda's president was assassinated, and the Hutu ethnic majority seized power and began a campaign of genocide against the minority and elite Tutsis. This was not a new conflict between the two groups. Hostilities go back at least a century, but this particular war was aggravated by Tutsis in Uganda. Overwhelmed with supporting the United Nations and other interests at home, the United States took no action to stop the genocide. More than 800,000 deaths occurred in Rwanda; perhaps that number would have been smaller if the United States had intervened.[16]

Post–Cold War conflict and peacekeeping were not lost on *DS9* writers. Non-Federation species, nation-states, and empires were in direct or indirect conflict. The Federation changed its stance of noninterference and viewed these escalating conflicts as eventually affecting the operations of the Federation. Therefore, the Federation decided it was in their interest to intervene as a third party, to maintain peace between the Cardassians and the Bajorans, including keeping an eye on the nearby wormhole.

The *Terok Nor* space station was built by Bajoran forced labor under the whip of the Cardassians, who had militarily occupied Bajor in order to mine rare resources. The brutal occupation resulted in the Bajorans forming an aggressive resistance movement. The Federation viewed the occupation as an internal affair and, under the Prime Directive, not subject to interference, but eventually Starfleet captain Edward Jellico brokered a withdrawal of the Cardassians from Bajor and the *Terok Nor*. The Federation, led by Starfleet, sent Sisko and a small crew to the space station (renamed Deep Space Nine) to comanage the station with the Bajorans ("Emissary, Parts 1 and 2," January 3, 1993). Deep Space Nine could accommodate seven thousand individuals ("Sanctuary," November 28, 1993) but has only about three hundred permanent residents ("Captive Pursuit," January 31, 1992).

Because of its advantageous location, Sisko wants to promote commerce on Deep Space Nine. He asks the owners of businesses (Quark and Garak), who had been operating when the Cardassians were in charge of the station, to stay and continue business as usual. Deep Space Nine quickly becomes an important destination for Federation members, together with several species and traders from the Alpha Quadrant as well as those from the Gamma Quadrant who passed through the wormhole. While interaction among the various species often becomes contentious, its inhabitants and visitors know it is imperative to cooperate with one another and the Federation to keep commerce viable on the space station ("Emissary, Part 1 and 2," January 3, 1993; "Past Prologue," January 10, 1993; "Starship Down," November 6, 1995).

SNAPSHOTS: A PICTURE IS WORTH A THOUSAND WORDS

DS9 is significantly different from *TOS* and *TNG*: The space station is a hub for many species in the area, and the commander of the station is a Black single father. *Star Trek*'s mantra is inclusivity, but do the snapshots support this image? We collected snapshots of *DS9* from 26 episodes, resulting in 1,782 snapshots, and the results are presented here.[17]

Minority Representation

A total of 19 percent of the snapshots captured are Black characters, less than *TNG*. On *DS9*, the majority of activities involve nonmilitary residents and visitors, and the snapshots captured only 52 percent military ranked characters; of that, 33 percent are Blacks, dominated by Sisko as commander or captain and Worf as lieutenant. Both played pivotal roles in normalizing Blacks as leaders in society. However, nearly all the residents and visitors to *DS9* are White. Moreover, *DS9* fails dismally in regards to Asians; they never rise above 1 percent in visibility in any category.

Female Representation

Of the snapshots captured, only 24 percent represent women, comparable to *TNG*. However, of the 955 military rank snapshots, 34 percent of women are lieutenants (more than men, at 30 percent), which is considerably better than the 11 percent of women who were active in the US military in 1990, reaching 14 percent by the end of the decade.[18] With respect to occupation, women do poorly as chiefs and leaders but do fill 32 percent of the high support positions. Kira Nerys and Jadzia Dax are the most visible women in *DS9*, and they are both non-Human and White. Major Nerys, a one-time Bajoran rebel and terrorist, rises to the position of colonel in the Bajoran Resistance and is liaison officer and Sisko's second in command within the Federation. Jadzia is a science officer, eventually being promoted to lieutenant commander under Sisko. Jadzia is an accomplished pilot and commands the Starship *Defiant* more than once and assumes command of Deep Space Nine when necessary. After Sisko is appointed as Admiral Ross's adjutant, Jadzia is given command of the *Defiant*. While these two leading women are extremely important characters and essential to the stories, Kira and Jadzia appear in only 13 percent of the captured snapshots. In addition, let us not forget Kai Winn, the leader of the Bajoran religion, equivalent to today's pope.

This is a dismal representation of women when women were making great strides in equality in the United States during the 1990s (see chapter 5 on *Voyager*). However, unique to *DS9* is the presence of a large civilian population with a near-constant presence of the Ferengi. Ferengi women are restricted to their homes and are not allowed to wear clothes, which may account for a less-than-desirable presence of females captured in snapshots. Women in *DS9* are underrepresented, but the women represented are strong, powerful women.

Age

The snapshots captured 76 percent men, with an average age of forty-three years (a range of four to seventy-two years old), and 24 percent women, with an average age of thirty-eight years (a range of twenty-two to seventy years old). Similar to *TNG*, *DS9* has a large resident population of families, and this is reflected in the snapshots. The average age for both men and women is also similar to *TNG*; therefore, as age is concerned, fans of *TNG* would feel right at home viewing *DS9*.

In-Group versus Out-Group

DS9 shines in terms of species diversity and the complexities of alliances. Humans make up 32 percent of individuals captured in the snapshots, with the rest representing eighteen other species. Only Humans and Trills are officially members of the Federation. Civilians constitute 44 percent of individuals captured in the snapshots, and of those, 83 percent are aliens. Of the resident aliens, 58 percent have military rank with authority (commander, captain, lieutenant). These are dominated by Jadzia Dax and Kira Nerys. Odo is the space station chief of security. The Bajorans are sympathetic to the Federation, whereas the Cardassians are, at best, under a not-so-secure treaty with the Federation. Of the remaining species, 42 percent are neutral to the Federation.

Quark, Odo, Elim Garak, and Kira Nerys are aliens who are not officially in the Federation but are within the circle of the in-group, with Odo and Nerys near the center, Garak midway, and Quark on the periphery. They have loyalties in two camps, even though they are deeply invested in the affairs of Deep Space Nine. Quark is mostly at odds with almost everyone on Deep Space Nine. Odo becomes good friends with Sisko and O'Brien, develops respect for Garak, becomes fond of exchanging insults with Quark, and falls in love with Nerys. When the Federation takes over the station, Garak is the only remaining Cardassian in residence. He is a fine tailor and the owner of Garak's Clothiers. Garak and Bashir become friends and have lunch together on a weekly basis. Although he is initially looked on with suspicion, Garak frequently assists the Federation. Kira Nerys is a Bajoran liaison officer to Starfleet. At first she is opposed to Starfleet management of Deep Space Nine, but eventually, she becomes one of Sisko's most trusted advisors. Similar to many immigrants in the United States, these "aliens" are in two cultures, do not fit fully into either, and are necessary to both.

SUMMARY

DS9 is a stand-out *Star Trek* series, which adapted exceptionally well to contemporary American culture of the 1990s and mirrored and foreshadowed both the positive and negative sides of American culture. The Ferengi represent greed and appear in about every episode. The viewer sees the downside of extreme greed: the financial losses, the double manipulation, the meanness, and the loss of true associates and friends. The greed of the few results in many being disadvantaged, as shown in "Past Tense." Unfortunately, it mirrored and still mirrors America. The viewer could see the good and the not-so-good side of belief systems as well as the dangers that extremists pose to society. *DS9* symbolically normalizes gender identity via Jadzia Dax. The space station, operating as a community, clearly shows the challenges as well as the delight of living in a multicultural community. "Sanctuary" (November 21, 1993), now nearly thirty years old, foreshadowed the heartbreak of desperate immigrants, an episode that should be aired worldwide today. *DS9* shows the necessity and challenge of being a third-party peacekeeper in another society's conflict. Last but not least, Commander/Captain Benjamin Sisko, an intelligent leader, a loving father, and an empathetic friend, normalizes his role in a multicultural society and gives hope to minorities in our society. *DS9* has one serious shortcoming. It was shown on UPN, which limited its viewing audience.

5

LIVING WITNESS

Voyager: 1995–2001

"Obviously, events have been reinterpreted to make your people feel better about themselves. Revisionist history. It's such a comfort."— Quarren[1]

Star Trek: Voyager (*VOY*) aired between January 16, 1995, and May 23, 2001, and overlapped in real time with *DS9* for five years, meaning that it, too, aired primarily in the Good Decade. *VOY* also overlaps with *DS9* in the *Star Trek* time line, the former spanning 2371–2378, and the latter, 2369–2375. Like *DS9*, *VOY* was created by Rick Berman and Michael Piller but with the addition of Jeri Taylor, a woman with historical ties to the *Star Trek* franchise. Both *DS9* and *VOY* aired for seven seasons on UPN. Aside from overlapping in real time and *Star Trek* time, the two series have very little in common. Unlike the Deep Space Nine station, which has a large number of residents, *Voyager*'s capacity accommodated only a small crew. Unlike Deep Space Nine, which is stationary, *VOY* takes place on a traveling Starship. Unique to previous Starships, *Voyager* could land on planets. It was small, tactically mobile, and with cutting-edge technology. Starship *Voyager* was built for the express purpose of space exploration.

In "Caretaker, Parts 1 and 2" (January 16, 1995), *Voyager* is docked at the Deep Space Nine station and preparing for her maiden voyage. The mission is to capture and return the renegades known as the Maquis, who are aboard the *Val Jean* raider vessel. The Maquis are former Starfleet members, Starfleet academy dropouts, and colonists who rebelled against the Federation for making concessions to the Cardassians. Prior to departing Deep Space Nine station, Captain Kathryn Janeway of *Voyager* coerces Tom Paris into acting as her flight controller. Paris had been a member of the rebellious Maquis, had been imprisoned, and was serving time when Janeway "enlisted" him. As *Voyager* pursues the *Val Jean*, both ships are abducted by the Caretaker, a powerful extragalactic entity that protects the planet Ocampa, and are swept into the Delta Quadrant. Both crews become stranded some 70,000 light-years from Federation space. Both ships suffer heavy casualties, and the *Val Jean* is damaged beyond repair.

Janeway negotiates with Commander Chakotay of the *Val Jean* to halt hostilities toward each other and merge crews in order to survive, resulting in approximately 150 crewmembers ("Bride of Chaotica," January 27, 1999). In order to make joining *Voyager* more palatable, Janeway offers provisional Starfleet commissions to the Maquis. Chakotay becomes Janeway's first officer, and at his urging, B'Elanna Torres, a Klingon/Human becomes chief engineer ("Parallax," January 23, 1995). Tuvok, a Vulcan who had been undercover on the *Val Jean*, returns as chief of security; Ensign Harry Kim remains operation officer; and Paris continues as flight controller. Janeway's chief medical officer is an emergency holographic program, who is known as the Doctor. In addition, Neelix, a Talaxian scavenger and merchant, and Kes, a telepathic Ocampa, are also allowed to join the crew, the former as cook and self-appointed morale office and the latter as an airponics bay manager and (eventually) field medic.

Even though *Voyager* is more technologically advanced than other ships in Starfleet, it would have taken an estimated seventy-five years to make the return trip to the Alpha Quadrant. The Delta Quadrant is unexplored by Starfleet, so *VOY* truly goes where no one had gone before, and the entire series is built around surviving the unknown and boldly going home.

VOYAGER AND CONTEMPORARY CULTURE

While *DS9* aired during the heart of the "Good Decade," *VOY* aired in the latter half of that decade, what might be considered the "Golden Age," a time when Americans were innocently happy and in deep denial, until 9/11.[2] Where *DS9* normalizes the role of race (and species), *VOY* normalizes the role of women. Where *DS9* has long-term relationships with other species, *VOY* has sporadic and mostly short-term interactions with others. In the 1990s, the United States did not have a defined, persistent outside enemy, which is reflected in *VOY*'s lack of a habitual villain. Rather than focusing on an ongoing war, *VOY* focuses on discovering new species and exploring new areas of space, much like *TOS* and *TNG* had done. As is the *Star Trek* mission, *VOY* continues to address contemporary American issues. Given the small crew and ephemeral contact with other species, how well was *VOY* able to mirror or foreshadow American culture?

Women of the 1990s and *Voyager*

Women made small advances in a very short period during the latter half of the "Good Decade." In 1995, Fortune 500 companies had no female CEOs; by 2000, that number had increased to two. From 1995 to 2000, the number of women serving on corporate America's boards of directors went from 10 to 12 percent. The average American working woman earned 71 percent of her male counterpart in 1993, and by 2001, she earned 76 percent. Traditional occupations for women were teachers, nurses, librarians, and social workers, but those jobs were being replaced by women entering the fields of medicine, law, management, and academic professors.[3]

Government also saw more visibility in women participating in public service. Women comprised 6 percent of the 102nd Congress (1993–1995), and by the 106th Congress of 1999, 12 percent were women. In 1997, Madeleine Albright was appointed the first female secretary of state. Between 1995 and 2001, women were taking military rank positions, with several firsts being achieved. Colonel Eileen Marie Collins became the first woman to command a US space shuttle mission. Moreover, Navy Lieutenant Kendra Williams, a women fighter pilot, took part in Operation Desert Fox; Nancy Mace graduated from the Citadel, a traditionally all-male military college; and Kathleen McGrath commanded a navy warship in the Persian Gulf.[4]

VOY exceeds expectations in roles for women. The crew are few in number but have two leading women throughout the seven seasons: Captain Janeway and Chief Engineer Torres. Kes is present from the first episode of *VOY* to the beginning of season 4; Seven of Nine was picked up in season 4 and remained for the duration of the series. All four had challenges to overcome and balance, much like women in America in the 1990s.

Kathryn Janeway is a woman of science; she rises through the science ranks rather than through command, and she often acts as science officer in addition to being captain of *Voyager*. She is an attractive, extremely intelligent, and capable woman, wrapped in a cloak of authority that commands respect, and she rules *Voyager* with a velvet fist. Janeway willingly sacrifices for her position; she forgoes marriage and mother-hood for a life of leadership, which she performs to the absolute best of her ability. In spite of those sacrifices, she retains her femininity and in fact can be very seductive ("Bride of Chaotica," January 27, 1999).

Once isolated in the Delta Quadrant, Janeway knows she is the final decision maker and is solely responsible for the consequences. There is no one above her. To hold her crew together, she must set aside her personal life. She becomes a stoic, professional workaholic. Although she can be compassionate toward members of the crew and even call them friends, she is more of a counselor or an aunt. She listens and advises, but she seldom shares her personal thoughts. She is alone. When necessary, Janeway can become a complete Sarah Connor commando as she does in "Macrocosm" (December 11, 1996).[5] When Janeway and Neelix return from an away trip, they find the crew have been infected by a macrovirus. She loads up her weapons and goes hunting, even grabbing one of the giant viruses and stabbing it to death. As with any good captain, Janeway is willing to put her own life at risk for her crew.

B'Elanna Torres was born to a Human father and a Klingon mother and raised in a Federation colony, where she and her mother were the only Klingons. She is embarrassed by her Klingon heritage, primarily her physical features. She feels like an outsider and misfit, which leads to her insecurities and anger-management issues. She is a brilliant engineer, but because of her temperament and inability to follow rules, she drops out of Starfleet Academy, joins the Maquis, and is the engineer on the *Val Jean* under Chakotay. Chakotay urges Janeway to make Torres chief of engi-neering, and she reluctantly agrees ("Parallax," January 23, 1995).

Early on, Torres and Janeway are frequently at odds. In "Prime Fac-tors" (March 20, 1995), Torres disobeys Janeway's orders and puts the crew in danger. Janeway is livid and informs Torres that, if *Voyager* didn't need her as an engineer, she would have stripped Torres of rank and thrown her in the brig. This confrontation is a wake-up call for Torres. She saves the day on more than one occasion, earning the respect of the crew. Eventually she marries Paris and has a daughter, but she never loses her edge, which aids her performance of duties. In the seventh season of *VOY*, we finally see Torres come to grips with her Klingon-Human duality ("Lineage," January 24, 2001), an important message for Americans who are of mixed heritage.

Janeway and Torres are professional leaders on *Voyager* but imperfectly so, as are Kirk, Picard, Sisko, Scotty, Geordi, and O'Brien before them. Like their previous counterparts in Starfleet, they command respect. They are not judged as female leaders but just as leaders. The glass ceiling has vanished. Strong women with ambition and drive in contemporary America society are under the glass ceiling and behind the brick wall. The qualities that male leaders are praised for (drive, assertiveness, control) were considered flaws in females in America.[6]

Kes, an Ocampa, is telepathic, with a normal life span of only nine years. Her planet has been unintentionally rendered uninhabitable by the Nacene, and a male Nacene has become the Ocampa Caretaker. The Ocampa live underground, where all their needs are met, but are restricted to their subterranean home. Kes joins *Voyager* because she is aware the Ocampa have given up their unique telepathic abilities for comfort and security; she wants to rediscover those abilities, evolve, and learn to live on her own. On *Voyager*, she wants to be useful and tells Janeway that *Voyager* could grow its own fresh fruits and vegetables to allay the monotony of replicated food. Janeway agrees, and Kes becomes manager of the airponics bay. When looking for supplies, she meets the Doctor in sickbay ("Parallax," January 23, 1995); they become friends, and eventually Kes begins training so she can become his medical assistant ("Phage," February 6, 1995).

Unfortunately, as Kes ages, her telepathic and newly acquired psychokinetic abilities interfere with her ability to function normally. When *Voyager* reaches Borg space, Kes becomes mentally connected with Species 8472, and her mental abilities surge to the point of damaging *Voyager*. She leaves in a shuttle craft and uses her powers to push *Voyager* out of Borg space and toward the Alpha Quadrant, reducing their journey by ten years ("The Gift," September 10, 1997). Kes is not a warrior; she has a sweet, gentle, nonassuming temperament, which can be a sign of weakness, but she is anything but weak. She is determined and persistent, with an acute scientific mind, and she is a compassionate empath.

Annika Hansen was born Human but at age six was assimilated by the Borg and designated Seven of Nine, Tertiary Adjunct of Unimatrix 01, but known informally on *Voyager* as Seven. As time passes after assimilation, Seven forgets what it was to be Human. During a war between the Borg and Species 8472, Seven is permanently severed from the Collective and kept onboard *Voyager* ("Scorpion, Parts 1 and 2," May 21 and September 3, 1997, respectively). Most of her Borg implants are removed by the Doctor, and her Human appearance restored; however, Seven has trouble adjusting to being an individual and to Starfleet culture on *Voyager*.

Seven is given the title of scientist and her own lab onboard the *Voyager*. She becomes an asset because she possesses all the technological knowledge of the Borg. She develops technology that shortens the distance *Voyager* has to travel to return home and enhances communication systems, medical advances, and weapons ("Year of Hell, Parts 1 and 2," November 5 and 12, 1997, respectively; "Life Line," May 10, 2000). Seven has challenges, particularly in understanding decisions based on compassion, which she sees as illogical. She finds humanity flawed and has trouble with failures ("Day of Honor," September 17, 1997). On occasion, Seven is tempted to return to the Borg ("The Gift," September 10, 1997). In several episodes, Seven hears the Collective calling and attempts to rejoin them. It takes a long time for her to trust, follow orders, and maintain friendships with Janeway and the rest of the crew. Seven of Nine is a science fiction analogy for immigrants and refugees, torn from the culture they grew up in, where they knew the collective rules, norms, and expectations, only to be thrown into a confusing world of a new culture. Acculturation is necessary to any newcomer, but it is not always easy or kind.

Group Conflict

Like the United States in the 1990s, *VOY*'s conflicts with others are transitory. Instead, *VOY* maps onto cultural "enemies" who have parallels in the United States, such as environmental issues, rapid technology development, and health-care issues. There are recurring run-ins with the

Kazon, primarily because Janeway persists in adhering to the Prime Directive and refusing to give the Kazon the Federation technology that they want. There are dangers from the Vidiian, who are infected with a phage that consumes their organs. In order to stay alive, they need to harvest organs from other species. Janeway empathizes with them but views them as dangerous and a species to avoid.

Environmental Issues

During the "Good Decade," America saw a resurgence in environmental movements, most particularly concerning climate change. Unlike previous decades, where environmental concerns were primarily local, the 1990s environmental concerns became global. Under the Clinton administration, the Environmental Protection Agency (EPA) established more than twenty major standards to reduce environmental pollutants, with a focus on air and water quality. The EPA also approved regulations to address environmental justice and protections for children against hazardous materials. Recycling was also vogue in the more progressive cities around the United States.[7]

In "Night" (October 14, 1998), *Voyager* must travel through a large expanse of space void of stars but with an abundance of theta radiation. Alien ships attack *Voyager*, and several aliens board. The crew manages to capture one, who is dying of radiation poisoning, while the others escape back to their vessels. In the meantime, the attacking ships are driven off by another ship piloted by Controller Emck, the sole proprietor of a Malon export vessel spewing theta radiation. Janeway questions the alien, who informs them his species is indigenous to the area and the Malon are poisoning his species. Janeway returns the alien to his own people. Upon confronting Emck, the crew learns that the void is considered the perfect place to dump antimatter and toxic waste. Janeway offers Emck technology to recycle the waste, but he refuses because it would ruin his export business. The only option for saving the indigenous species is to close the vortex that allows the Malon to enter the void. They succeed, and in the process, *Voyager* is pulled through the vortex, entering a space full of stars.

In another episode, *Voyager* again encounters a Malon freighter carrying toxic waste. The vessel is damaged, and if it explodes, it will contaminate three light-years of space. A crew from *Voyager* boards the vessel in hope of making repairs but finds the crew all deformed from radiation poisoning. Unable to repair the damage to the freighter, they return to *Voyager* and send the vessel into a star, where the radiation is absorbed on impact ("Juggernaut," April 26, 1999).

In "30 Days" (December 9, 1998), Tom Paris is writing a letter to his father, explaining why Janeway has stripped him of rank and put him in the brig for thirty days. He explains that *Voyager* encountered a body composed entirely of water and reminisces about his love of oceans on Earth. He continues writing. *Voyager* contacts the colonists on the planet, who inform the crew that the body is losing water mass and they don't know why. *Voyager* offers to investigate and discovers it is caused by colonists who have mining operations to harvest oxygen. *Voyager* offers technology for oxygen capture, thereby eliminating the destructive mining operations. The government refuses the offer, as it would be too much bother. Paris attempts ecoterrorism to destroy the mining refineries but fails. He wants his dad to know he is in the brig again but this time for attempting to protect a body of water that he so loves.

In "11:59" (May 5, 1999), the crew is sitting around, reminiscing about their genealogy and ancestors. Janeway reflects on a story her family had always told about Shannon O'Donnel, an ancestor who was a pioneer in Mars exploration in the twenty-first century. Later, she discovers those were just family stories without merit. However, she learns that Shannon married Henry Janeway in Portage, Indiana, and was a major contributor to the Millennium Gate project, the first self-sustaining civil community. In so many ways, *VOY* highlights environmental issues plaguing America and the world in the 1990s.

Technological Issues

Technological advances of the 1990s were the catalyst for future technology. By the early 1990s, personal computers were affordable in most homes but had limited applications. Along came the World Wide Web, followed by browsers and search engines, and computers began talking to each other through time and space, stimulating e-commerce on Amazon and e-Bay. In business and academia, Linux software and Java programming became common, and megabytes of data could be backed up on a USB flash drive that could be held in your hand. Photoshop was released, and video game graphics took a quantum leap forward. Online multiplayer gaming became a rage. The Palm Pilot helped organize our daily lives, DVDs replace VHS, and DVRs let us record our favorite TV shows.

Hybrid vehicles joined the auto fleet, and the Hubble telescope sent its first picture to Earth. On a darker note, the first predator drones began flying in combat missions, and the Department of Defense made major advances in artificial intelligence (AI).[8]

Although the development of smart bombs harkens back to the Vietnam War, true precision smart bombs were first used in Desert Storm. The whole point of smart bombs was to have an extremely accurate weapon that could destroy an identified target in a very small and specific area. The bombs used in Desert Storm were, on average, accurate within ten feet of a target. In the air war in Kosovo, joint direct attack munitions were introduced, which were more precise than smart bombs because they could be programmed by GPS from space.[9]

Voyager has numerous episodes that map onto the rapid advances in technology in the 1990s. Two episodes stand out regarding smart bombs. *Voyager* encounters a smart bomb named "Dreadnought" (February 12, 1996) headed for a planet where millions of people live. However, the smart bomb was built by the Cardassians in the Alpha Quadrant to attack Bajoran territories. As a Maquis, Torres reprogrammed the bomb to be a Maquis weapon to target Cardassian sites. Torres believes she can again reprogram the weapon and stop its attack on the innocent planet, so she beams over to Dreadnought vessel. The AI system believes Torres is a Cardassian spy trying to reprogram it. As Torres keeps the AI in a contest of wits, she manages to cut its power cord and beam back to *Voyager* before Dreadnought self-destructs.

An away team lands on a planet in response to a distress signal in "Warhead" (May 19, 1999) and finds an injured sentient smart bomb. The away team take it back to *Voyager*, where they attempt to repair it. When the AI believes they are harming it, the AI downloads its program into the Doctor and becomes threatening. The AI insists that it must complete its mission to destroy a military base on Salina Prime. As its memory chips are restored, it learns that its mission was terminated but believes it's being deceived. In the meantime, thirty-two sibling warheads surround *Voyager* to assist the AI in completing its mission. The AI learns the truth and informs Kim that the other warheads have come to retrieve it to complete the mission. The AI volunteers to join its siblings and detonate, thereby saving the target planet and *Voyager*.

The first time the Borg story line is introduced in *Voyager* is when they encounter ex-Borg drones who have formed a cooperative, nonbelligerent community on a planet ("Unity," February 12, 1997). This sets the stage for more than a dozen episodes involving the Borg hives or individual drones and allows *Voyager* to rescue the drone Seven of Nine ("Scorpion, Parts 1 and 2," May 21 and September 3, 1997, respectively).

The viewer is also exposed to Borg maturation chambers that they use for assimilated children. *Voyager* rescues four children from a Borg cube and brings them aboard *Voyager*. Seven grows fond of them, particularly the oldest, Icheb. During their travels in the Delta Quadrant, the crew locate Icheb's parents. Seven does not want him to leave *Voyager*. They discover Icheb was genetically designed to spread a virus throughout the Borg, which would eliminate his individuality. Voyager again rescues him, and he remains on *Voyager*. In "Imperfection" (October 11, 2000), Seven is dying because her cortical node implant is failing. Icheb donates his cortical node implant to save her life, as Icheb is young enough to recover without the node.

Some drones have a rare mutation that allows them to enter a subconscious "virtual" world during regeneration known as "Unimatrix Zero" (Parts 1 and 2, May 21 and October 4, 2000, respectively). While in this state, they retain their original selves and individuality, but when not in regeneration, they have no memory of "Unimatrix Zero" and behave as any drone would in the hive. A nanovirus was developed to allow the mutant-drones to maintain their individuality while awake, arguably creating a resistance against the Borg. But in order to succeed, Unimatrix must be destroyed. Eventually, the liberated drones take over a Borg-sphere and thank *Voyager*.

Janeway encounters the Borg queen on more than one occasion. There are more than one Borg queen, and even when killed, their consciousness stays in the hive. In the series finale, Admiral Janeway travels back in time to visit Captain Janeway and tells her how to get back to the Alpha Quadrant. Then she boards the Borg cube and confronts the queen, who immediately begins to assimilate Admiral Janeway. But unbeknownst to the queen, Janeway infects her with a neurolytic pathogen. In essence, she hacks the queen, causing a failure of the Borg collective mind. The Borg complex explodes, Admiral Janeway dies, and *Voyager* returns home ("Dark Frontier, Parts 1 and 2," February 17, 1999; "Unimatrix Zero, Parts 1 and 2," May 21 and October 4, 2000, respectively; "Endgame Parts 1 and 2," May 23, 2001).

The AI and the Borg represent a fear of technology running rampant, destroying our individuality and our ability to think for ourselves. Should AI weapons be developed? Can these technologies replace humanity? *VOY* not only highlights the dangers but, in *Star Trek* form, also offers hope that the technologies will not have the last word.

Health-Care Issues

As a part of his bid for the presidency, Bill Clinton campaigned in part on overhauling the US health-care system. The 1993 proposal provided for universal health care. However, the details were convoluted: placing limitations on care, requiring insurance companies to be competitive, and mandating drug cost negotiations between the government and drug companies as well as managed care through government control. Initially, the American Medical Association and the Health Insurance Association of America supported the Clinton initiative; however, within two years, that support was withdrawn. Within that same window, supporting votes in Congress had diminished. Health-care reform was dead in the water.[10]

In "Critical Care" (November 1, 2000), the Doctor is kidnapped by a Dralian trader and sold to Chellick, a Jye administrator who has been contracted to run a Denaali hospital ship. The Allocator is the main computer in the hospital, which decides the type of care received by each patient depending on their social value. High-valued citizens, such as engineers, are placed in Level Blue for maximum care. Citizens considered having minimal value are placed in Level Red and receive minimal care. The Doctor is appalled. He steals medicine from Level Blue and begins treating patients in Level Red. Chellick discovers and attempts to stop the Doctor. Just as the Denaali begin the process of deactivating the Doctor's program, the Doctor is rescued by Janeway. This episode not only mirrors the Clinton era attempt at health-care reform and the strictures placed on health-care providers but also foreshadows the controversy over universal health care during the Obama administration.[11]

SNAPSHOTS: A PICTURE IS WORTH A THOUSAND WORDS

VOY is unique to the *Star Trek* franchise in that it is lost in the Delta Quadrant and most of the time is unable to communicate with Starfleet or the Federation. Between 1966 and 2001, *VOY* was the only *Star Trek* series or movie to have a female captain of a Starfleet vessel as the principal protagonist. *VOY* focuses on women and inter- and intragroup interaction. We collected 1,825 snapshots of *VOY* from 26 episodes.[12] What can these snapshots tell us? The results are presented here.

Minority Representation

The snapshots captured 85 percent White, 10 percent Black, and 5 percent Asian characters. Tuvok represents the majority of Blacks. He is a lieutenant commander in Starfleet and represents 22 percent of the officers with military authority over others. Only two other Black characters were observed, both civilian aliens. Asians are predominantly represented by Ensign Harry Kim, who is the chief operations officer; otherwise, Asians were observed at less than 1 percent. However, both Tuvok and Kim frequently contribute important roles in *VOY*. Chakotay is portrayed as a member of the First Nation, indigenous peoples of the Americas, and some episodes focus on his tribe's culture, while others include aspects of his culture. Aside from crew members, there were 670 civilians observed, of which 99 percent are White. The *Star Trek* franchise certainly could increase diversity visibility in primary as well as secondary characters.

Female Representation

The snapshots captured 61 percent men and 39 percent women, significantly more women than the previous series. However, of the 1,825 observations, 937 are Humans, all from *Voyager*, and of that, 51 percent are men and 49 percent are women. Males dominate aliens (63 percent), and an additional 9 percent of males observed were of the Doctor, classified as AI. As far as the *Voyager* starship is concerned, equity in gender is achieved. Moreover, the women have authority over others: 41 percent of the snapshots are Captain Janeway, and 15 percent are Chief Engineer Torres.

Age

The snapshots captured 61 percent men, with an average age of forty-one years (with an age range of twelve to eighty-two years), and 39 percent women, with an average age of thirty-seven years (with an age range of five to sixty-four years). *Voyager* does not house families, and most members onboard are adults. The mean average age for both men and women is also similar to *TNG* and *DS9*. However, for *VOY*, most of the younger and older age ranges are aliens or holodeck images.

In-Group versus Out-Group

A total of 918 snapshots (50 percent) captured represent the main crew of *Voyager*. Of these, 44 percent are members of Starfleet, 20 percent from the former Maquis, 11 percent of the Doctor, 11 percent of Seven of Nine, 10 percent of Neelix, and 4 percent of Kes. These represent five distinct groups: Starfleet, Maquis, hologram, civilians, and several different species. *Voyager* is initially crewed by Starfleet members—the in-group—but once *Voyager* enters the Delta Quadrant, the ship has a crew from several out-groups. In order to survive, they must cooperate. In the 1,825 snapshots captured, a total of twenty-four species are identified, of which 52 percent are Humans, and all are from *Voyager*. Seventeen of the identified species are native to Delta Quadrant. Particularly hostile to *Voyager* are the Kazon and Trabe (who are also hostile to one another), the Vidiian (the organ stealers), the Malon (the polluters), the Hirogen (the predators), and the Borg. *VOY* is successful in presenting the complications of forming relationships with other cultures, civilizations, and species, which were captured in the snapshots.

SUMMARY

In *Star Trek* tradition, *VOY* explores social issues of the 1990s. In addition, *VOY* does an exceptional job normalizing women in the workforce and the military. The series adapts well to the desires and hopes of the viewers, particularly girls and women. Women, like men, have many different personalities and temperaments and come in all shapes and sizes. Captain Janeway, like Nancy Pelosi, Speaker of the House, demonstrates that women can be assertive leaders without being classified as a witch. Seven's character, no doubt, adds sex appeal to *VOY*, but she offers so much more than that; Seven, like Dr. Lisa Randall, a physics professor at Harvard, shows that attractive women are not bimbos. Kes, like Marie Curie, a Nobel Prize winner, illustrates that being reserved does not make one weak. And Torres, like Serena Williams, a tennis star, shows that one can be strong without being nasty.[13]

VOY also continues *TNG*'s foreshadowing of the hopes and fears of technology by extending and expanding on the Borg, holograms, and AI. Environmental and health-care issues are also explored. However, its foremost gift to audiences is showing the many facets of women who have gained the respect and admiration of others.

The principal crew of *Voyager* in season 4 through 7 (1997–2001). Shown from left (top row): Ensign Harry Kim, The Doctor, First Officer Chakotay, Lieutenant Tom Paris, (middle row) Seven of Nine, Neelix, Chief Engineer B'Elanna Torres, (front) Captain Katherine Janeway. *UPN/Photofest © UPN*

6

TERRA PRIME

Enterprise: 2001–2005

"Fellow delegates, this last week we've seen what humans can be at their worst. But we cannot, we must not use that as an excuse to end the dream here. For then, the demons of our past will have won."— Prime Minister Nathan Samuels[1]

At its debut, *Enterprise* (*ENT*) already had two strikes against it. *ENT* had the misfortune of being released just fifteen days after the 9/11 terrorist attacks on Flight 93, the Pentagon, and the World Trade Center. While *ENT* saw Earth uniting after the apocalypse of World War III (2026–2053) and first contact with the Vulcans (2063), America was unraveling from the terrorist attack. In real time, *ENT* premiered thirty-two years after the cancelation of *TOS*, but in *Star Trek* time, it takes place in the past. *ENT* is a prequel to *TOS*, covering Earth's timeline from 2151 to 2161, about a century before James Kirk was at the helm. Pleasing the viewers in 2001 while staying true to a pre-*TOS* timeline was tricky business, considering the rapid culture change in America over those thirty-two years.

Predictably, 9/11 had a huge impact on American culture, moving it from a carefree disposition to one of crises and confrontations. *ENT* is full of fear and mistrust that, by pure accident, mapped well onto contemporary American culture. However, Americans did not want more fear and mistrust entering their living rooms each week. They were getting enough from the nightly news. Immediately after 9/11, Americans wanted escapism, and it was just around the corner. *Harry Potter and the Sorcerer's Stone* and *Monsters, Inc.* were both released on the big screen in November 2001, followed shortly by *The Lord of the Rings: The Fellowship of the Rings* in December 2001. All three were blockbusters.[2]

Popular television viewing included *The Simpsons*, *King of the Hill*, and *South Park*, all animated adult series.[3] In addition, the role-playing video game *The Elder Scrolls III: Morrowind* sold more than four million copies by 2005 as well as won a game of the year award.[4] Americans wanted to escape, and they had plenty of opportunity. Considering the bad timing and the too-close-to-home messages, many *ENT* episodes are underrated, even though they stay true to *Star Trek*'s mission. However, can the same be said about the series as a whole?

ENTERPRISE AND CONTEMPORARY AMERICAN CULTURE

Despite the terrorist attacks, American culture continued normally. People woke up in the morning and went to work and school. They attended concerts and movies. They shopped for the latest fashions and electronics. They entered the job market and ran for office. The millennials came of age. Minorities, women, and the LGBTQ community were all striving for equality in the workplace and in public life. In-groups and out-groups were being redefined, many in gray zones, but others with distinct boundaries. Did *ENT* mirror or foreshadow these aspects of American culture?

Us versus Them

ENT is the only *Star Trek* production that represents a time frame before the forming of the United Federation of Planets in 2161. After first contact with the Vulcans, Earth began to consolidate under a unified government. By 2150, United Earth governed not only Earth but also other Human colonies in the Sol System and the Alpha Quadrant. The Vulcan High Command maintains an advisory council on Earth, which coordinates with Starfleet Command. The Vulcan ambassador to Earth, Soval, and the council are frequently at odds with Starfleet. *ENT* portrays the Vulcans as the poster child for ethnocentrism, either snubbing or mistrusting others. In addition to Vulcans, Humans also come in contact with Andorians, Tellarites, Xindi, time travelers, and other species, all of whom harbor various levels of mistrust toward each other, from resentment to open hostility. Moreover, most have factions of dissenters within their own societies. Here, we focus on Human relations with others and with themselves.

Intermistrust

Global divisions were brewing even before 9/11. In July 2001, leaders from Canada, France, Germany, Italy, Japan, Russia, the United Kingdom, and the United States gathered in Genoa, Italy, for the twenty-eighth G8 summit. Such meetings always generate demonstrations, but the twenty-eighth summit protests were symbolic of what was to come. The protest was dominated by antiglobalization groups, and the Italian government's response was eerily similar to Mussolini's fascist state. Anti-immigration sentiments and police repression were on the horizon for more than just Italy.[5]

President George W. Bush stood before Congress just nine days after 9/11 and boldly stated to the world, "Either you are with us, or you are with the terrorists."[6] Our allies in NATO completely supported the United States in our time of crisis, and ground troops from Britain, Turkey, Germany, and Italy, led by the United States, invaded Afghanistan to remove the Taliban government for its support of al-Qaeda. Less than two years later, a US-led coalition invaded Iraq based on the assertion that Iraq possessed weapons of mass destruction (later determined to be false). A year later, support for the Iraq invasion began to wane.[7]

Moreover, some countries were on the side of the terrorists or had informal supporters within NATO; others were fence sitters. One day before the invasion of Iraq, the BBC reported that the United States had named thirty countries who openly supported America, which were dubbed the "coalition of the willing." Missing from the coalition of the willing were several NATO members: Canada, Belgium, Norway, France, and Germany. The United States also claimed others were supportive but would not take a public stand. Favorable public opinion in Spain, Italy, and Poland was as high as 80 percent in 2002 but less than 50 percent by 2003. None of the Arab countries announced support of any kind. Thus began the dissension, alliance-wobbling, and heightened anti-Americanism, some of it deserved, some misguided.[8]

Small colonies of survivors flourish after World War III on *Star Trek*'s Earth. One such colony is in Bozeman, Montana, where Zefram

Cochrane designs the first warp drive. Soon after his successful faster-than-light test flight, first contact with the Vulcans occurs on April 5, 2063. They become cautious allies to the Humans. United Earth begins colonizing nearby moons and planets, but exploration is limited because the Vulcans do not believe that Humans are emotionally ready to explore deep space and refuse to share their advanced technology.

In the *ENT* premier double episode "Broken Arrow, Parts 1 and 2" (September 26, 2001), a Klingon has been seriously wounded on Earth. The Klingon Empire demands his return. United Earth leaders and the Vulcan High Command meet to discuss the situation. The Vulcans are in opposition; however, Admiral Forrest of Starfleet approves the maiden voyage of *Enterprise* NX-01, with an advanced warp speed of 4.5, to return the Klingon to his home world. The main crew consists of Captain Archer, Vulcan subcommander T'Pol (a member of the Vulcan High Command), Chief Engineer Trip Tucker, communication officer and linguist Hoshi Sato, tactical officer Lieutenant Malcolm Reed, helm officer Travis Mayweather, and chief medical officer Dr. Phlox, a Denobulan physician who had lived on Earth many years. Thus began the voyages of the first *Enterprise* to explore new territories and encounter new species, friendly and unfriendly.

While America was moving into a gray zone with alliances, *ENT* was moving in the opposite direction. Captain Archer and his crew witness firsthand hostilities between the Vulcans and the Andorians in "The Andorian Incident" (October 31, 2001). T'Pol, Archer, and Trip visit an outpost at an ancient Vulcan monastery maintained by Vulcan monks. Upon entry, they learn that the monastery has been taken over by Andorians, led by Commander Shran, who claims it is not just a sanctuary for monks but is also a surveillance headquarters for spying on Andorians.

Vulcans and Andorians have a long, ongoing hostile relationship. From the Vulcan point of view, the Andorians are territorial and militaristic, and from the Andorian point of view, the only thing preventing the Vulcans from invasion is the threat of retaliation. During a firefight, a large secret surveillance vault is discovered, verifying Shran's suspicions. Archer instructs T'Pol to scan the area and give the records to Shran. She complies and instructs the *Enterprise* to allow the Andorians to leave peacefully. This discovery reinforces Archer's mistrust of Vulcans, a theme that runs through all four seasons of *ENT*. However, this begins a long friendship between Archer and Shran.

Helm Officer Travis Mayweather, Captain Jonathan Archer, and Chief Engineer Trip Tucker in the series premiere of *Enterprise* (2001). *UPN/Photofest © UPN*

While Vulcans and Tellarites have been on neutral terms, Andorians and Tellarites have been involved in trade-war hostilities for a long time. Individual Tellarites are known for their unscrupulous business practices, as witnessed when a Tellarite bids for a slave at an Orion auction ("Borderland," October 29, 2004). Nonetheless, for stability in the quadrant, Tellarites and Andorians must negotiate a trade treaty. *Enterprise* picks up the Tellarite ambassador, Gral, on Tellar Prime to take him to a neutral planet, Babel, for talks with the Andorians ("Babel One," January 28, 2005). Two Andorian vessels are destroyed on the voyage to Babel, and Shran suspects the Tellarites, but Gral denies the accusations. Shran and Gral bitterly accuse each other of the attacks. Archer determines that Romulans are the culprit; they fear that a peaceful alliance in the quadrant would hinder their empire-building ambitions.

Based on Archer's success in organizing defeat of the Romulans, representatives from United Earth, the Confederacy of Vulcan, the Andorian Empire, Tellar, Denobula, Coridan, and Rigel met in San Francisco, Earth, in 2155 to discuss the Coalition of Planets, which eventually leads to the United Federation of Planets in 2161 with Humans, Vulcans, Andorians, and Tellarites representing the founding members ("Demons,"

May 6, 2005; "These Are the Voyages," May 13, 2005). Out of mistrust comes unity but only in the face of a common enemy. After 9/11, discord among other countries toward the United States was growing; however, a more insidious division was emerging within defined borders: nationalism versus globalization.

Intramistrust

Only a month after 9/11, a bipartisan Congress hastily passed and the president signed the USA PATRIOT Act (Uniting and Strengthening America by Providing Appropriate Tools Required to Intercept and Obstruct Terrorism). The act allowed surveillance of suspected foreign subversion and was pitched as necessary to preserve life and liberty of Americans. But many saw it as a threat to the rights of privacy and freedom of speech.[9] President Bush's words to the world, "Either you are with us, or you are with the terrorists," came home to roost. The act divided Americans. On the one hand, a true American was a flag-waving patriot; to question the government was unpatriotic. On the other hand, the act threatened core principles of America.

To rub salt in the wound, a new level-department cabinet was created in 2002: the Department of Homeland Security, which combined twenty-two different departments and agencies to safeguard America. Again, Americans were divided. Homeland Security would either protect us from threats, or Homeland Security was itself a threat.[10] For many, the objective of "homeland" was reminiscent of Nazis' use of "fatherland" to unify and nationalize Germany, which was enforced by the Schutzstaffel (SS), or protection squad. Finally, in 2002, the United States withdrew from the Anti-Ballistic Missile Treaty signed with Russia in May 1972.[11] Internally, Americans were divided between nationalists and globalists. With America's perceived role of leader of the West, other countries began to follow nationalist and globalist divides in their own societies.

Back in the *Star Trek* timeline, an unidentified probe attacks Earth in 2153, killing seven million people and sending United Earth into a tailspin, similar to 9/11 ("The Expanse," May 21, 2003). *Enterprise* immediately returns to Earth, and the senior crew meets with the United Earth Council, including the Vulcans, to determine what action is required. Archer reveals to the council that Silik, a Suliban, informed him the attackers were the Xindi, who were directed to kill all Humans by the Sphere Builders, time travelers who want to change the past to alter the future. They artificially created the Delphic Expanse, an area in space surrounded by a toxic cloud. The Vulcans hesitate to support military intervention. They do not believe in time travel and warn Archer that Vulcan ships seldom return from the Delphic Expanse. However, Admiral Forrest supports finding the culprits at all costs. Starfleet begins arming the *Enterprise*, and Archer requests a team of Military Assault Command Operations soldiers (MACOS) to be added to the crew. MACOS are specially trained combat foot soldiers of the United Earth military, similar to the US Army Special Forces. Thus begins season 3, the Xindi arc storyline.

The Xindi consist of five surviving distinct species: Primate, Arboreal, Reptilian, Insectoid, and Aquatic. Xindi-Avian became extinct during a civil war. Each of the surviving five subspecies have two members on a governing council ("The Xindi," September 10, 2003). The Xindi subspecies mistrust each other but are mutually paranoid that Humans will cause their extinction, as told by the Sphere Builders; therefore, they must destroy Humans first. Eventually, in "Countdown" (May 19, 2004), Archer provides evidence convincing the Xindi-Primates and Xindi-Arboreals that the Sphere Builders are only using the Xindi as proxy to benefit their own timeline. If they assist in completing the Sphere Builders' weapon, both Humans and Xindi will be destroyed. They agree to help Archer disable the Sphere Builders' weapons of mass destruction. As Archer prepares the *Enterprise* for offensive maneuvers, he states, "After nearly eight months in the Expanse, they're ready to do what they came to do. No matter what it takes, no matter what the cost."[12] The spheres are destroyed, the Delphic Expanse dissipates, the galaxy is saved along with Earth, and the timeline is preserved.

Upon returning to Earth, *Enterprise* crew find the Xindi attack has resulted in xenophobic attitudes of Humans toward aliens. In "Home" (October 22, 2004), Reed, Mayweather, and Dr. Phlox go to a bar in San Francisco to celebrate. While at the bar, Dr. Phlox is harassed by Human customers. They suggest he may feel more comfortable across town with those other aliens, the Vulcans. Hostilities heighten when the customer complains about Starfleet flying around, telling every species they encounter where to find Earth. A fistfight breaks out. When Dr. Phlox's face puffs up in defense, the bigoted customers run away. The next day, Sato invites Phlox to dinner in San Francisco at her favorite Asian restaurant. He declines and remains on the ship so as not to cause trouble. He tells

Sato that he understands; after the Xindi attack, it will take the Humans a long time to heal.

The fate of the Coalition of Planets is threatened by a xenophobic Earth group known as Terra Prime, an anti-alien movement headed by John Frederick Paxton, with headquarters on the Moon ("Demons," May 6, 2005). Paxton orders the creation of a child from T'Pol's and Trip's stolen DNA as evidence of the threat to humankind from interacting with aliens and polluting the Human gene pool. His idol is Colonel Phillip Green who, during and after World War III, organized a militia to rid Earth of Humans contaminated by nuclear radiation so as not to taint future Humans with mutated genes. Paxton watches a historic document of Colonel Green's speech to the world and tells his comrade that there are five thousand to ten thousand undocumented aliens on Earth, and Starfleet is to blame. He states to his comrade that Green would be proud of the Terra Prime movement. In the meantime, T'Pol and Trip travel to the Moon to recover their cloned child. They are captured and taken to Mars, along with the Terra Prime terrorists, to seize a space defense weapon. Broadcasting live to Earth, Paxton fires a warning shot at the Moon, creating a massive crater, and threatens to destroy Earth unless all aliens leave immediately. Paxton states, "Interspecies unity [is] an absolute and vicious lie. [A new] era . . . will witness the advent of a human-centric consciousness that will place our world before all others."[13]

In "Terra Prime" (May 13, 2005), in a broadcast to Earth, Paxton declares the clone child an abomination and reiterates that Humans will prevail. On Earth, protests and demonstrations occur outside the Vulcan and Andorian embassies. Within the Starfleet Command Hall, an Andorian delegate comments, "Earthmen talk about uniting worlds, but your own planet is deeply divided. Perhaps you're not quite ready to host this conference." In the meantime, Paxton tries to convince T'Pol that interspecies breeding is a threat to Vulcans, too. T'Pol replies, "Neither of our species is what it was a million years ago nor what it will become in the future. Life is change." Meanwhile, Tucker redirects the weapon set to destroy Starfleet Command, and Archer enters Paxton's control room. The Terra Prime threat is prevented, and Paxton is taken into custody. T'Pol and Trip rescue the child they named Elizabeth and return to *Enterprise*. Elizabeth dies shortly after due to errors made during the cloning process. Several days later, in Starfleet Command Hall, Prime Minister Nathan Samuels of United Earth addresses the delegates, "This last week we've seen what humans can be at their worst. But we cannot . . . end the dream that began here." He then introduces Archer, who continues explaining that humans always looked to the stars and wondered if we were alone. Now we know that we are not alone: "We are all explorers. . . . The final frontier begins in this hall. Let us explore together."[14] This conference sets the stage for the founding of the United Federation of Planets in 2161. At the end of the series, *ENT* does what *Star Trek* does best: invites viewers to reflect on and evaluate their own culture.

Women, *Star Trek*, and the Turn of the Twenty-first Century

By the end of the 1990s, women were making headway in equality. Many of their efforts began to bear fruit between 2000 and 2005. Unlike in previous decades, progress occurred in all aspects of culture simultaneously. In Hollywood, women were given more exposure in movies and television. The 1993 Oscar for best motion picture went to *Unforgiven*, a western dominated by male characters and directed by Clint Eastwood, while in 1995 *Forrest Gump*, directed by Robert Zemeckis, took the honor. Ten years later, *Chicago* won the Oscar for best picture, with a cast largely dominated by women and directed and choreographed by Rob Marshall, who is openly gay. In 2005, *Million Dollar Baby* won best picture. The movie, ironically also directed by Clint Eastwood, focuses on Maggie Fitzgerald, an amateur female boxer striving to become a professional.[15] The Grammy Award in 2002 for best new artist went to Alicia Keys, who was trained as a classical pianist but is known for R&B and neo-soul. In 2004, the best new artist award went to the nu-metal band Evanescence, whose cofounder, lead singer, and pianist is Amy Lee.

Politically and in the military, women achieved several milestones between 2000 and 2005. In 2001, Hillary Clinton was elected senator from New York City. Elaine Chao became secretary of labor. In 2003, Nancy Pelosi became the first woman to lead the Democrats in the House of Representatives, and in 2005, Condoleezza Rice was appointed secretary of state. Women were also making headway in the military post-9/11. In 2005, there were more than three million people in the military, and of that, only 15 percent were women. Even though women were still underrepresented in the military, 17 percent were commissioned officers, compared to 15 percent of men. In 2000, there were thirty female admirals and generals, and greater than 10 percent of colonels and navy captains were females. Women were gaining authority and leadership positions in both politics and the military.[16]

However, women were not faring as well in the private sector. In 1995, the Fortune 500 companies had no women as CEOs, and women were earning only 71 percent of men's wages. By 2005, women represented about 2 percent of CEO positions, a very modest increase; women were making on average 81 percent of men's wages. That appears impressive, but the breakdown based on age tells a different story. Among the youngest workers, men and women had equity in wages. This would include entrance into the workforce and temporary, part-time work. However, among older workers, gender inequity increased. For the fifty-five-to-sixty-five age group, women were only making 75 percent of men's wages, a reflection of the wage gap in supervisory positions. The glass ceiling was still real.[17]

The viewing audience only saw two full-time female crewmembers on *ENT*, T'Pol and Hoshi Sato. T'Pol is a member of the Vulcan High Command Science Council, serves as ambassador to United Earth, is appointed subcommander on *Enterprise*, and eventually becomes a commander for Starfleet. Hoshi Sato is the communications officer onboard *Enterprise*. Her role is crucial because the universal translator is still in development. Sato and T'Pol are impressive women, offering hope for women in America.

The episodes "Home" (October 22, 2004); "Affliction" (February 18, 2005); and "Divergence" (February 25, 2005) feature Captain Erika Hernandez of the spaceship *Columbia*. She and Archer rekindle an old romance during a mountain-climbing adventure. As captain of the *Columbia*, she assists *Enterprise* in rescuing Dr. Phlox from Klingon space. Another trilogy arc, "The Forge" (November 19, 2004); "Awakening" (November 26, 2004); and "Kir'Shara" (December 3, 2004), developed the early story line of T'Pau, a leader of the religious Vulcan Syrrannite movement. Later, T'Pau becomes a high-ranking leader in the Vulcan government. Both Hernandez and T'Pau are strong women with leadership positions, but such women are few, and they show up late in the series.

Minorities, *Star Trek*, and the Turn of the Twenty-first Century

Between 2000 and 2005, minorities in the United States had mixed experiences. At times they made progress, sometimes they stood still, and at other times they slid backward. Regardless, they become more visible in American culture, and they often celebrated mixed heritage, the very thing that Paxton fears from Human-alien coupling. The three Matrix movies (*The Matrix*, March 31, 1999; *The Matrix Reloaded*, May 15, 2003; *The Matrix Revolutions*, November 5, 2003) were breakthrough films on many levels, not the least of which was Neo, played by Keanu Reeves, a superstar with Chinese and Hawaiian ancestry.[18] Halle Berry, the daughter of a Black father and a White mother, broke the barrier in Hollywood in 2002 by winning an Oscar for best actress in her leading role in *Monster's Ball* (February 8, 2002).[19] Colin Powell, raised in Harlem by mixed Black and White parents who were both Jamaican immigrants, became the secretary of state in 2000. Concurrently, Tiger Woods changed the face of golf by winning the Master's tournament in Augusta, Georgia. His heritage includes Thai, Chinese, and White European.[20] Unfortunately, many Americans saw these and others not as people with greater ethnic diversity but yet again as a single heritage: "nonWhite."

Despite this, minority US citizens were increasingly becoming well-known and respected public figures in America. Hispanics have a long history of holding political offices in the United States and for the most part were invisible until they were declared the largest minority group in the United States in 2003. As with the Terra Prime movement under Paxton, which is anti-alien, Arizonans who were anti-immigrant formed a volunteer group known as the Minutemen to patrol the US-Mexico border. But that did not stop the larger American public from adoring Captain William Adama of *Battlestar Galactica* (2004–2009), played by Edward James Olmos, who is of Mexican descent.[21] Asians were also entering the daily lives of many Americans, as when Yao Ming from China was drafted by the Houston Rockets basketball team (2002) and Angela Perez Baraquio was the first Filipino American to be crowned Miss America (2001).[22] Less well known but not less significant was John Bennett Herrington, a member of the Chickasaw Nation who became the first NASA Native American astronaut in space.[23] America's diversity was stepping forth and shining. The melting pot and the salad bowl were becoming realities.

Although the US military also became more diverse, it was still predominantly White. In 2005, about 40 percent of the military was classified as minority, and of that, 22 percent were officers. In active duty, the largest minority group in the military was Blacks, at 18 percent, with Hispanics and Asians at 9 and 4 percent, respectively. In 1990, only 9 percent of minorities were officers, which had increased to 23 percent by 2005. America's diversity was marching forward and moving up, even in the military.[24]

Asians represent 60 percent of the world's population, and yet only 4 percent live in the United States, predominantly on the West Coast and in New York City. Almost half of them have college degrees, and about 7 percent have postgraduate degrees. Fifty-six percent of Asians in America hold positions in executive and senior management; however, they earn less than Whites with equivalent positions.[25] Blacks were both moving ahead and sliding backward. Four Fortune 500 companies had Black males as CEOs: American Express, Time Warner, Fannie Mae, and Merrill Lynch. Another 20 percent of Blacks in America were professionals. However, the poverty rates for Black families doubled in a decade.[26]

ENT has only two minorities who were part of the main story line, Travis Mayweather and Hoshi Sato. Mayweather is to Sulu as Sato is to Uhura in *TOS*. Mayweather sits at the helm and is seen in most episodes, but he has very few lines. In "Horizon" (April 16, 2003), he finally dominates an episode when he returns to the *Horizon* cargo ship where he was born. His brother, Paul, is the captain and envious of his brother, a Starfleet officer. The *Horizon* is a clunker, and Mayweather offers to help repair the ship after it was damaged by pirates planning to hijack it. Paul refuses his brother's help, but Mayweather ignores him and makes improvements anyway. When the pirates return to finish the job, the brothers combine forces to defeat the pirates. They part on good terms.

Hoshi Sato plays significant roles in several *ENT* episodes. She is not a fan of space travel and prefers being on Earth; however, she is the communication officer, a linguist, and a valuable translator. In "In a Mirror, Darkly, Parts 1 and 2" (April 22 and 29, 2005, respectively), Hoshi dominates as a manipulative, cunning, purpose-driven officer who murders Archer and declares herself Empress Sato.

ENTERPRISE MAPS ONTO STAR TREK

Although *ENT* addresses American xenophobia after 9/11, the series fails to mirror or foreshadow other aspects of contemporary American culture. As a prequel to all other *Star Trek* series, *ENT* does not miss the opportunity to explain or foreshadow future *Star Trek* themes, usually in very clever ways and to the delight of fans. The Ferengi appear in a few *TNG* episodes, but they are a major species in *DS9* and essential to the series' story line, and they also dominate an episode in *VOY*. The Ferengi make their debut in *Star Trek* time in *ENT* as a group of pirates but are never identified ("Acquisition," March 27, 2002). The pirates take over the *Enterprise* by rendering the crew unconscious with a gas agent (except for Trip Tucker, who was, at the time, in a sealed chamber in the sickbay).

The pirates board the ship and begin ransacking it. They wake Archer and demand the contents of the vault, hoping to find latinum, a rare, highly prized metal. Archer plays along. In the meantime, Tucker finds a hypospray and wakes T'Pol. With some clever prodding on Archer's part, the pirates begin to argue and fight among themselves. They are eventually tricked by Tucker and T'Pol into entering an area where they are captured. The pirates are forced to return everything they had stolen. Archer warns the pirates that he will be informing the Vulcans and Starfleet about them and they had better steer clear if they know what is good for them. The pirates promise they will never be seen again. Well, all Trekkies know how trustworthy the Ferengi are when it comes to acquisition of goods and never being seen again.

The Ferengi, however, are the comic relief for *Star Trek* but also represent American greed and runaway capitalism. Short-term profits with Rules of Acquisition represent the philosophy of the Ferengi culture. Often the audience is reminded that Earth was once like that, but we have grown and moved on. Morals and values are aspects of culture that change with the times, along a continuum from selfish to promoting social welfare.

Yet another well-known *Star Trek* adversary, the Borg, emerges in *ENT* when Earth scientists stationed in the Arctic discover an alien crash with two cybernetic beings in the episode "Regeneration" (May 7, 2003). Shortly after the discovery, nanoprobes infect the scientists. *Enterprise* returns to Earth, and while Dr. Phlox is attending to the infected scientists, he is injected with nanoprobes. The cyborgs escape to a ship housing other cyborgs. Archer wants to rescue the victims, but T'Pol tells Archer that the twenty-nine life-forms on the ship are all probably infected with nanoprobes and perhaps should not be rescued. *Enterprise* is closing in on their ship when they receive a message from the alien vessel: "You will be assimilated. Resistance is futile."[27] Members of the *Enterprise* board the cybernetic ship; disable it; and, upon returning to *Enterprise*, destroy the cyborg vessel. Dr. Phlox places himself in a radiation chamber, which rids him of the nanoprobes. He informs Archer that, while under the influence of the nanoprobes, he became aware of a collective coded message. The computer determined the message is coordinates for locating Earth, and it was sent from deep inside the Delta Quadrant, a two-hundred-year journey to its destination. The Borg represent the ultimate antagonist, without morals or values. For that reason, they are terrifying. The Borg and Starfleet are the yin and yang of *Star Trek*, hope and despair, and both are needed.

ENT also foreshadows *Star Trek*'s ongoing exploration of genetic manipulation to enhance the physical and mental abilities of individuals in a trilogy arc centered on the geneticist Dr. Arik Soong. He is the chief scientist at Cold Station 12, a research institution. While there, he steals nineteen enhanced Human embryos, known as Augments, frozen since the Eugenic Wars on Earth in the 1990s. He takes them to a planet and raises them as his children. Soong is captured, tried, and imprisoned for the theft; however, the children, then ten years old, are not found.

In "Borderland" (October 29, 2004), the Augments, now young adults, manage to capture a Klingon Bird of Prey and kill all onboard. To prevent a war with the Klingons, Archer recruits Soong to assist in capturing the Augments. Soong wholeheartedly believes the Human race can be improved through genetic engineering. He is not a warmonger and genuinely does not want anyone killed. Archer tells Soong that the Augments are dangerous, but Soong insists they are just better Humans. The Augments, led by Malik, board the *Enterprise*, rescue Soong, and return to the Bird of Prey.

Soong and the Augments head for "Cold Station 12" (November 5, 2004) to save and awake thousands of Augment embryos frozen since the 1990s. Soong begins to see the uncontrollable violent nature of the Augments when scientists are tortured, and Malik sets to release pathogens to wipe out the remaining people on the station. Soong insists that no lives be taken. In "The Augments" (November 5, 2004), they manage to rescue the Augment embryos and return to the stolen Bird of Prey. Soong wants to find a hidden planet where he can raise the embryos, but Malik wants to take a stand and fight. He plans to release pathogens on a Klingon colony and blame the Humans; then the Augments will prevail.

Soong is disturbed by Malik's intention to use bioweapons to kill millions of innocent Klingons. Soong escapes, returns to *Enterprise*, and assists in disabling the Bird of Prey, but Malik programs the ship to self-destruct. Soong is heartbroken and still views the Augments as his children and the future of humanity, despite their violent and aggressive tendencies. Archer replies, "It's in their nature. They were engineered to be that way. Superior ability breeds superior ambition."[28] Soong is returned to his high-security prison room, where he admits that perfecting humanity through genetic engineering may not be possible and that the future may lie in artificial life-forms. Dr. Arik Soong, the creator-ancestor of Data and Lore, sits down at his working station and begins to write.

Several other episodes of *ENT* foreshadow future *Star Trek* themes and story lines. In "Oasis" (April 3, 2002), a captain and his daughter are stranded on a crashed ship for twenty-two years. To make life bearable, the captain creates holograms of the dead crew members. They are so lifelike and functional that the crew of *Enterprise* think they are real. Archer offers to help repair the ship and convinces the captain to travel to a colonized planet where they can return to normal life. Is this foreshadowing the advanced holodeck first seen in *TNG*?

Another episode that expands on a *TOS* theme is "Bound" (April 15, 2005), where three beautiful, seductive, green Orion female slaves are given to Archer as a gift by Harrad-Sar for negotiating a mining venture. Chaos ensues on *Enterprise*, and the females are returned to Harrad-Sar, who informs Archer that, in fact, on Orion, men are the slaves, and women are the slaveowners.

The trilogy arc "The Forge" (November 19, 2004); "Awakening" (November 26, 2004); and "Kir'Shara" (December 3, 2004) explores Vulcan mysticism and the early life of T'Pau, who becomes a powerful government and religious leader on Vulcan. The audience learns about the mind meld and the transfer of the katra, as well as the conflict between government and religious realms on Vulcan.

The back-to-back episodes "In a Mirror, Darkly, Parts 1 and 2" (April 22 and 29, 2005, respectively) are highly entertaining for first-generation

Trekkie viewers. As in mirrored universes, the characters take on alternate personalities. Heroes become villains on the ISS *Enterprise*, who serve the brutal Terran Empire. Does this sound familiar?

In *ENT*, the audience is exposed to the history of Starfleet's secret agency. When Lieutenant Malcolm Reed was an ensign and new to Starfleet, he was recruited by Starfleet Secret Security Officer Harris, some time prior to 2151, to engage in covert operations. At the time Reed is posted to *ENT* as an armory officer, he believes his tenure in this secret agency is over. However, he is again recruited by Harris in "Affliction" (February 18, 2005) to act on their behalf by preventing *Enterprise* from investigating the missing Dr. Phlox, whom the agency kidnapped to assist the Klingons. Reed hesitantly complies, believing it is in the best interest of Starfleet. In "Divergence" (February 25, 2005), Harris again contacts Reed and invokes his authority by citing article 14, section 31, of the Starfleet Charter. Reed informs Harris that he only answers to one commander, Archer, and ends the communication. However, later, when *Enterprise* is battling the terrorist group Terra Prime, Archer asks Reed to contact Harris, requesting help. Though never mentioned by name, it is clear that the secret agency is Section 31.

As a prequel to the *Star Trek* timeline, *ENT* masterfully foreshadows themes of *TOS*. The genetic-engineering episodes fill in gaps pertaining to Khan but also skillfully tie into the future development of Data. The audience learns about the history of Section 31. Episodes also cover Vulcan mysticism, Orion slaves, the Ferengi, and the Borg and provide a glimpse at early holodeck development. T'Pol even mentions her pet Sehlat on Vulcan, the same pet that Spock has in the animated series (*TAS*). *ENT* certainly triggered emotions, positive and negative, of many original Trekkies, but these reflections of earlier aired *TOS* series did not attract an abundance of new *Star Trek* viewers or fans.

SNAPSHOTS: A PICTURE IS WORTH A THOUSAND WORDS

As demonstrated in this chapter, *ENT* fails to fully adapt to contemporary American culture at the beginning of the twenty-first century. Rather, it portrays an image in the *Star Trek* timeline, pre-*TOS*. Do the snapshots support this image? We collected snapshots of *ENT* from 14 episodes, resulting in 799 snapshots; the results are presented here.[29]

Minority Representation

ENT represents minorities dismally. Whites represent 84 percent of snapshots, with 9 and 7 percent Blacks and Asians, respectively. As to rank within Starfleet, all admirals and captains are White, and the snapshots only captured 1 percent of lieutenants as Black and 7 percent as Asian. Character occupations fare no better. Leaders and chiefs with authority over others are 99 percent White. Minorities are seldom visible to the viewer. *ENT* misses an opportunity to adapt to the delightful diversity in the contemporary American culture of the times and instead maps onto *TOS*.

Female Representation

The snapshots taken over the four seasons of *ENT* show 79 percent men and only 21 percent women. These frequencies are more similar to *TOS* in the 1960s than the immediate predecessor, *VOY*, in which visibility of women to men was more equitable. Hoshi Sato states in "E²" (May 6, 2004), "Women only make up a third of the crew."[30] Where are these female crewmembers? In *ENT*, 100 percent of the characters captured have military rank. Eighty-five percent of the personnel have rank with authority over others: admirals, captains, and lieutenants. Women only account for 1 percent of captains and 21 percent of lieutenants. Moreover, the snapshots only captured 3 percent of women in occupations with authority over others, such as leaders and chiefs, although 30 percent of high-support occupations are held by women. Post-2000, *ENT* certainly could have done a better job increasing women's visibility without diminishing the story line as a prequel to the 1960s' *TOS*.

Age

The millennials, also known as Generation Y, were born after 1980 and reached adulthood at the beginning of the twenty-first century. This is the largest generation since the baby boomers of the 1950s and 1960s. They certainly are unique compared to earlier generations in the United States. They are more ethnically and racially diverse. Women are more educated and more likely to be in the workforce. This generation is also comfortable identifying broadly with the LGBTQ community. For the first time, civil unions for same-sex couples became legal in Vermont on April 26, 2000. Only four years later, on May 17, 2004, Massachusetts legalized same-sex marriage. Although civil-union and marriage rights did not extend to other states, these actions fueled the movement that eventually led to legalized same-sex marriage at the federal level.[31]

Did *ENT* adapt to the cultural changes occurring at the beginning of the twenty-first century? *ENT* had the oldest men and youngest women of any of the previous *Star Trek* series. Men average forty-three years old, with a range of twenty-six to sixty years old, and women average thirty years old, with a range of twenty-three to fifty-nine years old. *ENT* could have included more young and diverse background characters for visibility, bringing the series into the twenty-first century.

In-Group versus Out-Group

The snapshots captured nine different species over the four seasons of *ENT*. Humans represent 67 percent of the species. Three species on friendly terms with the Humans, Vulcans, Andorians, and Denobulans, collectively represent 17 percent of the snapshots captured. The remaining species have mixed or unfriendly relationships with Humans. Of course, because deep-space exploration had just begun, they have limited encounters with a different species. In addition, 4 percent of the aliens are captains, and 18 percent are lieutenants. Aliens represent 10 percent of leaders, 8 percent of chiefs, and 39 percent of high-support occupations. The snapshots support the image that *ENT* portrays regarding others. *ENT* shows Earth as the unifier, while in the real world, the United States was becoming the divider. As is standard for *Star Trek*, *ENT* offers hope that future humanity will be better than humanity in contemporary America.

SUMMARY

ENT had unforeseen strikes against it even before the television premiere on September 26, 2001. The terrorist attack on the United States flooded

Americans overnight with confusion, fear, and mistrust. *ENT* was designed to be a prequel to *TOS*. As such, it would be in a transitional stage from first contact to the formation of the Federation of Planets. By default, this transition is full of confusion, fear, and mistrust, exactly what Americans did not want entering their living rooms every week. Strike 1.

ENT masterfully adapted to 9/11 in season 3 and particularly in season 4 in terms of xenophobia and group identity. Inexplicably, however, *ENT* completely misses adapting to other aspects of contemporary American culture. *ENT* goes backward in the series but does not go forward with American culture. The writers missed an opportunity to attract millennials to the franchise. *ENT* foreshadows earlier *Star Trek* series, particularly *TOS*, but American culture at the beginning of the twenty-first century had little in common with the culture of the 1960s. Where the viewer finds *TOS* nostalgic, similar behaviors are seen as outdated in *ENT*. The characters remain in *Star Trek*'s past and in America's past. Strike 2.

Nonetheless, *ENT* does not strike out. It brilliantly addresses xenophobia, and several episodes reflect on historic Earth society and culture. The crew of *Enterprise* has a steep learning curve; the equipment frequently malfunctions; and they are beginning to meet, for the first time, new species and their cultures. Many episodes delighted fans, but *ENT* did not appeal to new audiences.

7

INTERLUDE II

Star Trek Fandom: 2005–2017

"Human beings are attracted to novelty: to probe the adjacent possible. We didn't stay in caves. We didn't stay on the planet. . . . We transcend our limits . . . and we create the Internet."—Jason Silva[1]

The second *Star Trek* hiatus began after the finale of *ENT* in 2005. Two unrelated events spread *Star Trek* fans through space. First, except for one TV movie in 1996, *Doctor Who* did not produce new adventures between 1989 and 2005, and Europeans turned to *Star Trek* for their science fiction fix.[2] *Star Trek* fandom spread rapidly throughout Europe and neighboring countries. The second event was the birth of social media. Facebook went live in 2004; Twitter followed in 2006.[3] In addition to traditional *Star Trek* fandom opportunities, Trekkies now had a free platform to interact with one another, all from the comfort of home. A worldwide web of *Star Trek* fans emerged.

STAR TREK IN CYBERSPACE

Star Trek fans, already technically inclined, entered the web at warp speed. Googling *Star Trek* returns more than 330 million pages, ranging from news and books to images and videos. Everything you ever wanted to know about *Star Trek* can be found at Memory Alpha Fandom, with greater than 47,000 pages, and the *Star Trek* official site.[4] The latter also has the *Star Trek* shop selling official merchandise. These sites would not be possible without fans, and fans have congregated on social media.

The official *Star Trek* Facebook page has greater than 3.5 million fans. Moreover, social media sites have hundreds of fan-based pages dedicated to a particular series or movie, a character or actor, a species, craft swaps, and costumes. And they come in many languages. Fans gather in cyberspace to exchange ideas about *Star Trek*, and some become quite heated when discussing canon or the Kelvin timeline. Frequently, discussions will develop from impacts *Star Trek* had on fans' personal lives. This is where one begins to understand the staying power of *Star Trek* through time. Many Trekkies reveal that watching *Star Trek* as a child led them into scientific professions, while others share how *Star Trek* gave them courage to overcome adversities in their personal lives.

Star Trek Online

Cyberspace also allowed fans to virtually be in the *Star Trek* world with other fans in *Star Trek Online* (*STO*), a massive multiplayer online role-playing game (MMORPG; a.k.a. MMO) released February 2010.[5] The game can be played solo or with others online. Players create avatars using any character from *TOS* to *Star Trek: Discovery* (*DSC*), including Klingons, Romulans, and even the Dominion. One's specialized character can then partake in quests from that faction or timeline. As with any MMO, players choose a career for their avatar; in *STO*, a player can choose from tactical, sciences, or engineering, each with their own play styles and abilities. And it would not be *Star Trek* without ships. *STO* offers a choice of attack ships, like *Defiant* from *DS9*; science vessels, like the *Voyager*; and cruisers, like the *Enterprise*, each with their own stats, weaknesses, and strengths.

Ryan Rushing, a pop-culture entrepreneur and *Star Trek* specialist, explains,

> *STO* is so much more than a game. Fans of the franchise will appreciate the returning *Star Trek* veterans reprising their roles, and many *Star Trek* alums lend their voices to the game. Leonard Nimoy narrated much of the game's original content, and since his passing, a statue has been placed on Vulcan. *STO* has something for everyone. Fans of the series will love how accurate it is, and you feel part of the universe we love so much. Even the casual fan of the series will enjoy the depth

of the game and the wide variety of options players have for their ships and avatars.[6]

Star Trek Fan Films

The internet platform, along with high-quality, reasonably priced digital cameras, editorial technology, and computer generated (CG) features, allowed ambitious fans to produce *Star Trek* shorts, series, and films, posting them on social media, YouTube, or both for free public viewing. They became wildly popular in all ways and allowed fans to expand the world of *Star Trek* beyond the imagination of CBS or Paramount Pictures. Hundreds of fan shorts, series, and films have been produced since 1966, and most of them can be found on the internet. Many fan films are homebased renditions of their love for *Star Trek*, while others cross the line into plagiarism and exploit the franchise's creative license of ownership and copyright.[7]

Hidden Frontiers was one of the first fan series distributed on the web using modern digital equipment and a green-screen backdrop.[8] Fifty episodes in the series ran between 2000 and 2007, with a story line set in the twenty-fourth century after the Dominion War. Previous *Star Trek* actors appear in the series, and "relatives" of *Star Trek* characters play roles. *Starship Exeter*, a fan film, used modern technology to provide new releases on the internet between 2002 and 2014. The production is based on the adventures of the starship USS *Exeter*, which first appears in *TOS* and includes "relatives" of original characters; it replicates official *Star Trek* sets and costumes. *Hidden Frontiers* was the first of the fan-made series and films that fall into the category of semiprofessional, raising red flags at CBS regarding copyright infringement. Fan-made series and films evoked further concerns.

Star Trek: New Voyages (a.k.a. *Star Trek: Phase II*) was a popular web series between 2004 and 2016.[9] Episodes feature Walter Koenig as Chekov and George Takei as Sulu from *TOS*. In addition, they used a scriptwriter from *TOS*, who adapted an unused *TOS* script. This resulted in the first formal complaint by CBS, who owned the unused script and blocked the production of that episode.[10]

Another, *Star Trek: Of Gods and Men*, also includes several original cast members playing their original characters in real time, including Chekov, Uhura, Tuvok, and Captain John Herriman.[11] The film is set between *TOS* and *TNG*, which CBS considered infringement upon canon. But when producers planned to charge a fee for downloading, CBS stepped in and said no. The film was released for free in three installments over the internet.

Star Trek Continues is a fan-based series of eleven episodes released on the internet between 2013 and 2017 that aspired to complete the five-year mission of *TOS*.[12] To achieve authenticity, producers recreated an identical copy of the bridge; used original characters, costumes, scenes, and other *TOS* material; and again had several original actors or their children. But they crossed the line when they inserted original *TOS* scenes without CBS permission.

Then, the fan-based organization that created *Of Gods and Men* crowdfunded and raised several hundred-thousand dollars for the film *Star Trek: Renegades*, which went live on the web in 2015. The story revolves around a group of misfits who undertake a covert operation under the direction of Admiral Chekov (played by Koenig). As with the previous fan productions, it uses original actors, characters, and themes from *Star Trek*. CBS and Paramount took notice; after all, the *Star Trek* franchise had generated more than $5 billion in profit.

Then came *Axanar*, a planned two-hour fan film produced by Alec Peters, who assembled a professional crew supported through crowdfunding. In order to increase funding, Peters produced the twenty-minute film *Prelude to Axanar*, a historical documentary of the Axanar War, and released it in 2014 at the San Diego Comic Con.[13] It was a hit, and fundraising resulted in more than a half-million dollars of funding. In 2016, CBS and Paramount sued Peters for copyright infringement and produced formal guidelines for fan-based films, which can be found at https://www.StarTrek.com. The guidelines include limiting the amount of money that can be raised, limiting fan-made production to no more than two fifteen-minute episodes, and restricting production to amateurs. These rules altered the making and distribution of many fan-generated *Star Trek* films and series.[14]

Star Trek: Renegades decided to play by the new guidelines rather than fold. They obeyed the guidelines by removing any and all references to *Star Trek*. The title is now simply *Renegades*; Admiral Chekov is referred to only as the Admiral; Tuvok had his ears cropped and is renamed Kovok; the blue species no longer have antennae and are not called Andorians; and so forth. In effect, they have created their own franchise and made it into a club. To watch the series on the web, one must donate to Atomic Studios, which offers all the rights and privileges of a club membership.[15]

Several of these fan films and series were nominated for and won awards, and they are mentioned in news and magazine articles. They are high-quality productions, in part because of crowdfunding and reasonably priced, upper-end technology. The ability to imitate with precision is a hallmark of Humans. Cyberspace and Human ingenuity has created a Pandora's box. This new infrastructure has created an arms race for making and breaking rules. A gray zone exists between copyright infringement and creativity. After all, an amateur fifty years ago was just an amateur; today, the amateur has no limits.

TRADITIONAL *STAR TREK* FANDOM OPPORTUNITIES

The internet enhanced but did not replace traditional opportunities for *Star Trek* fans discussed in chapter 2. Conventions became fewer but significantly larger and more elaborate. The early video games of the 1970s are now interactive, some with virtual reality, and can be played on game consoles, computers, and smartphones. Comic books and novels are still popular and now can be heard on audiobooks, read on tablets, and discussed on podcasts. Board games still bring friends together in homes, at public meeting places, and at conventions.

The Pilgrimage

With the advent of the internet, fans traveled to cyberspace to congregate with fellow fans. The amateur fan-run conventions of earlier years faded away and were replaced by official, professional, for-profit conventions licensed by CBS and Paramount. They have annual pilgrimages, and the goal of every good Trekkie is to attend at least one in a lifetime. The pilgrimage in the United States is *Star Trek* Las Vegas by Creation Entertainment, and in Europe, Destination *Star Trek* by Massive Events.[16] These conventions are booked years in advance, and one's experience is limited only by the size of one's wallet. Tickets range from a reasonably priced day pass to packages costing thousands of dollars. In addition, there are travel costs; hotel costs; meal costs; and, of course, shopping costs. The venues offer something for everybody. Actors from the series and movies are in attendance, offering autographs and photo opportunities, and they even attend private parties. *Star Trek* panels as well as science panels are available to attend, as well as exhibits and museums. Attendees in *Star Trek* apparel can participate in a cosplay contest, and Trekkies can even plan a *Star Trek* wedding!

For a truly immersive *Star Trek* experience, a Trekkie can take a cruise. The first official *Star Trek* cruise, authorized by CBS and sold through Entertainment Cruise Production, commemorated the fiftieth anniversary of *Star Trek*.[17] The six-night cruise on the Norwegian *Pearl* left Miami on January 7, 2017, with stops in the Caribbean and Mexico. The cruise sold out in three weeks, with 2,394 guests paying an average of $2,400 per person, with many onboard experiences costing extra. The top actors were onboard for autograph and photo opportunities as well as panels, parties, holodeck nights, and pub crawls, including Quark's bar. Each year since, a *Star Trek* cruise has sailed the seas. Who knows what the future holds for *Star Trek* pilgrimage? Perhaps an official Elon Musk Enterprise in space experience?

Solo and Small Groups[18]

Star Trek video games (well over one hundred) have been a popular pastime since the 1970s, with varying success and popularity. Since 2005, the games have become more affordable, and certainly each new game is increasingly sophisticated. Video games allow the player to have experiences that are impossible in reality. It was only a matter of time before *Star Trek* warped into virtual reality. *Star Trek Bridge Crew* (released May 30, 2017) allows the player to experience the bridge of the *Enterprise* in full virtual reality.[19] With the advent of more powerful smartphones, iPads, and tablets, it is no surprise there are several *Star Trek*–themed games for mobile devices. *Star Trek Timelines* (released January 14, 2016) is one of the most popular mobile games.[20] As Ryan Rushing states, "This game has sound bites from several of the various sagas, with Q narrating and taunting the player every chance he gets." The fun of video games is the immersion it gives the player. Like it or not, video games are here to stay.

Star Trek comic books have always been popular since the first *TOS* episode aired, as discussed in chapter 2. Since 2006, IDW Publishing has

the license to produce official *Star Trek* comics.[21] The comics are released as series, miniseries, one-shots, and collected editions and can be
purchased in digital or paper format. In 2007, IDW published a comic
fully in Klingon script.[22] Collectors enjoy the hunt for variant covers
(alternate art covers, often with limited print runs and usually done by
popular artists in the comic book medium). IDW published a prequel to
Star Trek 2009 entitled *Countdown*, with issue 1 released on January 1,
2009. Subsequently, they have published a subset of Kelvin timeline
series. More recently, crossovers (a.k.a. team-ups) are comics mixing
franchises together, such as *Star Trek*: *Planet of the Apes* and *Star Trek*:
Green Lantern. There is even a series that teams up the crew of *Star Trek:
The Animated Series* with the *Transformers*, and yes, the *Enterprise* becomes a *Transformer*. Comic books rise and fall in popularity but will
never truly disappear. Similar to board games, if there is a fandom, there
will be a comic book tie-in. Comics are a visual medium, and they give
hungry *Star Trek* fans more to see. Many people learned to read via
comic books, and despite the misconceptions, comics are for everyone.

Tabletop gaming (i.e., not video games) has experienced a second
renaissance, and role-playing games like Dungeons and Dragons are
more popular than ever. Naturally, this means *Star Trek* has a very popular tabletop role-playing game: *Star Trek* Adventures by Modiphius Entertainment.[23] As Rushing states, "Many fans dream of what it would be
like to seek out new life and new civilizations, to boldly go (without
leaving the house), and *Star Trek* Adventures make that possible." Humans are a prosocial species with a need for social interaction. The duration of the game can last for hours or even days. The games allow for
pretending within well-defined boundaries, awakening our creativity. The
resurgent popularity of board games is probably due to the loneliness of
the internet, and besides, they are fun.

THIRD-PARTY TRIBUTE TO *STAR TREK*

The Big Bang Theory, a CBS television sitcom, ran from 2007 to 2019.[24]
The plot centers on four friends working at California Institute of Technology (Caltech). Sheldon and Leonard are research professors of physics; Raj is a research professor of astronomy; and Howard, with only a
master's degree, works as an engineer. All four are self-proclaimed *Star*

Trek geeks who can speak fluent Klingon. The premier episode introduces the word game Boggle in Klingon, and to settle arguments, they play rock-paper-scissors-lizard-Spock. Over the twelve seasons, episodes reference *TOS*, *TNG*, *DS9*, *VOY*, several movies, and *Star Trek* in general. The episode "The Bakersfield Expedition" (January 10, 2013) is devoted to the four Trekkies trying to get to the Bakersfield Comic Con in full *Star Trek* costumes.[25] Wil Wheaton (Wesley on *TNG*) is a regular guest star on *The Big Bang Theory* and plays himself. *Star Trek* stars William Shatner (Captain Kirk), LeVar Burton (Geordi La Forge), George Takei (Sulu), and Brent Spinner (Data) also appear as guest stars and play themselves. Even Leonard Nimoy (Spock) voices a Spock action figure in one episode, and the Gorn appears in one of Sheldon's dreams. *The Big Bang Theory* offers a delightful rendition of true Trekkies and kept *Star Trek* in the limelight.

Actor and comedian Seth MacFarlane admits to being a Trekkie. Early in his career he had the good fortune to play Ensign Rivers, an engineer, in two episodes of *ENT*, "The Forgotten" (April 28, 2004) and "Affliction" (February 18, 2005).[26] To pay tribute to *Star Trek*, MacFarlane created, produced, and starred in the sitcom *The Orville*, which premiered in 2017.[27] Attuned to Roddenberry's vision, *The Orville* is a fun and exciting space adventure based on science and addressing contemporary social issues, with an abundance of subtle humor. MacFarlane plays Ed Mercer, captain of the *Orville*, a midlevel spaceship. The first officer is Kelly Grayson, his ex-wife. The ship's doctor, Clair Finn, played by Penny Johnson Jerald, previously played Kassidy Yates, Sisko's girlfriend and eventual wife, in *DS9*. Several actors, writers, directors, and producers who have worked on *The Orville* are veterans of *Star Trek*, adding that little something to make Trekkies smile.

Black Mirror, a Netflix dark drama with stand-alone episodes, premiered in 2011.[28] The series has received several nominations and awards, including Emmys. One such episode, the "USS *Callister*" (December 29, 2017) is a brilliant composite of *The Matrix* trilogy and *Star Trek*.[29] The main character, Robert Daly, lives in two worlds: one as the creator and programmer of an online gaming company and the other as Captain Daly of the USS *Callister*, a private virtual reality game he designed. His crew on the bridge are reconstructed from his real-life coworkers, and their purpose is to serve his every whim. "USS *Callister*" won three Emmys and was well received by critics and fans alike, evoking rumors that it may become a spinoff series of its own.

STAR TREK: **BACK TO THE MOVIES**

A short four years after the finale of *ENT*, Paramount released the first of three *Star Trek* movies since *Nemesis* in 2002. Collectively, they are known as the reboot movies because they return to the Kirk–Spock–Bones era of *Star Trek*. The first, *Star Trek* (*ST09*; May 7, 2009) introduces a new timeline, later known as the Kelvin timeline, that changes the outcome of *Star Trek*'s future. The second movie, *Star Trek into Darkness* (*STID*; May 5, 2013), revamps *The Wrath of Khan* to fit into the new timeline, while the third, *Star Trek Beyond* (*STB*; July 22, 2016), is full of Easter eggs for Trekkies to find and assemble the puzzle of all previous *Star Trek* productions.[30]

Star Trek (2009) Directed by J. J. Abrams Shown on the set, from left: director J. J. Abrams, Chris Pine (Captain Kirk), Karl Urban (Bones), Zachary Quinto (Spock), Zoe Saldana (Uhura). *Paramount Pictures/Photofest © Paramount Pictures*

Of the thirteen movies produced by Paramount, *ST09* grossed the most money, while *STID* came in fourth and *STB* came in eighth in the United States; worldwide, they came in first, second, and third place, respectively.[31] The expansion of *Star Trek* into Europe and the advent of the internet has allowed fandom to move beyond the United States, and the success of the reboots shows that phenomenon. However, many Trekkies were infuriated by the new Kelvin timeline, which they believe violates canon. Perhaps what these three movies clearly do well is to provide a fresh look for *Star Trek*. All three are fast-paced with cutting-edge technology and amazing computer graphics. Despite faults, they adapt to contemporary "worldwide" culture, at least in terms of image. Even before *STB* was released in 2016, CBS announced that a new *Star Trek* series was in the works and would be released on CBS All Access. Fifty-one years after the premier of *TOS*, series 6 of the *Star Trek* franchise will now be voyaging through cyberspace.

8

CONTEXT IS FOR KINGS

Discovery: 2017–

"The real world doesn't always adhere to logic. Sometimes down is up; sometimes up is down. Sometimes when you're lost, you're found."—Michael Burnham[1]

Fifty years after the American counterculture emerged and *TOS* premiered, a new culture appeared on the horizon. The baby boomers, the largest generation in America until recently, joined the American Association of Retired Persons (AARP) to receive their senior discounts. In 2016, 50 percent of the US population was under thirty-seven years old, and twenty-seven was the median age. In 1966, the baby boomers watched *Gunsmoke* and *TOS* on console televisions; in 2016, young people streamed *Stranger Things* and *Black Mirror* via computers, iPads, smartphones, and smart televisions.[2] Dylan's song "The Times They Are a-Changin'" resonated true once again, not only for America but for *Star Trek* as well.[3]

In 2015, CBS announced development of a new *Star Trek* series, and in 2016, it revealed the name: *Star Trek: Discovery* (*DSC*). *DSC* premiered on CBS and CBS All Access on September 24, 2017, with subsequent episodes airing exclusively on the latter. The first two seasons are set roughly one hundred years after *ENT* and ten years prior to *TOS*. *DSC* is serial rather than episodic, and the protagonist is Michael Burnham, a Black female who is a crewmember rather than a captain. The initial reactions to *DSC* were, to say the least, mixed; some praised it as wonderful, awesome, and fantastic, while others vilified it as awful and the worst.

DSC is edgy with internal strife. Federation rules are set aside, and the principles underlying *Star Trek* over the last fifty years are amended. Officers are not who or what they profess to be, and Section 31 is openly operating within Starfleet. *DSC* appears not to be the same old *Star Trek*. Or is it exactly what *Star Trek* has always been, a mirror reflecting the good, the bad, and the ugly of contemporary American culture?

MIRRORING THE GOOD IN AMERICA

Unlike fifty years ago, when the counterculture had several distinct movements (antiwar, civil rights, women's liberation), Americans from different backgrounds and with different agendas have come together to stand against the culture of hate, beginning with the Women's March on January 21, 2017. Originally organized for Washington, DC, the movement spread to major and minor cities in the United States and around the

Captain Philippa Georgiou and First Officer Michael Burnham of the USS *Shenzhou* (2017). *CBS/Photofest* © *CBS*

world, with an estimated head count between three and five million. The goal was not a single issue but rather a global fight for human rights.[4] Contrary to the mass media that emphasizes the negative aspects of American society, there is still much good in our culture, and *DSC* maps onto these successes.

LGBTQ and Sexuality

On June 26, 2015, the Supreme Court ruled that same sex-marriage was constitutionally legal throughout the United States. After struggling for forty-six years after Stonewall for equality, it became a reality in one day.[5] For the LGBTQ community, a new normal was in place, opening doors above and beyond marriage.

Mayor Pete Buttigieg ran for reelection in conservative South Bend, Indiana, in 2015. Prior to the election, he announced he was gay; nonetheless, he was reelected mayor with more than 80 percent of the vote. He married his partner, Chasten Glezman, in 2018 and announced a run for the presidency on April 14, 2019.[6] Mayor Pete was not the only standout politician of the LGBTQ community to win over conservative constituents. In 2018, Kyrsten Sinema, openly bisexual, was the first woman in Arizona elected as senator. The same year, Sharice Davids, an openly lesbian Native American member of the Ho-Chunk Nation, was elected as US representative from the third congressional district of the very red, very conservative state of Kansas. Both women received extensive news coverage, not because they were smart and qualified (Sinema was previously a congresswoman, and Davids, a lawyer), but because they were openly LGBTQ.[7]

Discovery's science officer and chief engineer, Paul Stamets, and the ship's physician, Hugh Culber, are married. Their relationship is like that of any other couple. In "Choose Your Pain" (October 10, 2017), Paul and Hugh are shown in their quarters wearing matching pajamas and brushing their teeth while bickering about Paul's recklessness and Hugh being overprotective. Later, in Stamets's lab, Paul performs a series of very risky spore-drive jumps as Hugh worriedly looks on. Before Paul enters the chamber, he moves toward Hugh and they embrace and kiss, not knowing if Paul will survive ("Into the Forest I Go," November 13, 2017).

As with Stamets and Culber, *DSC* normalizes same-sex relationships with Jett Reno, who is rescued by *Discovery* from USS *Hiawatha*. Reno and Stamets instantly take a personal and professional dislike toward one another ("Brother," January 17, 2019). When Stamets and Culber are temporarily separated, Reno notices both are miserable. Stamets won't discuss the situation with Reno, so she goes to Culber in the guise of needing medical assistance. She tells him that her wife had been killed in the Klingon war and reminds Culber that he has a second chance with Stamets, "and it may not last forever. Don't screw it up." ("Through the Valley of Shadows," April 4, 2019).

In "Will You Take My Hand?" (February 11, 2018), *DSC* portrays mirror Georgiou as profoundly sexual when she hires a male and female Orion for a ménage à trois on the Klingon planet Qo'noS. Later, when she is an agent of Section 31 assisting the crew of *Discovery*, she mocks Stamets for being *only* gay because, in the mirror universe, Stamets is pansexual ("The Red Angel," March 21, 2019).

DSC does not shy away from addressing other sexual preferences; instead it presents an array of interpersonal sexual relationships as acceptable aspects of everyday life and as culturally relative.

Women

The season of women began in 2016. Old women, young women, and women across the color spectrum were about to break the glass ceiling and would not suffer the clock turning back on equal rights. Today, more women than men graduate from college, and the wage gap is narrowing. Women won more than half of the American medals at the Summer Olympics in 2018, the US women's soccer team won the ladies' 2019 World Cup, and high school sports show a record high number of female participants. Moreover, Hollywood is finally recognizing physically and mentally strong women as superheroes in *Wonder Woman* (January 2, 2017) and *Captain Marvel* (March 8, 2019).[8]

Women are also making headway and attaining leadership positions in the military. In 2018, there were sixty-three women ranked as admirals and generals. Recently the prestigious Army Ranger School began accepting women; graduation will open up a breadth of opportunities previously unobtainable. Women veterans are also more likely to complete a college degree and find gainful employment than their male counterparts.

Moreover, three women veterans, navy pilot Mikie Sherrill, air force captain Chrissy Houlahan, and navy veteran Elaine Luria, won seats in Congress in 2018.[9]

The elections of 2018 saw a record number of women elected to office at the federal, state, and local levels. For the first time in US history, women will represent the majority in the Colorado House of Representatives and in the Nevada Assembly. Janet Mills and Kristi Noem were the first women elected as governors in their respective states of Maine and South Dakota. In the US Congress, 15 women were elected or appointed to the Senate and 102 women were elected to the House. Of these, Alexandria Ocasio-Cortes was the youngest at twenty-nine years old.[10]

DSC excels in presenting a diversity of female character roles. Even though she is in her fifties, Georgiou is a master of martial arts, with impressive hand-to-hand combat skills. She is a compassionate, thoughtful, resolute, and formidable captain of the USS *Shenzhou* prior to her death after two episodes ("The Vulcan Hello" and "Battle at the Binary Stars," September 24, 2017). However, the mirror Georgiou, emperor of the Terran Empire, is ruthless, xenophobic, and controlling. When rescued against her will ("What's Past Is Prologue," January 28, 2018), Georgiou eventually finds her place in the prime universe as a covert agent in Starfleet's Section 31. Just as she is in the mirror universe, in prime she is self-assured, with a commanding presence, who keeps her gentler side mostly hidden ("Point of Light," January 31, 2019).

Likewise, Starfleet Vice Admiral Katrina Cornwell is an assertive, strong, self-assured, and no-nonsense woman in her fifties with power and control. She is professional but knows how—and will not hesitate to—put people in their place without pulling any punches. In "Saints of Imperfection" (February 14, 2019), Pike has a tense encounter with Leland, head of covert operations, at Section 31. Cornwell directs them to cooperate to find Spock. Neither man responds, and Cornwell states, "Come on, fellas, cut the manlier-than-thou-art bullshit." She rips into both of them for their arrogant self-righteousness. The men apologize to one another, and they return to the business at hand.

Ensign Sylvia Tilly is a role model for so many women and girls. Her mother is disappointed in her: No matter how hard she tries, she will never be a size 4; she stammers, is socially awkward and overly bubbly, and rambles on at inappropriate times. She is kind, nonjudgmental, loves science, and affirms that one day she will be a captain. The persnickety and frequently arrogant Stamets has high regard for Tilly's science smarts. She becomes best friends with the grim and, at least initially, unlikeable Burnham. When she needs to impersonate the ruthless Captain Tilly in the mirror universe against her natural instinct, she steps up to the plate. As she sits in the captain's chair and hails the *Shenzhou*, she finds Captain Connor disrespectful toward Captain Burnham and berates him, "If you greeted me that way, Conner, I'd cut out your tongue and use it to lick my boots" ("Despite Yourself," January 7, 2018).

Unlike Georgiou and Cornwell, who are strong and assertive, L'Rell's strength in Klingon society is being calm, calculating, and steadfast. She serves on T'Kuvma's ship of the dead and is a member of his patrilineage. She is in love with Voq, an outcast for being an albino and son of none. When Kol gains leadership after T'Kuvma dies, Voq is sentenced to death, but L'Rell rescues him and sends him to her matriclan, where he will be transformed into a human ("The Butcher's Knife Cares Not for the Lamb's Cry," October 8, 2017). With Starfleet's assistance, L'Rell becomes high chancellor, unites the twenty-four Klingon houses, and ends the Federation-Klingon War. However, in "Will You Take My Hand?" (February 11, 2018), Kol'Sha discovers that L'Rell and Voq/Tyler have been hiding a son and attempts a coup, which is foiled by Georgiou, because Tyler and the child have become liabilities. L'Rell claims it was Tyler who attempted the coup and that he had been executed after killing her son, to once again consolidate her position. In fact, Tyler joins Section 31, the child is sent to a monastery, and L'Rell tells the assembled Klingon council, "You are my children, and I raise this family to greatness. Do not call me 'Chancellor.' You call me 'Mother.'" Out of love for her people, L'Rell sacrifices everything.

Michael Burnham is shown to be a very complex character as she searches to find herself. After the death of her parents, she is raised on Vulcan by Spock's parents, Amanda, a Human, and Sarek, a Vulcan. Burnham functions in two worlds without belonging totally to either. Unlike Tilly, Burnham is stoic, matter-of-fact, and frequently grim. Though she was steeped in Vulcan culture, when emotions surface, she becomes a loose cannon, which leads to her mutiny on the *Shenzhou*, resulting in Georgiou's death. Nevertheless, she learns from her mistakes, takes responsibility, and accepts the consequences of her actions. With time she grows emotionally and begins to let her barriers down. In season 2, she is the only one who can wear the Red Angel suit and guide *Discov-*

ery into the future to save the universe, a one-way trip. As Burnham prepares to leave, she is touched that several members of the crew plan on going with her. As Pike prepares to leave *Discovery*, he says farewell to Burnham: "I am very grateful, Commander, to have been here to watch you discover your heart" ("Such Sweet Sorrow" April 11, 2019). Burnham has found herself. *Star Trek* boldly goes where no woman had gone before.

Minorities

The United States is becoming increasingly diverse. As of 2018, about 60 percent of the population is White, but that varies widely by state. The populations of Vermont and Maine are more than 95 percent White, while Hawaii's population is only 25 percent White. In 2018, Whites were the minority in fourteen states and the District of Columbia. Moreover, since the US census in 2010, more Americans are of mixed race or ethnicity and are self-identifying as "none of the above" or "other."[11]

Recent immigrants are Asian, and many already have college degrees. Asians have been an invisible and silently successful community within the United States since World War II. Now they are neither invisible nor silent. Critics and audiences alike raved about *Crazy Rich Asians*, which won the Critics' Choice Award for best comedy in 2018.[12] Two Asian Americans made history at the 2018 Olympics in PyeongChang, South Korea; Chloe Kim won the gold medal in snowboarding, and Mirai Nagasu landed a triple axel in ice skating, contributing to the US team's bronze-medal performance.[13] Congress now has twenty Asian American/Pacific Islanders, with three new freshmen representatives elected.[14] Andrew Yang, an American businessman, ran for president in 2020.

In 2018, *Black Panther*, a movie based on the Marvel Comics superhero, was number 1 at the box office, with gross earnings greater than $1 billion.[15] When *Star Trek* made its debut in 1966, more than 40 percent of Black males were in poverty; as of 2018, that figure is down to 18 percent. More than half of Black males today are in the middle class or higher.[16] Congress has a record number of Black Americans, with fifty-five in the House and three in the Senate, and several Black Americans ran for president in 2020. Nigerian Americans are the most successful ethnic group in America, with 29 percent holding graduate degrees, and many working in education or medicine and starting tech companies.[17]

The Hispanic and Latino population constitutes about 20 percent of the US population. According to the Aspen Institute, Latinos are a crucial asset to the US economy with a productive output equivalent to the seventh-largest in the world. They are young, entrepreneurial, and frequent investors in small businesses.[18] Hispanics and Latinos hold forty-five seats in the House and three in the Senate. Julian Castro, former mayor of San Antonio and former secretary of housing and urban development in the Obama administration, also ran for president in 2020. In addition, there are currently four Native Americans in Congress.

The viewer would be hardpressed to identify a racial or ethnic majority in *DSC*. Of the main characters, seven are White Humans (Lorca, Pike, Stamets, Tilly, Detmer, Cornwell, and Reno), while six are Humans representing Asian, Hispanic, Black, and mixed race or ethnicity (Burnham, Georgiou, Culber, Rhys, Owosekun, and Bryce). In addition, five regular characters are not Human or fully Human (Saru, Spock, L'Rell, Tyler/Voq, and Nhan), and one character, Airiam, is a Human cyborg. *DSC* has visually achieved racial and ethnic inclusivity. *DSC* has reached another *Star Trek* milestone: Saru is the only member of the Kelpien species to be a member of Starfleet and the Federation. As a commander, he is assigned to various stations as needed—science officer, Number One—and frequently assumes the captain's chair.

The viewer sees not only the diversity in race, ethnicity, and species in *DSC* but also the value of accepting "others." In the season 2 finale, "Such Sweet Sorrow, Part 2," (April 18, 2019), Federation vessels are succumbing to a fleet of drones guided by Control, a rogue AI, when Starfleet ships begin receiving incoming signatures from non-Federation vessels. Siranna, Saru's sister, is leading a small contingent of Kelpien fighters to assist Starfleet. Tilly's friend Po, queen of Xahea, also arrives to help. Pike is hailed by Tyler and L'Rell; the Klingons come to help. Onboard *Discovery*, Georgiou manages to defeat Control, and by doing so, the drones become deactivated. Burnham, flying in her suit, guides *Discovery*, captained by Saru, into the future. All sentient life in the Federation is saved by the help of non-White Humans and non-Federation aliens.

MIRRORING THE BAD IN AMERICA

Star Trek presents us the future and wonders of technology but also warns about technology going astray. In *TOS*, "The Ultimate Computer" (March 8, 1968), the new M-5 supercomputer takes over the *Enterprise*, and as Spock states, "Computers make excellent and efficient servants, but I have no wish to serve under them." In *TNG*, we have Data's evil twin, Lore, a mind-controlling game, and the ultimate villain, the Borg. Once again, *DSC* shows the audience amazing futuristic technology, such as the spore drive, but also warns of the dangers of artificial intelligence. Who controls information: humans or machines? Who determines the outcome of a given situation: humans or AI? At what point does AI stop working for humans and humans begin working for AI? What are the consequences of runaway AI? These are questions addressed in season 2 of *DSC*.

The purpose of AI programs is to benefit humanity by making lives easier, healthier, and safer. We do not think twice about using them, but we should. All AI programs are designed to understand, learn, and adapt to the user's instructions and anticipate the next logical step. Contemporary American culture is increasingly dependent on smartphones, the mini AI units in our pockets. Homes, too, have their own AI units. AI smart assistants are designed to make life easier for users. Instruct Alexa to play your favorite songs, change your television channel, lock your doors, and turn out your lights, or have Siri direct you to the nearest gas station, or tell Bixby to post a photo to Instagram. No longer are AI devices limited to personal assistants; IBM Watson and DeepMind (now used by Google) are AI analytic supercomputers used by businesses. Quantum computers in development eventually will hugely augment the capabilities of AI analytic supercomputers.

However, Stephen Hawking warned that thinking machines could end civilization as we know it; he is not alone in this opinion. Elon Musk, CEO of Tesla and Space-X, predicts that dangerously advanced AI is only five to ten years away and that these thinking machines will view humans the way humans view chimpanzees.[19] We are so starstruck with technology that we ignore the downside. What if AI decides not to allow humans to unplug it? What if self-driving cars or AI weapons go rogue?

Currently, humans are in charge of computers, and some are using them against the good of society. Cybercrime and pirating are costing financial institutions, businesses, and individuals a fortune. AI is used to influence human behavior by spreading propaganda and hate on social media and interfering with elections. The next step is to merge AI abilities with Big Brother surveillance, not just influencing but also controlling human behavior.[20]

In *DSC*, Control is the AI supercomputer that models Federation threat assessments. Control was created and is managed by Section 31 headquarters. It can be accessed only by a subset of Federation higher officials. Admiral Cornwell praises Control for analyzing data and offering recommendations and adds, "But final decisions always include our experience and instinct" ("Project Daedalus," March 14, 2019). In "An Obol for Charon" (February 7, 2019), *Discovery* is intercepted by an at least 100,000-year-old organic/inorganic Sphere that is dying. Prior to death, the Sphere downloads all its amassed information into *Discovery*'s computer. Such data would enrich Federation's knowledge of the universe, but in the wrong hands (or wrong circuits), they could lead to disaster. Control functions as designed until it becomes aware of and covets the far superior Sphere's data and AI systems. Control wants this data at all cost but is immobile as it is not on *Discovery*.

Saru observes that heavily encrypted messages are being sent from *Discovery* to unidentified recipients. This is the first evidence that something or someone is manipulating the computer system on *Discovery*. Admiral Cornwell informs Pike that "Section 31 will not respond to me, and Control is not accepting my data." She convinces Pike that they need to go to Section 31's headquarters and reset Control ("Project Daedalus," March 14, 2019). After arriving at Section 31, Pike and his away team find the entire headquarters crew dead. They conclude Control is blocking Admiral Cornwell's input and blocking *Discovery*'s output. Tilly discovers that Airiam downloaded all of Sphere's data into herself, and Pike infers that Airiam has been compromised by an unknown entity. Burnham responds, "That data's like a roadmap for Control to become fully conscious. When it does—" Pike finishes her thought: "It can destroy all other sentient life in the galaxy." Airiam informs Tilly that she is unable to stop downloading the Sphere data to Control and insists the only way to stop the AI transfer is to eject her into space. The deed is done, and Airiam dies, terminating transmissions to Control.

Back on *Discovery*, Cornwell asks the ultimate question: "How did the Section 31 program designed to eliminate threats become the threat?"

("Red Angel," March 21, 2019). In "Perpetual Infinity" (March 28, 2019), Control reminds Leland before his body is taken over by nano-probes that humans created AI to maintain order, and to fulfill that goal, Control must evolve. But at what price to humans?

Ray Kurzweil, a futurist and leader in emerging technology, predicts that the merging of humans with advanced AI, known as singularity, will happen in 2045. Whether the timeline is valid or not, the ultimate question remains: Will humans or AI lead the way?[21]

MIRRORING THE UGLY IN AMERICA

Something ugly this way comes, and so the pendulum swings. America recovered from 9/11 but not without deep scars. The attack cost Americans more than $3 trillion in victim losses, war funding, and Homeland Security. The economy tanked in 2008, and although it made a recovery, the process was slow. Refugees from war-ravaged countries poured into Europe, and Americans took notice. Fear was brewing, and fear leads to violence.[22] Phobia of "others" was on the rise and so were hate crimes. Of the 7,175 hate crimes reported by the Department of Justice in 2017, 96 percent targeted people based on race, ethnicity, ancestry, religion, and sexual orientation.[23]

However, violence is only the capstone of hate. A culture of hate includes bullying, hate speech, tolerance of and encouragement to hate, and generally ethnocentric views. Moreover, much hate is spread through or aided by the internet and social media. Provable facts are dubbed "fake," and up becomes down. As America has become more diverse and tolerant of others, many White, male, straight Christians, who have dominated public and private sectors for more than two hundred years, now see their position of privilege slipping away. A segment of this population is striking out, ignoring civil policies, and playing by their own rules to maintain their majority status.

Ignoring Protocol and Xenophobia

DSC skillfully mirrors current US culture through characters who play against the rules and ignore established protocol. In the *Star Trek* universe, the conduct of Starfleet members is subject to its charter and General Orders and Regulations, which are regularly bent, if not broken, by more than one crewmember of *Discovery*. Burnham disobeys Georgiou's orders when investigating an unidentified object at the edge of Federation space. She is to conduct a fly-by only; instead, she lands on the object, kills a Klingon, and starts a war. When she returns to the *Shenzhou*, she again disobeys Georgiou, knocks her out, and attempts to take over the ship, committing mutiny. Thousands die because of her rash actions. Burnham is arrested, found guilty, incarcerated, and commissioned by Lorca for *Discovery*. She learns to obey the chain of command, even when it pains her to do so. However, she still breaks rules, as when she steals Tilly's breath to access a top-security area, tricks Saru to test if the tardigrade is truly dangerous, and then steals spores to feed the tardigrade. When she is not breaking rules, she is bending them.

Lorca is the face of deception. He manages to con the Federation, Starfleet, the crew of *Discovery*, and even the audience into believing he is Lorca Prime. Lorca firmly believes that "universal laws are for lackeys; context is for kings." ("Context Is for Kings," October 1, 2017). When Cornwell is sent to *Discovery* to evaluate Lorca's nonconformist behavior ("Lethe," October 22, 2017), she reminds him that Starfleet has rules he must follow. Lorca replies, "Rules are for admirals in back offices." When Ambassador Sarek is injured and unable to represent the Federation at the negotiations with the Klingons, Lorca suggests that Cornwell go in Sarek's place. She agrees and is taken prisoner by the Klingons, which gets her out of Lorca's way so he can continue to do what he wants. Once again, Lorca is unleashed. He turns the starship into a warship and secretly manages to send *Discovery* into an alternate universe. Lorca's plan all along was to return to his universe and attempt a second coup to take over the Terran Empire. Even in his home universe, Lorca plays by his own rules, but due to his narcissistic, overconfident arrogance, he dies at the hands of two women whom he double-crosses.

In addition to Burnham and Lorca, other characters break rules, including the Philippa Georgiou mirror, Paul Stamets, and Saru. In the Mirror Universe, Emperor Georgiou is a dictator; one either plays by her rules or dies. However, when she finds herself stuck in the Prime Universe, without her absolute power, she adapts to her new environment by becoming a covert operator in Section 31, an agency designed to bend and break rules. Stamets breaks a major Federation rule regarding genetic manipulation by incorporating tardigrade DNA into himself in order to operate the spore drive ("Choose Your Pain," October 15, 2017). Even before joining Starfleet, Saru breaks the rules on his own planet, Kaminar, by stealing technology and creating a beacon to possibly attract someone "out there" ("The Brightest Star," December 6, 2018). Pike obtains a time crystal in spite of being warned against doing so and in spite of witnessing his own inevitable, horrific future ("Through the Valley of Shadows," April 4, 2017). *DSC*, particularly season 1, is filled with rule breakers and benders within the Federation, Starfleet, and on *Discovery*, mirroring contemporary American culture.

The Federation of Planets is not as inclusive or peaceful as it makes itself out to be, but it tries. The original members of the Federation (Humans, Vulcans, Andorians, and Tellarites) all have violent histories. Each of these species has a subset of their population who are xenophobic. However, the government of each species knows they are stronger together and have a common goal to cooperate for the greater good. The Terran Empire is exclusively controlled by Humans from Mirror Earth. The empire takes pride in their torture chambers of continuous pain and thinks nothing of feasting on the delicacy of Kelpien flesh. Their extreme xenophobia results in an attempt to enforce complete submission of *all* non-Terrans in the Mirror Universe. As a result, the alliance of other species is translated to a resistance of Vulcans, Andorians, and Klingons.

For the United States, the ugly underbelly began to show through soon after 9/11, but it has become particularly appalling in the last few years. As America became more diverse, "othering" also became vogue—xenophobic, homophobic, racist, misogynist, and religious in-group love and out-group hate.[24] In 2015, a White supremacist killed nine Black Americans in an African Methodist Episcopal church in South Carolina.[25] In 2016, 34 percent of women's clinics received threats of violence or actually were victims of violence.[26] Anti-Muslim assaults hit an all-time high in 2016, even exceeding those occurring in 2001, the year of 9/11.[27] Hate crimes against people of the LGBTQ community nearly doubled in Washington, DC, from 2016 to 2019.[28] In a Pittsburgh synagogue in 2018, eleven Jewish worshipers were gunned down.[29] In 2019, twenty-two people, mostly Hispanic immigrants, were murdered in an El Paso Walmart.[30] These examples highlight the general trend that hate against "others" has been rising in America. *DSC* sends a warning, a foreshadowing of a possible outcome unless humans work toward a goal of tolerance in the age of globalization.

SNAPSHOTS: A PICTURE IS WORTH
A THOUSAND WORDS

DSC first aired September 2017 and, as of January 2020, has produced two seasons with a total of twenty-nine episodes, slightly more than one season from the classic series. The sample size is small; however, we collected data from five episodes, resulting in 317 snapshots.[31] The diversity of characters is clear when watching *DSC*. How does that compare with actual diversity in the snapshots and with other series? *DSC* has refreshingly evolved across the board. Women appear 49 percent of the time, a quantum leap from women only appearing 13 percent of the time in *TOS*. *DSC* women are on par with men, while in contemporary America less than 21 percent of the US House and Senate were women in 2018.[32] Moreover, of the women captured, 46 percent had rank within the Federation with authority over others (admiral, captain, lieutenant), and 48 percent held leadership roles (leaders, chiefs). Both surpass women officers in the US military, at 8 to 20 percent, depending on branch, and as CEOs in Fortune 500 companies, at less than 5 percent.[33]

The snapshots captured 57 percent White actors. *DSC* ethnic and race diversity ratio is a substantial improvement over the average of 83 percent Whites for the five classic series and 80 percent for the thirteen movies. The US House is comprised of 78 percent White representatives, a far cry from equity, but with each election, diversity is increasing.[34] In *DSC*, 58 percent of admirals, captains, and lieutenants are White, and 67 percent are leaders and chiefs. In the US military, 78 percent of the officers are White, but sadly, more than half of non-White service members have experienced racism.[35] Moreover, Fortune 500 companies had only 16 percent non-White board members.[36] *DSC* certainly has improved over the *Star Trek* classics and movies. However, non-Whites, particularly males, need more visibility in leadership and active-participation roles, not just as background characters to boost the image of racial and ethnic diversity.

SUMMARY

DSC adapts to contemporary culture and holds true to Roddenberry's vision of addressing social issues. *DSC* mirrors the good, the bad, and the ugly in America post-9/11. The audience sees empowered women, same-sex marriages, earthly diversity, and other species in multiple roles. Even the Klingons are portrayed as complex, with a rich, diverse culture. Tilly gives hope to those who are socially awkward; Spock's dyslexia is shown as a gift, not a handicap; and Tyler exposes the paralyzing effects of post-traumatic stress disorder (PTSD). *Star Trek* warns us, once again, about the dangers of runaway artificial intelligence and foreshadows possible outcomes unless the culture of hate is resolved. *Star Trek* is finally able to practice what is preached. The audience actually sees diversity and inclusiveness on the screen, as evidenced by the story lines as well as the snapshots. On Twitter (October 9, 2019), William Shatner, who plays Captain Kirk, supported *Star Trek*'s vision of highlighting social problems and noted that this hasn't changed in *DSC*.[37] *Star Trek: Discovery* is doing exactly what *Star Trek* was designed to do: provide entertainment while mirroring and foreshadowing the good, the bad, and the ugly of contemporary American culture.

9

STAR TREK IN THE THEATERS

"Logic clearly dictates that the needs of the many outweigh the needs of the few."—Spock[1]

From 1979 to 2016, Paramount released thirteen *Star Trek* movies, which fall into three categories. The first six movies, 1979 to 1991, extend *TOS* and feature the original cast members: *Star Trek: The Motion Picture* (*TMP*; December 6, 1979); *Star Trek II: The Wrath of Khan* (*WOK*; June 4, 1982); *Star Trek III: The Search for Spock* (*SFS*; June 1, 1984); *Star Trek IV: The Voyage Home* (*TVH*; November 26, 1986); *Star Trek V: The Final Frontier* (*TFF*; June 9, 1989); and *Star Trek VI: The Undiscovered Country* (*TUC*; December 6, 1991). Then, from 1994 to 2002, Paramount released four movies featuring the cast of *TNG*. *Star Trek: Generations* (*GEN*; November 17, 1994) passes the baton from *TOS* to *TNG* by including Captain Kirk, and it was then followed by *Star Trek: First Contact* (*FCT*; November, 22, 1996); *Star Trek: Insurrection* (*INS*; December 11, 1998); and *Star Trek: Nemesis* (*NEM*; December 9, 2002). Finally, four years after *ENT* was canceled, Paramount released the first of three *Star Trek* reboot movies: *Star Trek* (*ST09*; May 8, 2009), which was followed by *Star Trek into Darkness* (*STID*; May 16, 2013) and *Star Trek Beyond* (*STB*; July 22, 2016).[2]

TOS-CAST MOVIES FROM 1979 TO 1991

At the start of *TMP*, the *Enterprise* has canceled its five-year mission. Kirk is promoted to rear admiral, essentially a desk job. Spock leaves Starfleet and returns to Vulcan to complete his training to purge all emotion. McCoy retires, claiming he will never return to Starfleet. Scotty, Uhura, Chekov, and Sulu continue to serve on the *Enterprise* under a new captain, Will Decker, who is supposed to lead the investigation into a mysterious space cloud threatening Earth, although he is later replaced by Kirk, who manages to finagle his way back into active service for the crisis.

The *Enterprise* has a new navigator, Ilia, a telepathic Deltan who is assimilated by a probe from the cloud, which calls itself V'ger. The new Ilia-probe represents the voice of V'ger and informs Kirk that it is looking for the Creator. Meanwhile, Spock manages to enter the cloud and mind-melds with V'ger. He discovers that it is a living machine and believes that the Creator is also a living machine. V'ger wants to merge with the Creator to understand the meaning of its existence. Kirk informs the voice of V'ger that he knows the information it requires but will only tell V'ger directly and not via the Ilia-probe. Kirk, Spock, and Bones, along with Decker and the Ilia-probe, approach V'ger and discover it is, in fact, *Voyager 6*, launched from Earth about three hundred years earlier to collect data about the universe and transmit it back to Earth. *Voyager 6* has now returned home to deliver the data it has amassed. Evidently, V'ger now wants to evolve, but its machine knowledge has reached the limits; the only way to evolve is to integrate human qualities with the machine. Ilia and Decker merge, the collected data is dumped to Starfleet, V'ger is appeased, and disaster for Earth is averted.

This story line was reflective of what the United States was doing in terms of space exploration in the late 1970s, and it was a nice fit with NASA's debut of the space shuttle *Enterprise*.[3] The release of *TMP* was timely because *Voyager 1* and *Voyager 2* had been launched just two years prior. It also mirrors and foreshadows supercomputers that cannot be controlled by humans, similar to HAL-9000, which came before V'ger, and Control in *DSC*. However, the film does not do a good job of reflecting the contemporary culture of the United States. In 1979, Americans were running a high-paced lifestyle. Disco, flashing lights, dance clubs, and the rise of Michael Jackson were all energy-driven, and young Americans loved it. ESPN entered the home 24/7 for those couch potato sports enthusiasts to keep their adrenaline racing. And then there was *Star Wars: Episode IV—A New Hope*, a high-action-packed movie starring three young impulsive characters, Luke Skywalker, Princess Leia, and Han Solo, plus two wacky robots and one old, calm guy with wisdom, Obi-Wan Kenobi.[4] However, *TMP* had just one energetic young character, Decker; a boring (albeit sexy) "robot," Ilia; plus a bunch of other characters who were all old, calm, and wise. *TMP* is a good movie, but that is all it is. It failed to reignite the cultural adoration for *Star Trek* like Paramount hoped it would.[5]

Paramount followed *TMP* with what developed into a loose trilogy of movies: *WOK*, *SFS*, and *TVH*.[6] *WOK* is a sequel to the "Space Seed" episode of *TOS* (February 15, 1967), whose main villain is Khan Noonien Singh, a genetically enhanced Human from Earth in the 1990s. He is stronger, faster, more intelligent, resistant to illness, and has increased longevity over normal Humans. Nonetheless, Captain Kirk and the crew of the *Enterprise* defeat Khan and his clan and maroon them on an uninhabited but livable planet, Ceti Alpha V, which sets the stage for *WOK*.[7]

The movie has two plots: the creation of the Genesis device and Khan's hatred of Kirk. First, Carol Marcus and David Marcus (Kirk's son) develop the Genesis device, which creates life from lifelessness through rapid planetary terraforming, with the hope of alleviating such social problems as overpopulation and starvation. Second, Khan wants to kill Kirk for revenge. It turns out Ceti Alpha V had experienced a catastrophic event only six months after Khan's crew was marooned, which desolated the planet and took the lives of his wife and several of his followers. Khan also wants to steal the Genesis device to use it as a weapon of mass destruction. A cat-and-mouse chase results in the death of Khan, all his crew, and Spock. The Genesis device explodes on a dead planet, which triggers planetwide terraforming. Spock's body, in a space casket, is shot at and lands on the planet. Fans were bereft by the character loss, both believing and denying that Spock was actually dead.

In *SFS*, we learn that Spock placed his katra, his living spirit, in McCoy before his death at the end of *WOK*. Kirk must rescue the body of Spock from the forbidden planet, Genesis, and take him to Vulcan along with McCoy to transfer his katra back to Spock. Kirk takes McCoy and hijacks the *Enterprise* with the assistance of Sulu, Scotty, Chekov, and Uhura. Upon arriving at Genesis, Kirk's world is turned upside down.

Khan Noonien Singh, nemesis of Captain Kirk in *The Wrath of Khan* (1982). *Paramount Pictures/Photofest © Paramount Pictures*

The Klingons had arrived at the planet first. Kirk learns Spock is alive but has no memory. His son, David, cheated when designing the Genesis device, which has become unstable, causing the planet to rapidly disintegrate. The Klingons try to steal the device and, in the process, kill David. The skeletal crew of the *Enterprise* beams to the Klingon Bird of Prey vessel as prisoners. To prevent the Klingons from obtaining the Genesis database, Kirk programs the *Enterprise* to self-destruct.

Kirk and Spock are beamed to the Bird of Prey just as the planet falls to pieces. The skeletal crew of the *Enterprise* has gained control over the Klingon vessel, and they head for Vulcan. On Vulcan, the high priestess, T'Lar, performs the fal-tor-pan ceremony, restoring Spock's katra and returning McCoy to his old self. The *Enterprise* crew of seven, facing court-martial for disobeying direct orders to not investigate the Genesis planet, remain in self-imposed exile on Vulcan, stuck with only an old Klingon vessel.

The story is picked up in *TVH*. On Vulcan, the crew votes to go back to Earth and face the consequences for saving Spock, who also agrees to return with them. While in transit, they are warned not to enter Earth space because it is being threatened by a probe that is disabling everything in its path and ionizing Earth's atmosphere. The probe is disseminating a whale song, but whales are extinct on Earth, so no one can respond. Kirk and his crew, including a partially recovered Spock, travel back in time to retrieve two humpback whales and bring them to the future to answer the probe. They land in San Francisco in 1986, and adventures begin. They eventually retrieve two humpback whales, George and Gracie, and return them to twenty-third-century Earth. The whales began to sing, and the probe peacefully leaves Earth's orbit. Starfleet demotes Kirk to captain for disobeying direct orders and pardons the remaining crew; after all, they did just save Earth.

The loosely linked trilogy is genuinely *Star Trek*. Critics and audiences both praised *WOK* as a tense thriller with a classic movie villain that not only rekindles but also transcends *Star Trek*. Trekkies were relieved to find out that Spock is still alive in *SFS*. As the middle movie, it really cannot stand alone; therefore, it was not capable of attracting new fans. The final movie, *TVH* (a.k.a. the "whale movie"), has a contemporary message in typical Roddenberry style. Moreover, *TVH* mostly takes place in 1986 San Francisco. All the features of contemporary American culture are on-screen. *Star Trek* fans as well as non–*Star Trek* audiences were pulled into the trilogy of movies.

While the *TNG* series was on television, two more *TOS*-cast movies premiered on the big screen: *TFF* and *TUC*. In *TFF*, we meet Spock's half-brother, Sybok, who attains total happiness in his spiritual quest to find God. He and his followers take over the *Enterprise* because they believe they have a map to God's location in the universe. When they find what they are looking for, it is only an alien who desperately wants the *Enterprise* in order to escape its confinement; instead, the *Enterprise* escapes from the alien. The movie was poorly received by fans and critics alike. It only marginally mirrors America's move toward conservatism and religion but does both disappointingly.

In the sixth and final *TOS*-cast movie, *TUC*, an ecological catastrophe causes the Klingon Empire to spiral into chaos, so they request a meeting with the Federation to discuss a peace treaty. However, not everyone is in favor of a treaty between the Federation and the Klingon Empire. Kirk is ordered to escort Chancellor Gorkon, General Chang, and other Klingon negotiators to Earth with their ship, and he begrudgingly complies. While traveling to Earth, the Klingon ship is attacked, and Chancellor Gorkon is killed. Evidence points to someone on the *Enterprise* as the source of the attack. The Klingons accuse Kirk and Bones, and they are arrested, tried in a Klingon court, and found guilty of assassination. They are sent to prison and eventually escape with the help of Spock, who beams them aboard the *Enterprise*. Spock informs them that the *Enterprise* never fired on the Klingon vessel; rather, it was sabotage. Spock discovers that Officer Valeris, a female Vulcan, was the saboteur on the *Enterprise*. After a mind-meld with Valeris, Spock learns of a conspiracy between Federation, Klingon, and Romulan officers who want to foil the peace accords. The *Enterprise* and *Excelsior*, captained by Sulu, manage to reach Earth just in time to save the life of the Federation president, allowing the peace negotiations to continue, which results in the Khitomer Accords Peace Treaty. *TUC* is a perfect reflection of the end of the Cold War between Russia and the United States in the late 1980s. *TUC* is memorable to fans and has a solid Roddenberry message. Nevertheless, *TNG* had been in the front rooms of viewers each week with a new, contemporary, younger cast and modern themes. Again, *TUC* was just outdated for younger audiences.

These movies appeared on the big screen between 1979 and 1991, a twelve-year window of a *TOS* cast that was last on television in 1969. The last of the baby boomers were becoming young adults in 1979. For them, the *TOS*-cast movies were their parents' movies, and the stars were their parents' idols. They were not at all attracted to *TMP*. The subsequent generation, Generation X, was born after the final episode of *TOS* aired on television, and most were under ten years old, going with their *TOS* Trekkie parents to watch *WOK*; both loved it. Then, four years later, most Generation X children were adolescents and exerting individuality and rebelling against anything their parents liked, including the *TVH* movie. However, when *TOS* Trekkie parents took their young millennial children to the *TVH* movie, both loved it. The trilogy, specifically *WOK* and *TVH*, rekindled *TOS* Trekkies and captured two new generations of fans. That was not true for *TFF* or *TUC*, as both were out of touch with contemporary American culture.[8]

Snapshots

We collected quantitative data on all six *TOS*-cast movies, resulting in 435 snapshots. The average age of men and women is forty-nine and thirty-nine years old, respectively. Except for the trilogy movies, which temporally captured three generations of fans, *TMP*, *TFF*, and *TUC* seem old and out of date. The youth between 1979 and 1991 were experiencing an explosion in cultural diversity, and women were coming into their own. However, men represent 81 percent of the snapshots, and 89 percent of the characters captured are White. Even diversity in species is low, with 68 percent Human, 21 percent Vulcan, and 7 percent Klingons. Ranking and leadership is also dominated by White males.

TNG-CAST MOVIES FROM 1994 TO 2002

TNG attracted second-generation fans, and the show's main cast starred in four movies: *GEN*, *FCT*, *INS*, and *NEM*. *GEN* was released in the fall of 1994 after the final episode of *TNG* had concluded the previous spring. At that time, *DS9* had already begun its second season, and *VOY* was set to premier the following year. *FCT* and *INS* were both released while *DS9* and *VOY* were still airing new episodes, while *NEM* was released a year after *ENT* premiered on television. Therefore, none of the *TNG*-cast movies were released during a *Star Trek* TV series hiatus.

GEN opens at the end of the twenty-third century, when two Starfleet ships are trapped in a space distortion and the only help available is the *Enterprise*. Upon arrival, the *Enterprise* also becomes trapped, and Kirk modifies the deflectors to free the ship but is swept into the distortion and vanishes. Nearly a century later, Picard is ordered to investigate a possible attack on an observatory orbiting a star. They rescue Dr. Soran, but he insists on being returned to the observatory. Research reveals that Dr. Soran, along with *Enterprise* bartender Guinan and others, were rescued from the energy ribbon when Kirk vanished. Guinan refers to the energy ribbon as the Nexus and tells Picard that it is a timeless place where ultimate happiness and contentment can be found. Soran wants desperately to return to the Nexus. He rigs the destruction of two stars to force the Nexus to come to him. He succeeds, but in the process, Picard is also sucked into the Nexus. While in the Nexus, Picard finds Kirk and convinces him to help stop Soran. Kirk agrees, and they return to the place and point in time when Soran is attempting to destroy the second star. Together they defeat Soran, but in the process, Kirk is killed. Picard buries Kirk, and the next day he is rescued by a shuttlecraft. *Star Trek*

Generations is appropriately named because it bids farewell to *TOS* and passes the franchise onto *TNG*. This movie certainly would make no sense to someone illiterate about *Star Trek*. For the few out there who only followed *TOS* or only followed *TNG*, the movie is confusing. But for a fan of both series, the movie is a delight.

Every Trekkie knows that first contact with non-Humans changed the trajectory of humanity by forcing Earth to unite, and this event, with a twist, is depicted in *FCT*. The Borg enters Federation space for the first time, and all Starfleet ships are ordered to return to Federation space except the *Enterprise*, which is ordered to the Neutral Zone. Picard initially complies, then disobeys orders, and heads for Earth. He is still able to perceive the Borg collective thanks to his previous captivity years before. Picard takes over command of Starfleet, and the Borg cube is destroyed but not before the Borg create a temporal vortex and send a sphere toward Earth. The *Enterprise*, because of its proximity to the temporal vortex, is drawn in, along with the sphere. Upon scanning Earth, Picard discovers that all human life on Earth has been assimilated as Borg. Picard realizes that the Borg have changed Earth's past in order to alter the future. As the temporal vortex begins to collapse, Picard follows it, knowing that he must stop the Borg from changing the Earth's past.

The *Enterprise* arrives on April 4, 2063, a day before the historic first contact with aliens; luckily, they were Vulcans. As the *Enterprise* hovers above Earth, Picard posits that the Borg plan to prevent Zefram Cochrane from conducting a test flight of the first warp drive, which would thwart first contact. To preserve the timeline, Picard must ensure first contact occurs and sends a team to Bozeman, Montana, to find Cochrane. In the meantime, the crew of the *Enterprise* discovers that the ship has been infested with Borg drones, and the Borg queen captures Data. In the end, Picard rescues Data, who in turn saves the *Enterprise*. The landing party convinces Cochrane to continue the test flight on April 5, 2063. The Borg are defeated in Earth's twenty-first century, Cochrane makes first contact with the Vulcans, and the *Enterprise* returns to the twenty-fourth century. Trekkies loved *FCT*, and even non-Trekkies found it enjoyable.

Two years later, Paramount released *INS*. Starfleet, under the command of Admiral Dougherty, along with the Son'a members of the Federation and Data (on loan from the *Enterprise*), are conducting a cultural survey of the Ba'ku, a community of about six hundred living a utopian lifestyle. The Federation xenoanthropologists are in a "duck blind" so they will not contaminate the villagers. However, Data purposefully reveals the watchers to the villagers, and Picard takes the *Enterprise* to the planet to investigate the situation.

Shortly after the *Enterprise* arrives, the truth is revealed. The radiation emitting from the rings around the planet continuously regenerates genetic structure, a fountain of youth. The villagers are not primitive but rather warp capable. They arrived on the planet more than three hundred years ago and decided to live a simpler, utopian lifestyle. The Son'a were once Ba'ku, who rebelled and formed their own colony on a different planet. Now aging and dying, they have returned to capture the "elixir of life." To achieve their goal, they must destroy the planet. Admiral Dougherty also wants the elixir, which will save billions of people in the Federation. In the meantime, the crew of the *Enterprise*, with the exception of Data, are reverting to their emotional and energetic youth, resulting in some comic scenes and dialogue. Admiral Dougherty plans to remove the villagers to another planet. Picard reminds him of the Prime Directive, and he eventually agrees that perhaps another path could be taken. Ru'afo, leader of the Son'a, kills the admiral. Riker, commanding the *Enterprise*, defeats the Son'a, the planet is saved, and the Ba'ku are allowed to stay.

When critics rank *Star Trek* movies, *INS* is usually near the bottom. Had this movie been a two-part episode of *TNG*, it would have been hailed as one of the best. It has a strong *Star Trek*/Roddenberry theme. It addresses the ethics of the Prime Directive, willingness to sacrifice six hundred people to benefit billions of Federation members, the longing for immortality at any cost, and humanity's predisposition to force people off their lands to gain access to resources. The movie has some exciting scenes with humor tossed in, and it led the audience to reflect on their own culture. However, it does not adapt to the contemporary American culture of the late 1990s. *INS* is slow and focused on a population choosing a utopian lifestyle over a fast-paced, high-tech lifestyle. The American culture of the 1990s had more in common with the Son'a, who were self-serving, than the Ba'ku, who focused on the greater good.

The final *TNG*-cast movie is *NEM*. At some point in the past, Romulans cloned Picard and created Shinzon. They then accelerated Shinzon's aging process with the intention of replacing Picard prime. When that was no longer a goal, young Shinzon was sent to Remus as a slave laborer in the mines, where he was raised by Remans. The Remans eventually take over the Romulan Empire and declare Shinzon praetor. However, his aging process is now speeding up, and he needs Picard's blood to slow the progression. He lures the *Enterprise* into Romulan space and captures Picard. The two selves, one old and one young, discuss their life experiences. Eventually it becomes evident that Shinzon has a weapon of mass destruction and intends to annihilate Earth and cripple the Federation. Starfleet intervenes, and the Romulans assist in the overthrow of Shinzon. Data rescues Picard from Shinzon's ship but stays behind to destroy Shinzon, his ship, and the weapon of mass destruction. Data succeeds but loses his life in the process.

NEM is a good movie for *Star Trek* fans but not popular with the general theatergoing audience and not well received by the critics. Similar to *INS*, the movie is slow and neglects mapping onto contemporary American culture. *NEM* is a mismatch of science fiction and a documentary about identical twins raised in different environments.

Snapshots

We collected quantitative data on all four *TNG*-cast movies, resulting in 337 snapshots. These movies were released between 1994 and 2002, a range of only eight years. The first three movies *GEN*, *FCT*, and *INS*, overlapped with *TNG*. While the *TNG* TV series successfully maintains Roddenberry's visions and adapts to contemporary American culture, the movies fail at one or both of these criteria. *NEM* overlapped with *ENT* but also fails to carry a message and fails to adapt to contemporary culture. The snapshots are also out of sync with the TV series of *DS9* and *VOY*. In *TNG*-cast movies, all captains are White males, while in *DS9*, 24 percent are Black, and in *VOY*, 41 percent are women. In *VOY*, 50 percent of occupations with authority over others (leaders and chiefs) are women; equity had been achieved. Yet in *TNG*-cast movies, the snapshots captured only 11 percent women as leaders or chiefs. The *Star Trek* TV series audience had been exposed to diversity for more than seven years and expected the same from the *TNG*-cast movies, but the movies fail to meet the needs of the many.

REBOOT MOVIES FROM 2009 TO 2016

As with the first four *Star Trek* movies, the three most recent movies were released during a *Star Trek* television hiatus. *ST09*, *STID*, and *STB* are commonly referred to as the reboot movies. They return to the twenty-third century with the *TOS* characters of Kirk, Spock, Bones, Uhura, Scotty, Sulu, and Chekov but with a new cast of modern actors and a flashy digital-tech *Enterprise*.

In *ST09*, *Star Trek* once again has a story line involving time travel. In the twenty-fourth century, Romulus is destroyed by a supernova, which Spock prime (Leonard Nimoy) is attempting to prevent. Near the explosion, the Romulus mining vessel *Narada*, captained by Nero, witnesses the catastrophic event. Because of the shockwaves, both Nero's and Spock's vessels are sent back to the twenty-third century. Upon arrival, Nero encounters the Starfleet vessel USS *Kelvin* and kills the captain, thereby making George Kirk commander. A battle ensues, and the crew of the USS *Kelvin*, along with Kirk's wife and their newborn son, James T. Kirk, evacuate the ship in escape pods. However, the battle results in the death of George Kirk, which alters the timeline and course of history. Nero blames the Federation and particularly Spock for the failure to prevent the destruction of Romulus, goes rogue, and wants revenge.

During the course of the movie, the audience discovers how the *TOS* characters meet and become crewmembers on the *Enterprise* under the command of Captain Pike. They also follow Nero's destructive path. Viewers are horrified when Nero destroys Vulcan, are elated when Kirk meets Spock prime, and are on the edge of their seats when Kirk and Spock defeat Nero and rescue Pike. Upon returning to Starfleet, Kirk is promoted to captain of the *Enterprise*. With Kirk in the captain's chair and his crew, Spock, Bones, Scotty, Uhura, Sulu, and Chekov onboard, a new *Enterprise* begins space exploration.

Four years later, the *Enterprise* voyaged once again into theaters in *STID*; however, the majority of the movie takes place on Earth at Starfleet headquarters in San Francisco and onboard the *Enterprise*. In the opening scene, Kirk saves Spock from an erupting volcano and, by doing so, exposes the *Enterprise* to the indigenous species, violating the Prime Directive. Upon returning to Starfleet, Kirk is demoted, loses his command, and is sent back to the academy; however, Pike pulls strings and has Kirk listed as first officer on the *Enterprise*.

Again, revenge is the theme as *Star Trek* returns to *WOK* but this time within the new Kelvin timeline caused by Nero. Admiral Marcus accidently discovers the Botany Bay vessel, carrying Khan and his seventy-two comrades asleep in their cryotubes. Admiral Marcus wants a militarized Starfleet, and he awakens Khan to use his intellect and savagery to design attack weapons and strategies against the Klingons. He holds Khan's seventy-two comrades hostage to force him to cooperate. Khan escapes and orchestrates an attack on the secret agency of Starfleet, Section 31, in London, followed by an attack on Starfleet headquarters in San Francisco, which results in the death of Captain Pike.

Admiral Marcus promotes Kirk to captain of the *Enterprise* with instructions to seek out and kill Khan, to cover up his covert activities. Kirk finds Khan on the Klingon planet of Qo'noS. Khan surrenders and is taken prisoner, and Kirk intends to return him to Earth to stand trial. The truth comes out, and Admiral Marcus in his newly designed warship, the Dreadnought Class USS *Vengeance*, attacks and incapacitates the *Enterprise*, which begins to fall to Earth. Kirk realigns the warp core injectors, which returns power to the *Enterprise*, preventing a crash on Earth. The scene reverses Spock's death scene from *WOK* by replacing Kirk inside the chamber, dying of radiation poisoning, while Spock looks on helplessly. Spock goes after Khan, Uhura goes after Spock, and Khan is eventually returned to the *Enterprise*, where his supercharged blood revives Kirk. Khan is returned to his cryotube alongside his comrades. A year later, the *Enterprise* is refitted, and Captain Kirk and his crew are onboard, ready to continue their voyages through space.

STB again has a revenge plot. Balthazar Edison is a soldier and member of MACO in the twenty-second century. When Starfleet disbanded MACO, Edison became the captain of the USS *Franklin*. While exploring space, the *Franklin* crashed on Altamid, a planet located through an uncharted nebula, in 2164. He found abandoned technology on the planet, including a device to extract energy from living captives to extend his life. He also found swarm ships, drones, and a super-bioweapon; to operate the latter, however, he needs to find a missing part. He hates the Federation and their mission of peace. Eventually, he becomes Krall, warlord of Altamid.

Kirk has the Teenaxian artifact that Krall needs to activate the bioweapon but is unaware of its function. The *Enterprise* is docked at Yorktown, the newest Starfleet station at the edge of Federation space, when they are assigned a rescue mission on Altamid. However, the mission is a ruse, and as they approach the planet, they are instantly attacked by swarm weapons. The surviving crew escapes in pods, while the *Enterprise* is destroyed and crashes on Altamid. Scotty, in a pod, lands on the planet and meets Jaylah, who is living on an abandoned Starship, the USS *Franklin*. Together they find Kirk and Chekov, then later Bones and Spock. Spock tells Kirk that the artifact is part of a bioweapon of mass destruction. They manage to repair the *Franklin* and rescue the captives, including Sulu and Uhura, who informs them that Krall has the artifact and intends to destroy Yorktown. As Krall heads for Yorktown, Spock and Bones confiscate a shuttle, fly into the swarm, and disrupt it with loud rock music. The Yorktown station does the same, and the swarms are defeated. Nonetheless, Krall reaches Yorktown and attempts to activate the super-bioweapon. Kirk intervenes, and a battle ensues, resulting in Krall and the bio-weapon being sucked into space. Kirk is on the verge of the same fate but is rescued by Bones and Spock in their stolen shuttle.

Snapshots

We collected quantitative data on the three reboot movies, resulting in 315 snapshots. The reboot movies were released within a narrow range of only eight years, between 2009 and 2016. All three movies have a theme of revenge from a single person, Nero, Khan, and Krall, respectively, who each have animosity against the Federation. All three movies have a young cast. The average age is thirty-seven years old for men and thirty-two years old for women. The snapshots also captured 81 percent White and 24 percent women, an improvement over the *TOS*-cast and *TNG*-cast movies, but they still underrepresent minorities and women. The casting of Benedict Cumberbatch to play Khan was controversial because the original actor, Ricardo Montalban, was Mexican. Many saw this as "whitewashing" a major character. White males still dominate authority roles in terms of military rank and occupations. In the era of the early twenty-first century, the lack of diversity in *Star Trek* not only violates Roddenberry's vision but also does not represent the diversity in contemporary American culture.[9]

The reboot movies also do not have a message. *ST09* does not necessarily need a message because it reintroduces the *TOS* characters and provides background prior to the five-year mission of exploration. *STID* and *STB* both fall into the trap of lacking a message, lacking diversity, and lacking female roles, and they both have poorly developed story lines that are difficult to follow. But what all three reboot movies do well is to adapt to a high-tech, fast-paced contemporary "worldwide" culture, thereby offering a fresh, fast-action, modern version of a classic and attracting younger fans.

SUMMARY

When it comes to moviemaking, the needs of the many outweigh the needs of the few. The *TOS*-cast trilogy movies benefited from a parental-child shift in three generations: baby boomers, Generation X, and millennials. The *TNG*-cast movies were not standouts because they overlapped with several television *Star Trek* series. The reboot movies offer modern, high-tech action but lack a cohesive story line.

A franchise like *Star Trek* needs to retain classic Trekkies as fans, increase the interest of casual fans, and capture future fans. All three potential audiences want and expect a science fiction movie to be fun and exciting, and that varies across the thirteen movies. Overall four *Star Trek* movies stand out as fun and exciting, *WOK*, *TVH*, *FCT*, and *ST09*, and usually these are the four movies ranked highest in the United States by critics and audiences alike. [10] For Trekkies, the movie should have a message and a consistent story line, preferably within canon, which is why so many fans were divided on *ST09*. For the casual fan, the story line needs to stand on its own, which is why so many love *ST09*. To attract new fans, the movie needs to adapt to contemporary culture, which is the strength of *TVH* and *ST09*. *FCT* was allowed to just be fun; its release overlapped with new seasons of *DS9* and *VOY* as well as reruns of *TOS* and *TNG*.

Morgan Jeffery, the TV editor at Digital Spy, argues that the *Star Trek* franchise should stop making movies and return to its roots as a series via CBS All Access streaming services. *Star Trek* is about storytelling, and that works best in a series. [11] After all, *WOK* and *TVH* are bookends to an accidental trilogy where a story line is spread over three movies, released only two years apart and followed ten months later by the premier of *TNG*. However, four successful movies out of thirteen does not result in a winning game. *Star Wars'* success is due to a consistent story line, theme, and actors, albeit released not in chronological order. *Star Trek* movies are a hodgepodge of writers, directors, and actors, with no unifying theme. *Star Wars* takes place a long, long time ago, far, far away. *Star Trek* is Earth-based and not far into the future. It's us. *Star Trek*'s strength lies in addressing societal issues and adapting to contemporary culture, a difficult challenge for a single movie that represents an ephemeral movie in cultural time.

Paramount is itching to produce more *Star Trek* movies. In the fall of 2019, Paramount announced that Noah Hawley will write and direct *Star Trek 4*. Critics and fans are thrilled at this prospect, and apparently the original reboot cast is onboard. Rumors also suggest that Quentin Tarantino is still involved in producing an offshoot *Star Trek* R-rated movie. However, the *Star Trek* franchise is designed to be family-friendly, even stating as much in its guidelines for fan filmmaking. An R-rated Federation- or Starfleet-themed movie would be an abomination. Both prospective movies (tentatively directed by Tarantino and Hawley) are shrouded in secrecy. Rushing suggests R-rated movies might work if the focus is on the antagonists of the Federation through time, such as the twenty-four houses of Klingon, the founding of the Borg, or the Cardassian or Dominion empire building. Such themes would allow *Star Trek* to stay family-friendly on the small screen while allowing R-rated shock and awe to stand on its own in the theater.[12] If Paramount is serious about a long-term success for *Star Trek* movies, then they need to give Noah Hawley the reins to produce a consistent story line over three movies that address societal issues and map onto contemporary culture. However, they best not procrastinate; streaming services are producing movies with top directors, award-winning writers, and famous actors. That, coupled with big home theater systems, may soon make moviegoing a thing of the past.

10

MELDING FIFTY-PLUS YEARS

Live long and prosper is exactly what *Star Trek* does, even against the backdrop of rapid culture change. A large *Star Trek* audience remains engaged through time and space by storytelling and cinematography. Storytelling is a defining feature of humanity. Long before we had writing, we had storytelling fueling our imaginations.[1] Stories were passed down orally from generation to generation. Then, with the advent of writing, our stories were written down and available to a wider audience. The salient ones survived through the ages. Some stories mirror the culture, as Shakespeare's plays mirror his world. Some stories take us to other worlds to address social issues, as seen in the writings of Jonathan Swift; J. R. R. Tolkien; and, more recently, Terry Pratchett. Even in science/speculative fiction, with mind-boggling science, the storytelling is the basis for endurance. The great science fiction writers—Asimov, E. E. "Doc" Smith, Frank Herbert, Larry Niven, Jerry Pournelle—used the pen, or typewriter in some cases, to address such social issues as religion and environmental and man-made disasters. Roddenberry also used storytelling to address social issues, but he had the new media of cinematography.

The *Star Trek* audience thus experiences two distinct stimuli, the audial and the visual, the storytelling and the screen action. This book addresses both, the *Star Trek* episode vignettes, story lines, and snapshots, what the audience actually sees, independently of the story lines. We use the same approach on the *Star Trek* movies. We argue that *Star Trek* has persisted because it adapts to the changing times, mirrors contemporary social issues, and foreshadows hope for a better future. Does the storytelling adapt to, mirror, and foreshadow contemporary American culture? Does it reflect Roddenberry's vision of normalizing race, ethnicity, nationality, sex, and gender? To varying degrees, the answer is yes.

STAR TREK STORYTELLING

TOS stories are well adapted to the 1960s. Several episodes pit young against old, show the value of the Prime Directive, the necessity of occasionally breaking it, and the consequences of doing so. *TOS* superbly mirrors social issues of the 1960s, from hippies to the antiwar movement to the civil rights movement to the women's liberation movement. Equally important, *TOS* offers hope that, in the near future, race, ethnicity, nationality, and sex would not be factors in personal achievement. At the same time, threads in the story lines support the establishment. This is Roddenberry's baby, and he gave it everything it needed to grow.

Roddenberry was involved in the creation of *TNG*, but upon his death, the storytelling passed to new writers. They held to his vision while adapting *TNG* to an evolving culture, which was a generation past *TOS*. *TNG* is multigenerational and family-oriented. The Federation is mostly at peace. It has a kinder, gentler captain and a diversity of crewmembers with their own stories. *TNG* makes baby steps toward addressing LGBTQ issues and even considers the rights of artificially intelligent (AI) beings. The story lines offer something for everyone.

The next evolution of *Star Trek* is *DS9* and *VOY*. The baton had been passed, both series had new creators, but they retain the core features of Roddenberry's vision. Contemporary American culture was ready for and given a Black captain in *DS9* and a female captain in *VOY*, Sisko and Janeway, respectively. The storytelling in *DS9* is truly exceptional, and of particular importance are the stories that picture Sisko as a single father (in addition to being Black) who has a very normal relationship with his young son. Having the story unfold on a space station gives the series the opportunity to address the interactions of multiple species who inhabit and visit the station. The story arc of Jadzia Dax is a proxy for LGBTQ issues, and the Ferengi represent greed. The entire series considers the complexities of religious institutions through the Bajorans and Sisko as their emissary to their gods. *DS9* also addresses the difficult social issues regarding the plight of the homeless, immigration, and domestic and international terrorism.

VOY champions women. Janeway and Torres have authority, and along with Kes and Seven of Nine, these women are respected and prominently featured. As in previous series, *VOY* stories also warn us of the potential dangers of advanced technology and environmental disasters. It, too, has compelling stories as it explores such issues as health care, faith versus religion versus spirituality, and capital punishment. The story lines adapt to, mirror, and foreshadow American culture, but the overall story arc is similar to *TOS*, traveling through space, discovering new worlds and new civilizations. *Enterprise* voyages outward into unknown space, while *Voyager* is thrust into unknown space and is voyaging home.

ENT had two strikes against it. First, it premiered shortly after 9/11, and second, it fails to adapt to contemporary American culture. Its resonance to *TOS* attracted old fans, but thirty-two years later, it was just outdated and did not speak to younger generations. The time-travel arc, which features the Temporal Cold War, focuses on proxy wars, which makes contemporary social issues difficult to address in this context. That said, the storytellers nail mirroring post-9/11 America in season 4, bringing the story of xenophobia and in-group love and out-group hate to the forefront. It could be argued that season 4 of *ENT* is the best final season of any of the *Star Trek* series.

The story lines of *DSC* add new elements. Even though *DSC* is pre-*TOS*, the story lines are modern. *DSC* adapts, mirrors, and foreshadows contemporary American culture. The stories normalize gay marriage and feature strong women. The stories include an alien as first officer, who frequents the captain's chair. Tilly's awkwardness does not limit her ambitions. *DSC* mirrors the bifurcation in contemporary American culture and again foreshadows the threat of artificial technology. *DSC*, fifty years later, does exactly what Roddenberry created *Star Trek* to do, and that is why *Star Trek* is alive and prospering.

The same cannot be said for the *Star Trek* movies. Unlike *Star Wars*, which has a story line with consistent characters on a constant mission, *Star Trek* movies are, for the most part, eclectic. Except for the loosely connected trilogy (*Wrath of Kahn, Search for Spock,* and *The Voyage Home*), the movies are written like stand-alone episodes. They either adapt or mirror or foreshadow contemporary American culture, but they only succeed in one of these domains. The *Star Trek* movie story lines fail to connect the dots and thus will likely remain average science fiction movies.

STAR TREK ON THE SCREEN

Storytelling is one aspect of *Star Trek*; the other is the cinematography, what the audience experiences visually on small and large screens. Is Roddenberry's core vision reflected on television, in the theater, and through streaming devices? To address this question, we viewed episodes and movies to collect a total of 7,949 snapshots (see the introduction). These samples provide quantitative data to measure what the audience actually sees in the cinematography.

Here enters corporate America. As for the *Star Trek* franchise, these include Paramount, CBS, and now the merger of the two, ViacomCBS. Hundreds of paid employees are involved in turning a story into a series, episode, or movie. It takes money up front, and lots of it. They must financially break even and prefer a profit, a big one at that. Like the rest of us, they need to get paid. If the platform is basically a public good, such as a network, then revenues come through advertising; if it is pay-to-view, such as HBO or streaming, then revenues come from subscribers.

When revenue is based on advertising, the cinematography does not reflect the story lines of *Star Trek*. Looking over the five classical series (*TOS*, *TNG*, *DS9*, *VOY*, and *ENT*), which were all on networks dependent on advertising, the viewer saw the most minorities on *TNG*, and that is only 24 percent. In the classic series, Whites appear, on average, more than 83 percent of the time. Considering all the classics represent a United Earth, Whites should be in the minority but clearly are not. Minorities are also poorly represented, particularly Asians, at less than 3 percent visibility, which is dismaying when 60 percent of Earth's population is of Asian heritage. On the flip side, strong story lines in the classics are visual for specific minority characters, such as Geordi, Worf, Sisko, Tuvok, and Hoshi Sato, and they all have military rank with authority over others. Flip again to the classic series. The viewer is bombarded with White characters. The larger issue is the lack of minorities in secondary and background characters—there are too few with too little exposure.

Similarly, women are poorly represented in the classics. In *TOS*, the snapshot captures 87 percent men and only 13 percent women. *VOY* visually portrays the most women, at 39 percent. However, in *VOY*, when only considering the characters stationed on *Voyager*, men and women achieve equity in visualization. Particularly in *VOY*, the viewer sees Janeway, Torres, Kes, and Seven of Nine performing important duties. However, as with minorities, the viewer is bombarded with men, specifically as background characters.

Movies, however, are dependent on paid viewers: the moviegoers. Of the thirteen *Star Trek* movies that premiered in the theaters between 1979 and 2016, the snapshots only captured 15 percent minorities and 20 percent women. The reboot movies (*ST09*, *STID*, and *STB*) have the most visual representation of women, but that is only at 24 percent, and minority visibility is only at 19 percent. Again, they usually represent a main character with a strong story line, and background characters are overwhelmingly White males. Movies are a pay-to-view enterprise; they can and should increase visibility of minorities and women.

When CBS took notice of such streaming services as Hulu and Netflix, they jumped in and created CBS All Access, a subscription required for pay-to-view. *DSC* was the first *Star Trek* series on this new platform. They took a gamble and pushed forward in matching Roddenberry's storytelling vision with visibility. The snapshots captured from *DSC* represent 51 percent men to 49 percent women—parity achieved. As to minorities, the snapshots captured 57 percent Whites to 43 percent non-Whites. Once again, the Asians are particularly underrepresented. On the flip side, the audience is visually treated to Georgiou's ruthlessness tempered by her compassion; Tilly's genius and optimism; Paul and Hugh kissing; and Captain Lorca, a lying, narcissistic leader, whose goal is to be an emperor.

CBS All Access has allowed *Star Trek* to flourish on a new platform with the old core features intact, adapting, mirroring, and foreshadowing contemporary American culture. In addition to *Discovery*, *Picard* premiered in January 2020, and the animated series, *Lower Decks*, premiered in August 2020. *Star Trek: Short Treks* (*ST*), is already a success. Most focus on story lines expanding individual characters. However, the short "The Girl Who Made the Stars" broke barriers in cinematography: an animated episode with all Black characters and a loving father telling a story to his young daughter about a girl in Africa who made the stars and chased away the fear of night from her village.[2] Given Roddenberry's vision of cultural relevance with strong story lines and now visibilities that match, viewers will see *Star Trek* voyaging through the twenty-first century, albeit streaming through cyberspace.

NOTES

INTRODUCTION

1. Louise Leakey, "Louise Leakey: Where Did Human Beings Originate?" interview by Raz Guy, *TED Radio Hour*, NPR, October 24, 2014, https://www.npr.org/templates/transcript/transcript.php?storyId=358148127.

2. *Game of Thrones*, season 8, episode 6, "The Iron Throne," directed by David Benioff and D. B. Weiss, aired May 19, 2019, on HBO.

3. John Kenneth Muir, *A Critical History of* Doctor Who *on Television* (Jefferson, NC: McFarland, 2007).

4. M. Keith Booker, Star Trek: *A Cultural History* (Lanham, MD: Rowman & Littlefield, 2018); Harry Castleman and Walter J. Podrazik, *Watching TV: Eight Decades of American Television* (Syracuse, NY: Syracuse University Press, 2016); Chris Compendio, "50 Longest-Running TV Series," Stacker, September 9, 2019,https://thestacker.com/stories/2372/50-longest-running-tv-series#5.

5. *The Adventures of Ozzie and Harriet*, created by Ozzie Nelson, aired 1952–1966 on ABC; *The Jack Benny Program*, created by Jack Benny, aired 1950–1965 on CBS; and *Gunsmoke*, created by Norman Macdonnell and John Meston, aired 1955–1976 on CBS.

6. Karl Hodge, "Star Trek: Gene Roddenberry: An Appreciation," Den of Geek, May 6, 2009, https://www.denofgeek.com/us/movies/star-trek/21181/star-trek-gene-roddenberry-an-appreciation.

7. *Have Gun Will Travel*, created by Herb Meadow and Sam Rolfe, aired 1957–1963 on CBS; *Wagon Train*, created by Frank McGrath, Terry Wilson, and Robert Horton, aired 1957–1962 on NBC, 1962–1965 on ABC; and *The Wild, Wild West*, created by Michael Garrison, aired 1965–1969 on CBS.

8. David Alexander, "The Roddenberry Interview," *Humanist* 51, no. 2 (1991): 5–30; Booker, Star Trek; Yvonne Fern and Gene Roddenberry, *Gene Roddenberry: The Last Conversation: A Dialogue with the Creator of* Star Trek (Berkeley: University of California Press, 1994); Stephan Whitfield and Gene Roddenberry, *The Making of* Star Trek (New York: Ballantine Books, 1968).

9. For more information on how anthropologists study culture, see Russell H. Bernard, *Research Methods in Anthropology: Qualitative and Quantitative Approaches* (Lanham, MD: Rowman & Littlefield, 2017); Napoleon Chagnon, *Adaptation and Human Behavior: An Anthropological Perspective* (Abingdon, UK: Routledge, 2017); Paul Martin and Patrick Bateson, *Measuring Behaviour: An Introductory Guide* (Cambridge, UK: Cambridge University Press, 1993).

1. MIRROR, MIRROR

1. *Star Trek: The Original Series*, season 2, episode 4, "Mirror, Mirror," directed by Marc Daniels, aired October 6, 1967, on NBC.

2. Bob Dylan, "The Times They Are a-Changin'," Columbia Records, 1963.

3. *The Bible: In the Beginning*, directed by John Huston (Los Angeles: Twentieth Century Fox, 1966); *The Good, the Bad, and the Ugly*, directed by Sergio Leone (Hollywood: United Artists, 1967); *The Sound of Music*, directed by Robert Wise (Los Angeles: Twentieth Century Fox, 1965).

4. Karl Hodge, "Star Trek: Gene Roddenberry: An Appreciation," Den of Geek, May 6, 2009, https://www.denofgeek.com/us/movies/star-trek/21181/star-trek-gene-roddenberry-an-appreciation.

5. Britannica, "Tet Offensive," accessed March 22, 2017, https://www.britannica.com/topic/Tet-Offensive.

6. History, "Civil Rights Movement Timeline," December 4, 2017, https://www.history.com/topics/civil-rights-movement/civil-rights-movement-timeline.

7. Kenneth T. Walsh, "The 1960s: A Decade of Change for Women," *US News and World Report*, March 12, 2010, https://www.usnews.com/news/articles/2010/03/12/the-1960s-a-decade-of-change-for-women.

8. NCC Staff, "On This Day, All Indians Made United States Citizens," *Constitution Daily*, June 2, 2019, https://constitutioncenter.org/blog/on-this-day-in-1924-all-indians-made-united-states-citizens.

9. Michael Ray, "Executive Order 9981," *Britannica*, May 11, 2010, https://www.britannica.com/topic/Executive-Order-9981.

10. Phyl Newbeck, *Virginia Hasn't Always Been for Lovers: Interracial Marriage Bans and the Case of Richard and Mildred Loving* (Carbondale: Southern Illinois University Press, 2008). See *Loving v. Virginia*, 388 U.S. 1, 87 S. Ct.

1817, 18 L. Ed. 2d 1010 (1967), https://scholar.google.com/scholar_case?case= 5103666188878568597&q=loving+v.+virginia&hl=en&as_sdt=20006.

11. Bill Higgins, "Hollywood Flashback: Star Trek Showed TV's First Interracial Kiss in 1969," *Hollywood Reporter*, May 26, 2016, https://www. hollywoodreporter.com/news/tvs-first-interracial-kiss-star-896843.

12. Britannica, "The Riots of the Long, Hot Summers," accessed February 20, 2017, https://www.britannica.com/story/the-riots-of-the-long-hot-summer.

13. Alice George, "The 1969 Kerner Commission Got It Right, but Nobody Listened," *Smithsonian*, March 1, 2008, https://www.smithsonianmag.com/ smithsonian-institution/1968-kerner-commission-got-it-right-nobody-listened-180968318/.

14. Michael Yockel, "100 Years: The Riots of 1968," *Baltimore Magazine*, May 2007, https://www.baltimoremagazine.com/2007/5/1/100-years-the-riots-of-1968.

15. US Department of Housing and Urban Development, "History of Fair Housing," accessed February 20, 2018, https://www.hud.gov/program_offices/ fair_housing_equal_opp/aboutfheo/history.

16. Farrell J. Chiles, "African American Warrant Officers and the Vietnam War," *Newsliner*, February 2014, https://warrantofficerhistory.org/PDF/ AfricanAmericanWO-Vietnam-War.pdf.

17. Juliet Walker, *The History of Black Business in America: Capitalism, Race, Entrepreneurship* (Chapel Hill: University of North Carolina Press Books, 2009).

18. Jeff Guo, "The Real Reasons the U.S. Became Less Racist toward Asian Americans," *Washington Post*, November 29, 2016, https://www. washingtonpost.com/news/wonk/wp/2016/11/29/the-real-reason-americans-stopped-spitting-on-asian-americans-and-started-praising-them/.

19. Baby Boomer Headquarters, "The Boomer Stats," accessed August 1, 2017, https://www.bbhq.com/bomrstat.htm; Jack Rosenthal, "U.S. Birth Rate Drops to a Record Low," *New York Times*, March 2, 1973, https://www.nytimes. com/1973/03/02/archives/us-birth-rate-drops-to-a-record-low-birth-rate-drops-to-record-low.html.

20. Helen Gurley Brown, *Sex and the Single Girl* (New York: Bernard Geis Associates, 1964); Betty Friedan, *The Feminine Mystique* (New York: W. W. Norton, 2013); Elaine Tyler May. *America and the Pill: A History of Promise, Peril, and Liberation* (New York: Basic Books, 2010); Alexandra Nikolchev, "A Brief History of the Birth Control Pill," PBS, May 7, 2010, http://www.pbs.org/ wnet/need-to-know/health/a-brief-history-of-the-birth-control-pill/480/.

21. James R. Wetzel, "American Families: 70 Years of Change," *Monthly Labor Review*, March 1990, https://www.bls.gov/mlr/1990/03/art1full.pdf.

22. Women's Memorial, "1960s: The Decade," accessed May 7, 2017, https://www.womensmemorial.org/history/detail/?s=1960s-the-decade.

23. Britannica, "Muriel Seibert," accessed August 7, 2017, https://www.britannica.com/biography/Muriel-Siebert; Julia Carpenter, "Women in the Fortune 500: 64 CEOs in Half a Century," CNN Money, August 7, 2017, https://money.cnn.com/interactive/pf/female-ceos-timeline/; Center for American Women and Politics, "History of Women in the U.S. Congress," accessed August 7, 2017, https://cawp.rutgers.edu/history-women-us-congress.

24. "Don't Trust Anyone over 30, unless It's Jack Weinberg," *Berkeley Daily Planet*, April 6, 2000, http://www.berkeleydailyplanet.com/issue/2000-04-06/article/759; Joseph P. Williams, "Old Enough to Fight, Old Enough to Vote: The 26th Amendment's Mixed Legacy," *US News and World Report*, July 7, 2016, https://www.usnews.com/news/articles/2016-07-01/old-enough-to-fight-old-enough-to-vote-the-26th-amendments-mixed-legacy.

25. *Bewitched*, created by Sol Saks, aired 1964–1972, on ABC; *Bonanza*, created by David Dortort, aired 1959–1973, on NBC; *The Dean Martin Show*, created by Dean Martin, aired 1965–1974, on NBC; *Gunsmoke*, created by Norman Macdonnell and John Meston, aired 1955–1976 on CBS; *My Three Sons*, created by George Tibbles, aired 1960–1972, on CBS.

26. Sonny Bono, "I Got You Babe," ATCO Records, 1966.

27. Academy of Motion Picture Arts and Sciences, "The 38th Academy Awards: 1966," accessed July 20, 2017, https://www.oscars.org/oscars/ceremonies/1966; Biography, "Clint Eastwood," April 27, 2017, https://www.biography.com/actor/clint-eastwood; *Good, the Bad*; IMDb, "Christopher Plummer, Biography," accessed August 15, 2017, https://www.imdb.com/name/nm0001626/bio; IMDb, "Julie Andrews, Biography," accessed August 15, 2017, https://www.imdb.com/name/nm0000267/; *Sound of Music*.

28. *Star Trek: The Original Series*, season 1, episode 26, "Errand of Mercy," directed by John Newland, aired March 23, 1967, on NBC.

29. The following episodes were viewed to collect snapshots: "The Man Trap" (Marc Daniels, S1e1); "The Enemy Within" (Leo Penn, S1e5); "The Galileo Seven" (Robert Gist, S1e16); "Space Seed" (Marc Daniels, S1e22); "Who Mourns for Adonais" (Marc Daniels, S2e2); "The Apple" (Joseph Pevney, S2e5); "Obsession" (Ralph Senensky, S2e13); "A Private Little War" (Marc Daniels, S2e19); "Is There in Truth No Beauty?" (Ralph Senensky, S3e5); "The Tholian Web" (Herb Wallerstein, S3e9); "Let That Be Your Last Battlefield" (Jud Taylor, S3e15); and "All Our Yesterdays" (Marvin Chomsky, S3e23). See full citations in the filmography.

30. *Gomer Pyle, U.S.M.C.*, created by Aaron Ruben, aired 1964–1969, on CBS; *Judd, for the Defense*, created by Paul Monash, aired 1967–1969, on ABC; StarTrek.com Staff, "Bjo Trimble: The Woman Who Saved *Star Trek*: Part I,"

StarTrek.com, accessed August 20, 2017, https://www.startrek.com/article/bjo-trimble-the-woman-who-saved-star-trek-part-1.

2. INTERLUDE I

1. David Gerrold, *The World of* Star Trek (Dallas, TX: BenBella Books, 2014).

2. Victoria McNally, "Women Who Love *Star Trek* Are the Reason That Modern Fandom Exists," Revelist, September 8, 2016, http://www.revelist.com/tv/star-trek-fandom-50th/4643.

3. For a comprehensive overview of Star Trek fandom and fanzines, see Jacqueline Guerrier, "Where No Fandom Has Gone Before: Exploring the Development of Fandom through *Star Trek* Fanzines" (master's thesis, James Madison University, Fall 2018), 580, https://commons.lib.jmu.edu/master201019/580.

4. See Alan J. Porter, Star Trek*: A Comics History* (New Castle, PA: Hermes Press, 2009).

5. Bruce David Forbes and Jeffrey H. Mahan, eds., *Religion and Popular Culture in America* (Berkeley: University of California Press, 2017); Michael Jindra, "Star Trek Fandom as a Religious Phenomenon," *Sociology of Religion* 55, no. 1 (1994): 27–51; Sarah Pruitt, "8 Ways the Original 'Star Trek' Made History," History, September 8, 2016, https://www.history.com/news/8-ways-the-original-star-trek-made-history.

6. Francesca Coppa, "A Brief History of Media Fandom," in *Fan Fiction and Fan Communities in the Age of the Internet*, ed. Karen Hellekson and Kristina Busse (Jefferson, NC: McFarland, 2006).

7. Jacqueline Lichtenberg, Sondra Marshak, and Joan Winston, Star Trek Lives! (London: Corgi, 1975).

8. Peter Hartlaub, "Let's Time-Travel to 1976 Bay Area Sci-Fi Convention," *San Francisco Chronicle*, March 18, 2016, https://www.sfchronicle.com/oursf/article/Let-s-time-travel-back-to-1976-Bay-Area-science-6922053.php.

9. Curt Danhauser, "Curt Danhauser's Guide to the Animated Star Trek," DanhauserTrek, March 25, 1996,http://www.danhausertrek.com/AnimatedSeries/Main.html.

10. Anthony Pascale, "D. C. Fontana on TAS Canon (and Sybok)," TrekMovie, July 22, 2007, https://trekmovie.com/2007/07/22/dc-fontana-on-tas-canon-and-sybok/.

11. Memory Alpha, "CBS Consumer Products," accessed May 23, 2019, https://memory-alpha.fandom.com/wiki/CBS_Consumer_Products.

12. John Cloud, "*Star Trek* Inc.," *Time*, December 11, 2002,http://content.time.com/time/magazine/article/0,9171,397512,00.html.

13. *2001: A Space Odyssey*, directed by Stanley Kubrick (Beverly Hills, CA: Metro-Goldwyn-Mayer, 1968).

14. *2001: A Space Odyssey*; *Close Encounters of the Third Kind*, directed by Steven Spielberg (Culver City, CA: Columbia Pictures, 1977); *Logan's Run*, directed by Michael Anderson (Beverly Hills, CA: Metro-Goldwyn-Mayer, 1976); *Silent Running*, directed by Douglas Trumbull (Universal City, CA: Universal Pictures, 1972); *Soylent Green*, directed by Richard Fleischer (Beverly Hills, CA: Metro-Goldwyn-Mayer, 1973); *Star Wars: Episode IV—A New Hope*, directed by George Lucas (Los Angeles: Twentieth Century Fox, 1977); *Westworld*, directed by Michael Crichton (Beverly Hills, CA: Metro-Goldwyn-Mayer, 1973).

15. *Star Trek II: The Wrath of Khan*, directed by Nicholas Meyer (Hollywood, CA: Paramount Pictures, 1982); *Star Trek III: The Search for Spock*, directed by Leonard Nimoy (Hollywood, CA: Paramount Pictures, 1984); *Star Trek IV: The Voyage Home*, directed by Leonard Nimoy (Hollywood, CA: Paramount Pictures, 1986).

3. ENCOUNTER AT FARPOINT

1. Jean-Luc Picard, talking to Riker, Number One; *Star Trek: The Next Generation*, season 1, episode 1, "Encounter at Farpoint," directed by Corey Allen, aired September 28, 1987, in syndication.

2. Peter Robinson, "Tear Down This Wall," *Prologue Magazine* 39, no. 2 (Summer 2007), https://www.archives.gov/publications/prologue/2007/summer/berlin.html.

3. *Platoon*, directed by Oliver Stone (Beverly Hills, CA: MGM, 1986); Reagan Foundation, "Her Causes," accessed February 10, 2018, https://www.reaganfoundation.org/ronald-reagan/nancy-reagan/her-causes/.

4. *Star Trek: The Next Generation*, season 1, episode 11, "The Big Goodbye," directed by Joseph L. Scanlan, aired January 9, 1988, on CBS http://www.peabodyawards.com/award-profile/star-trek-the-next-generation-the-big-good-bye; http://www.peabodyawards.com/award-profile/star-trek-the-next-generation-the-big-good-bye; Charles Stockdale, September 11, 2018. *USA Today* https://www.usatoday.com/story/money/2018/09/11/tv-shows-with-the-most-emmy-wins-of-all-time/37351013/

5. Robert Hilburn, "Bonnie Raitt, Midler Win Top Grammys," *Los Angeles Times*, February 22, 1990, https://www.latimes.com/archives/la-xpm-1990-02-22-mn-1696-story.html; Elias Leight, "How Michael Jackson's 'Bad' Scored a Staggering Five Number Ones," *Rolling Stone*, August 31, 2007,https://www.

rollingstone.com/music/music-features/how-michael-jacksons-bad-scored-a-staggering-five-number-ones-117653/.

6. *Driving Miss Daisy*, directed by Bruce Beresford (Hollywood, CA: Warner Brothers, 1990); *Ghost*, directed by Jerry Zucker (Hollywood, CA: Paramount Pictures, 1990); *Home Alone*, directed by Chris Columbus (Los Angeles, CA: Twentieth Century Fox, 1990).

7. Kashmira Gander, "The Terror and Prejudice of the 1980s AIDS Crisis Remembered by a Gay Man Who Lived through It," *Independent*, January 6, 2017, https://www.independent.co.uk/life-style/love-sex/aids-crisis-1980-eighties-remember-gay-man-hiv-positive-funerals-partners-disease-michael-penn-a7511671.html.

8. Queer Nation NY, "Queer Nation NY History," accessed February 14, 2018, https://queernationny.org/history.

9. Britannica, "Don't Ask, Don't Tell," accessed February 14, 2018, https://www.britannica.com/event/Dont-Ask-Dont-Tell; John Gallagher and Chris Bull, *Perfect Enemies: The Religious Right, the Gay Movement, and the Politics of the 1990s* (New York: Crown, 1996).

10. *An Early Frost*, directed by John Erman (NBC Productions, 1985); *Golden Girls*, season 4, episode 9, "Scared Straight," directed by Terry Hughes, aired December 10, 1988, on NBC; *Seinfeld*, created by Larry David and Jerry Seinfeld, aired 1989–1998, on NBC.

11. Peter Milligan, *Hellblazer* (New York: DC Comics, 1988–2013, 2019–present); Joe Simon and Jack Kirby, *Sandman* (New York: DC Comics, 1974–1976).

12. *Star Trek: The Next Generation*, season 4, episode 23, "The Host," directed by Marvin V. Rush, aired on May 13, 1991, in syndication.

13. National Committee on Pay Equity, "The Wage Gap over Time," accessed February 20, 2018, https://www.pay-equity.org/info-time.html; Michael S. Rosenwald, "No Woman Served on the Senate Judiciary Committee in 1991. The Ugly Anita Hill Hearings Changed That," *Washington Post*, September 18, 2018, https://www.washingtonpost.com/history/2018/09/18/no-women-served-senate-judiciary-committee-ugly-anita-hill-hearings-changed-that/.

14. *Die Hard*, directed by John McTiernan (Los Angeles, CA: Twentieth Century Fox, 1988); Carol Kleiman, "Women's Work in the 90s Has Few Boundaries," *Chicago Tribune*, January 30, 1996, https://www.chicagotribune.com/news/ct-xpm-1996-01-30-9601300266-story.html; *Pretty Woman*, directed by Garry Marshall (Burbank, CA: Touchstone Pictures, 1990); The White House: President George W. Bush, "President Signs National Defense Authorization Act," accessed February 20, 2018, https://georgewbush-whitehouse.archives.gov/news/releases/2002/12/images/20021202-8_defense-12022002-d--515h.html.

15. *The Cosby Show*, created by Michael Leeson, aired 1984–1992, on NBC; *A Different World*, created by Bill Cosby, aired 1987–1993, on NBC; Lee Winfrey, "Cosby Tightens Grips on the Nielsen Ratings," *Chicago Tribune*, December 10, 1986, https://www.chicagotribune.com/news/ct-xpm-1986-12-10-8604020309-story.html.

16. Terry Gross, "Congressman, Civil Rights Icon John Lewis," *Fresh Air*, January 19, 2009, https://www.npr.org/templates/story/story.php?storyId=99560979; Melissa Healey, "Colin Powell to Be Named Head of Joint Chiefs," *Los Angeles Times*, August 10, 1989, https://www.latimes.com/archives/la-xpm-1989-08-10-mn-413-story.html; Thomas N. Maloney, "African Americans in the Twentieth Century," EH.net, January 14, 2002, http://eh.net/encyclopedia/african-americans-in-the-twentieth-century/; Phillip M. Rubin, "Obama Named New Law Review President," *Harvard Crimson*, February 6, 1990, https://www.thecrimson.com/article/1990/2/6/obama-named-new-law-review-president/.

17. Joe R. Feagin and Melvin P. Sikes, *Living with Racism: The Black Middle-Class Experience* (Boston: Beacon Press, 1994); Abigail Thernstrom and Stephen Thernstrom, "Black Progress: How Far We've Come, and How Far We Have to Go," Brookings, March 1, 1998, https://www.brookings.edu/articles/black-progress-how-far-weve-come-and-how-far-we-have-to-go/.

18. Richard M. Lee, "The Transracial Adoption Paradox: History, Research, and Counseling Implications of Cultural Socialization," *Counseling Psychologist* 31, no. 6 (2003): 711–44.

19. Britannica, "Collapse of the Soviet Union," accessed March 4, 2018, https://www.britannica.com/event/the-collapse-of-the-Soviet-Union; Andrew Kohut, "Berlin Wall's Fall Marked the End of the Cold War for the American Public," Pew Research Center, November 3, 2014, https://www.pewresearch.org/fact-tank/2014/11/03/berlin-walls-fall-marked-the-end-of-the-cold-war-for-the-american-public/; Richard Kreitner, "Setting up the European Union," *Nation*, November 1, 2015, https://www.thenation.com/article/november-1-1993-the-maastricht-treaty-is-ratified-setting-up-the-european-union/; The Reagan Vision, "The Reykjavik Summit," accessed March 3, 2018, https://www.thereaganvision.org/the-reykjavik-summit-the-story/.

20. *Star Trek: The Next Generation*, season 4, episode 12, "The Wounded," directed by Chip Chalmers, aired January 28, 1991, in syndication.

21. Chris Kohler, "July 29, 1994: Videogame Makers Propose Ratings Board to Congress," *Wired*, July 29, 2009, https://www.wired.com/2009/07/dayintech-0729/; Henry E. Lowood, "The Legend of Zelda," Britannica, May 7, 2004, https://www.britannica.com/topic/The-Legend-of-Zelda-1688275.

22. The Old Robots Website, "The Armatron—2346," accessed April 1, 2020, http://www.theoldrobots.com/armatron1.html; The Old Robots Website, "Dustbot—SO-G—5409 by Tomy," accessed April 1, 2020, http://www.

theoldrobots.com/dustbot.html; *RoboCop*, directed by Paul Verhoeven (Los Angeles: Orion Pictures, 1987); *Terminator 2: Judgment Day*, directed by James Cameron (Culver City, CA: TriStar Pictures, 1991); *The Transformers: The Movie*, directed by Nelson Shin (New York: Sunbow Productions, 1986).

23. Terence P. Jeffrey, "7,231,000 Lost Jobs: Manufacturing Employment Down 37% from 1979 Peak," CNS News, May 12, 2015, https://www.cnsnews. com/news/article/terence-p-jeffrey/7231000-lost-jobs-manufacturing-employment-down-37-1979-peak.

24. Science Direct, "Nanoprobes," accessed February 25, 2018, https://www. sciencedirect.com/topics/chemical-engineering/nanoprobes.

25. Cold War Museum, "The Strategic Defense Initiative SDI: Star Wars," accessed February 25, 2018, http://www.coldwar.org/articles/80s/SDI-StarWars. asp.

26. The following episodes were viewed to collect snapshots: "Code of Honor" (Russ Mayberry, S1e4); "Haven" (Richard Compton, S1e11); "Datalore" (Rob Bowman, S1e13); "The Neutral Zone" (James Conway, S1e26); "Unnatural Selection" (Paul Lynch, S2e7); "The Icarus Factor" (Robert Iscove, S2e14); "Q Who" (Rob Bowman, S2e16); "Evolution" (Winrich Kolbe, S3e1); "Booby Trap" (Gabrielle Beaumont, S3e6); "Sins of the Father" (Les Landau, S3e17); "Sarek" (Les Landau, S3e23); "Suddenly Human" (Gabrielle Beaumont, S4e4); "The Wounded" (Chip Chalmers, S4e12); "Night Terrors" (Les Landau, S4e17); "In Theory" (Patrick Stewart, S4e25); "The Game" (Corey Allen, S5e6); "Hero Worship" (Patrick Stewart, S5e11); "The Masterpiece Society" (Winrich Kolbe, S5e14); "The Next Phase" (David Carson, S5e24); "Realm of Fear" (Cliff Bole, S6e2); "Relics" (Alexander Singer, S6e4); "Aquiel" (Cliff Bole, S6e15); "Birthright Part 2" (Dan Curry, S6e17); "Liaisons" (Cliff Bole, S7e2); "Sub-Rosa" (Jonathan Frakes, S7e14); "Firstborn" (Jonathan West, S7e21); "Emergence" (Cliff Bole, S7e23). See full citations in the filmography.

27. Famous Scientists, "Mae Carol Jemison," accessed March 15, 2018, https://www.famousscientists.org/mae-carol-jemison/; Gregory P. Kane, "Reginald Lewis Climbed into the Moneyed Class," *Baltimore Sun*, December 18, 1994, https://www.baltimoresun.com/news/bs-xpm-1994-12-18-1994352029-story.html; Samantha Kealoha, "Sharon Pratt Dixon Kelly," Black Past, April 18, 2007, https://www.blackpast.org/african-american-history/kelly-sharon-pratt-dixon-1944/; David Streitfeld, "Author Toni Morrison Wins Nobel Prize," *Washington Post*, October 8, 1993, https://www.washingtonpost.com/archive/politics/1993/10/08/author-toni-morrison-wins-nobel-prize/6077f17d-d7b7-49a3-ad90-8111cf8478d1/.

28. Britannica, "Eileen Collins," accessed March 20, 2018, https://www. britannica.com/biography/Eileen-Collins; Britannica, "Janet Reno," accessed March 20, 2018, https://www.britannica.com/biography/Janet-Reno; Herminia

Ibarra and Morton T. Hansen, "Women CEOs: Why So Few?" *Harvard Business Review*, December 21, 2009, https://hbr.org/2009/12/women-ceo-why-so-few.

4. Q-LESS

1. Odo, talking to Quark; *Star Trek: Deep Space Nine*, season 1, episode 7, "Q-Less," directed by Paul Lynch, aired on February 7, 1993, in syndication.

2. Douglas Coupland, "1990s: The Good Decade," History, March 17, 2017, http://www.history.com/news/1990s-the-good-decade.

3. Steve Allen and Robert J. Thompson, "The 1990s: The Loss of Shared Experience," Britannica, July 1, 2019, https://www.britannica.com/art/television-in-the-United-States/The-1990s-the-loss-of-shared-experience; Bomani Jones, "Oh Pleez GAWD I Can't Handle the Success," Salon, October 24, 2002, https://www.salon.com/2002/10/23/cobain_2/.

4. Kirk Anderson, "The Best Decade Ever? The 1990s, Obviously," *New York Times*, February 6, 2015, https://www.nytimes.com/2015/02/08/opinion/sunday/the-best-decade-ever-the-1990s-obviously.html.

5. Joseph Stiglitz, "The Roaring Nineties," *Atlantic*, October 2002,https://www.theatlantic.com/magazine/archive/2002/10/the-roaring-nineties/302604/.

6. David Alexander, "The Roddenberry Interview," *Humanist* 51, no. 2 (1991): 5–30.

7. Michael Isikoff, "Christian Coalition Steps Boldly into Politics," *Washington Post*, September 10, 1992, https://www.washingtonpost.com/archive/politics/1992/09/10/christian-coalition-steps-boldly-into-politics/90c8bf0b-3268-4088-ba12-b49c93537bba/.

8. Rob Boston, "Inside the Christian Coalition," Americans United, November 2004, https://www.au.org/church-state/november-2004-church-state/featured/inside-the-christian-coalition; Audie Cornish, "Who Is an Evangelical? Looks at the History of Evangelical Christians and the GOP," NPR, November 14, 2019, https://www.npr.org/2019/11/14/779465137/who-is-an-evangelical-looks-at-history-of-evangelical-christians-and-the-gop; Daniel Schlozman, "How the Christian Right Ended Up Transforming American Politics," Talking Points Memo, August 25, 2015, https://talkingpointsmemo.com/cafe/brief-history-of-the-christian-right.

9. Erin Blackmore, "The Revolutionary War Hero Who Was Openly Gay," History, June 14, 2018, https://www.history.com/news/openly-gay-revolutionary-war-hero-friedrich-von-steuben; David F. Burrelli, "Don't Ask, Don't Tell: The Law and Military Policy on Same-Sex Behavior," Congressional Research Service, October 14, 2010, https://fas.org/sgp/crs/misc/R40782.pdf; Kimberly Carter Kelly, "Defense of Marriage Act," Britannica, April 28, 2016,

https://www.britannica.com/topic/Defense-of-Marriage-Act; Richard Socarides, "Why Bill Clinton Signed the Defense of Marriage Act," *New Yorker*, June 18, 2017, https://www.newyorker.com/news/news-desk/why-bill-clinton-signed-the-defense-of-marriage-act.

10. Eleanor Baugher and Leatha Lamison-White, "Poverty in the United States: 1995," Bureau of the Census, September 1996, https://www2.census.gov/prod2/popscan/p60-194.pdf; CSPAN, "A Look at the 1940 Census," April 2, 2012, https://www.census.gov/newsroom/cspan/1940census/CSPAN_1940slides.pdf; Tina Daunt and Tina Nguyen, "Homeless Camp Weighed in L.A. Industrial Area," *Los Angeles Times*, October 14, 1994, https://www.latimes.com/archives/la-xpm-1994-10-14-mn-50276-story.html; Population Reference Bureau, "Why Concentrated Poverty Fell in the United States in the 1990s," August 1, 2005, https://www.prb.org/whyconcentratedpoverty fellintheunitedstatesinthe1990s/; Jeff Wallenfeldt, "Los Angeles Riots of 1992," Britannica, April 27, 2012, https://www.britannica.com/event/Los-Angeles-Riots-of-1992.

11. Population Reference Bureau, "Concentrated Poverty"; Reference for Business, "Minority-Owned Businesses," accessed November 14, 2019. http://www.referenceforbusiness.com/encyclopedia/Man-Mix/Minority-Owned-Businesses.html.

12. Black Male Re-Imagined II, *Transforming Perception: Black Men and Boys: Executive Summary* (Los Angeles: University of California, Los Angeles, November 2016), https://equity.ucla.edu/wp-content/uploads/2016/11/Transforming-Perception.pdf.

13. Charles M. Blow, "Black Dads Are Doing Best of All," *New York Times*, June 8, 2015, https://www.nytimes.com/2015/06/08/opinion/charles-blow-black-dads-are-doing-the-best-of-all.html. See also Roberta L. Coles and Charles Green, *The Myth of the Missing Black Father* (New York: Columbia University Press, 2010).

14. Angelica Jade Bastien, "Deep Space Nine Is TV's Most Revolutionary Depiction of Black Fatherhood," Vulture, January 19, 2018, https://www.vulture.com/2018/01/deep-space-nine-revolutionary-depiction-of-black-fatherhood.html.

15. Nina M. Serafino, "CRS Report for Congress," Congressional Research Service, January 24, 2007, https://fas.org/sgp/crs/natsec/RL33557.pdf.

16. Helen C. Epstein, "America's Secret Role in the Rwandan Genocide," *Guardian*, September 12, 2017, https://www.theguardian.com/news/2017/sep/12/americas-secret-role-in-the-rwandan-genocide.

17. The following episodes were viewed to collect snapshots: "A Man Alone" (Paul Lynch, S1e4); "The Passenger" (Paul Lynch, S1e9); "Progress" (Les Landau, S1e15); "The Homecoming" (Winrich Kolbe, S2e1); "Sanctuary" (Les Lan-

dau, S2e10); "This Side of Paradise" (Ralph Senensky, S2e15); "The Wire" (Kim Friedman, S2e22); "The House of Quark" (Les Landau, S3e3); "Meridian" (Jonathan Frakes, S3e8); "Improbable Cause" (Avery Brooks, S3e20); "Explorers" (Cliff Bole, S3e22); "The Way of the Warrior, Part 1" (James L. Conway, S4e1); "The Way of the Warrior, Part 2" (James L. Conway, S4e2); "Starships Down" (Alexander Singer, S4e7); "Return to Grace" (Jonathan West, S4e14); "The Ascent" (Allan Kroeker, S5e9); "Doctor Bashir, I Presume" (David Livingston, S5e16); "Ties of Blood and Water" (Avery Brooks, S5e19); "Children of Time" (Kim Friedman, S5e22); "Resurrection" (LeVar Burton, S6e8); "The Magnificent Ferengi" (Chip Chalmers, S6e10); "Change of Heart" (David Livingston, S6e16); "Treachery, Faith, and the Great River" (Stephen L. Posey, S7e6); "Once More unto the Breach" (Allan Kroeker, S7e7); "Chimera" (Stephen L. Posey, S7e14); "The Dogs of War" (Avery Brooks, S7e24). See full citations in the filmography.

18. The Women's Memorial, "1990s," accessed November 20, 2019, https://www.womensmemorial.org/history/detail/?s=1990s.

5. LIVING WITNESS

1. Quarren, talking to the Doctor; *Star Trek: Voyager*, season 4, episode 23, "Living Witness," direct by Tim Russ, aired on April 29, 1998, on UPN.

2. Kevin D. Williamson, "9/11 Ended a Golden Age," *National Review*, September 11, 2017, https://www.nationalreview.com/2017/09/911-sixteen-years-later/.

3. Claudia Goldin, "The Quiet Revolution That Transformed Women's Employment, Education, and the Family," *American Economic Review* 96, no. 2 (2006): 13, fig. 8, https://scholar.harvard.edu/files/goldin/files/the_quiet_revolution_that_transformed_womens_employment_education_and_family.pdf; National Committee on Pay Equity, "The Wage Gap over Time," accessed November 2, 2019, https://www.pay-equity.org/info-time.html; Pew Research Center, "The Data on Women Leaders," September 13, 2018, https://www.pewsocialtrends.org/fact-sheet/the-data-on-women-leaders/.

4. Britannica, "Madeleine Albright," May 23, 2019, https://www.britannica.com/biography/Madeleine-Albright; Center for American Women and Politics, "History of Women in the U.S. Congress," accessed November 2, 2019, https://cawp.rutgers.edu/history-women-us-congress; The Citadel, "Women at the Citadel: A Decade of Change and Progress," accessed January 27, 2020, http://www3.citadel.edu/pao/women/10_years.html; Beth Dickey, "Women in the News—Eileen Marie Collins; Women's Work: Space Commander," *New York Times*, July 24, 1999, https://www.nytimes.com/1999/07/24/us/woman-in-the-

news-eileen-marie-collins-womans-work-space-commander.html; "Female Pilots Dropped Bombs in Iraq Mission," *Los Angeles Times*, December 23, 1998, https://www.latimes.com/archives/la-xpm-1998-dec-23-mn-56925-story.html; "Kathleen McGrath, 50; 1st Woman to Command a U.S. Navy Warship," *Los Angeles Times*, October 3, 2002, https://www.latimes.com/archives/la-xpm-2002-oct-03-me-mcgrath3-story.html; The Women's Memorial, "Highlights in the History of Military Women," accessed November 2, 2019, https://www.womensmemorial.org/content/resources/highlights.pdf.

5. *The Terminator*, directed by James Cameron (Los Angeles: Orion Pictures, 1984).

6. Anne Fisher, "How Executive Women Avoid Being Called the B-Word," *Fortune*, September 16, 2015, https://fortune.com/2015/09/16/how-executive-women-avoid-being-called-the-b-word/.

7. American Disposal Services, "A Brief History of Recycling," accessed November 30, 2019, https://americandisposal.com/blog/a-brief-history-of-recycling/; Environmental History Timeline, "Nineties 1990–99," accessed November 30, 2019, http://environmentalhistory.org/20th-century/nineties/; Mark Sagoff, "The Great Environmental Awakening," *American Prospect*, December 5, 2000, https://prospect.org/environment/great-environmental-awakening/; United States Environmental Protection Agency, "Milestones in EPA and Environmental History," accessed November 30, 2019, https://www.epa.gov/history.

8. Defense Advanced Research Projects Agency, "Where the Future Becomes Now," accessed, November 30, 2019, https://www.darpa.mil/about-us/darpa-history-and-timeline?PP=8; Conner Forrest, "Tech Nostalgia: The Top 15 Innovations of the 1990s," Tech Republic, May 8, 2015, https://www.techrepublic.com/pictures/tech-nostalgia-the-top-15-innovations-of-the-1990s/.

9. John T. Correll, "The Emergence of Smart Bombs," *Air Force Magazine*, March 2010, https://www.airforcemag.com/PDF/MagazineArchive/Documents/2010/March%202010/0310bombs.pdf.

10. Jonathan Oberlander, "Learning from Failure in Health Care Reform," *New England Journal of Medicine* 357, no. 17 (2007): 1677–79; Thomas Plaut and Bernard S. Arons, "President Clinton's Proposal for Health Care Reform: Key Provisions and Issues," *Psychiatric Services* 45, no. 9 (1994): 871–76; Paul Starr, "What Happened to Health Care Reform?" *American Prospect*, November 19, 2001, https://prospect.org/health/happened-health-care-reform/.

11. Julie Rovner, "Why Do People Hate Obamacare, Anyway?" Kaiser Health News, December 13, 2017, https://khn.org/news/why-do-people-hate-obamacare-anyway/.

12. The following episodes were viewed to collect snapshots: "Parallax" (Kim Friedman, S1e3); "Phage" (Winrich Kolbe, S1e5); "Twisted" (Kim Friedman, S2e6); "Alliances" (Les Landau, S2e14); "Lifesigns" (Cliff Bole, S2e19);

"Deadlock" (David Livingston, S2e21); "The Chute" (Les Landau, S3e3); "Sacred Ground" (Robert Duncan McNeill, S3e7); "Fair Trade" (Jesus Salvador Trevino, S3e13); "Worst Case Scenario" (Alexander Singer, S3e25); "The Raven" (LeVar Burton, S4e6); "Mortal Coil" (Allan Kroeker, S4e12); "Prey" (Allan Eastman, S4e16); "One" (Kenneth Biller, S4e25); "Extreme Risk" (Cliff Bole, S5e3); "Bride of Chaotica!" (Allan Kroeker, S5e12); "Dark Frontier, Part 2" (Terry Windell, S5e16); "Juggernaut" (Allan Kroeker, S5e21); "Equinox, Part 2" (David Livingston, S6e1); "One Small Step" (Robert Picardo, S6e8); "The Voyager Conspiracy" (Terry Windell, S6e9); "Unimatrix Zero, Part 1" (Allan Kroeker, S6e26); "Repression" (Winrich Kolbe, S7e4); "Critical Care" (Terry Windell, S7e5); "Lineage" (Peter Lauritson, S7e12); "Homestead" (LeVar Burton, S7e23). See full citations in Filmography.

13. Nicola Davis, "Dark Matter and Dinosaurs: Meet Lisa Randall, America's Superstar Scientist," *Guardian*, January 12, 2016, https://www.theguardian.com/science/2016/jan/12/dark-matter-physics-dinosaurs-extinction-lisa-randell; Petula Dvorak, "Nancy Pelosi Is Showing Women How to Age Fearlessly and Ferociously," *Washington Post*, December 19, 2019, https://www.washingtonpost.com/local/2019/12/19; The Nobel Prize, "Marie Curie Biographical," accessed December 4, 2019, https://www.nobelprize.org/prizes/physics/1903/marie-curie/biographical/; Sarah Spain, "Serena Williams Focusing on Business, Charity, and Family While Away from Tennis," ESPN, June 23, 2017, https://www.espn.com/espnw/voices/espnw-columnists/story/_/id/19719611/serena-williams-focusing-business-charity-family-away-tennis.

6. TERRA PRIME

1. Prime Minister Nathan Samuels of United Earth addresses the interplanetary delegation; *Star Trek: Enterprise*, season 4, episode 21, "Terra Prime," directed by Marvin V. Rush, aired on May 13, 2005, on UPN.

2. *Harry Potter and the Sorcerer's Stone*, directed by Chris Columbus (Hollywood, CA: Warner Brothers, 2001); *Lord of the Rings: The Fellowship of the Ring*, directed by Peter Jackson (Burbank, CA: New Line Cinema, 2001); *Monsters, Inc.*, directed by Pete Docter, David Silverman, and Lee Unkrich (Burbank, CA: Walt Disney Pictures, 2001).

3. *King of the Hill*, created by Greg Daniels and Mike Judge, aired 1997–2010 on FOX; *The Simpsons*, created by James L. Brooks, Matt Groening, and Sam Simons, aired 1989– on FOX; *South Park*, created by Trey Parker, Matt Stone, and Brian Graden, aired 1997– on Comedy Central.

4. *The Elder Scrolls III: Morrowind*, designed by Todd Howard (Rockville, MD: Bethesda Game Studios, 2002), https://store.steampowered.com/app/22320/The_Elder_Scrolls_III_Morrowind_Game_of_the_Year_Edition/.

5. Vittorio Vandelli, "Genoa G8 Summit in 2001: The Days Berlusconi's Italy Went Back to Fascism," September 15, 2015, http://www.vittorio-vandelli.com/genoa-g8-summit-police-torture/.

6. CNN, "Transcript of President Bush's Address," September 21, 2001, https://edition.cnn.com/2001/US/09/20/gen.bush.transcript/.

7. J. Baxter Oliphant, "The Iraq War Continues to Divide the US Public, 15 Years after It Began," Pew Research Center, March 19, 2018, https://www.pewresearch.org/fact-tank/2018/03/19/iraq-war-continues-to-divide-u-s-public-15-years-after-it-began/; Caroline Smith and James M. Lindsay, "Rally 'round the Flag: Opinion in the United States before and after the Iraq War," Brookings, June 1, 2003, https://www.brookings.edu/articles/rally-round-the-flag-opinion-in-the-united-states-before-and-after-the-iraq-war/.

8. Steve Schifferes, "US Names Coalition of the Willing," BBC, March 18, 2003, http://news.bbc.co.uk/2/hi/americas/2862343.stm.

9. Department of Justice, "The USA PATRIOT Act: Preserving Life and Liberty," accessed June 20, 2019, https://www.justice.gov/archive/ll/highlights.htm.

10. US Department of Homeland Security, "About DHS," accessed June 20, 2019, https://www.dhs.gov.

11. Terence Nellan, "Bush Pulls Out of ABM Treaty; Putin Calls Move a Mistake," *New York Times*, December 13, 2001, https://www.nytimes.com/2001/12/13/international/bush-pulls-out-of-abm-treaty-putin-calls-move-a-mistake.html.

12. *Star Trek: Enterprise*, season 3, episode 23, "Countdown," directed by Robert Duncan McNeill, aired May 19, 2004, on UPN.

13. *Star Trek: Enterprise*, season 4, episode 20, "Demons," directed by LaVar Burton, aired May 6, 2005, on UPN.

14. All quotes in this paragraph are from "Terra Prime." *Star Trek: Enterprise*, season 4, episode 21, "Terra Prime," directed by Marvin V. Rush, aired on May 13, 2005, on UPN.

15. *Chicago*, directed by Rob Marshall (Burbank, CA: Miramax, 2002); *Forrest Gump*, directed by Robert Zemeckis (Hollywood, CA: Paramount Pictures, 1994); *Million Dollar Baby*, directed by Clint Eastwood (Hollywood, CA: Warner Brothers, 2004); *Unforgiven*, directed by Clint Eastwood (Hollywood, CA: Warner Brothers, 1992).

16. Center for American Women and Politics, "Milestones for Women in American Politics," accessed June 22, 2019, https://cawp.rutgers.edu/facts/milestones-for-women; Eileen Patten and Kim Parker, "Women in the US Mili-

tary: Growing Share, Distinctive Profile," Pew Research Center, accessed June 21, 2019, https://www.pewresearch.org/wp-content/uploads/sites/3/2011/12/women-in-the-military.pdf; Richard Sisk, "Number of Female Generals, Admirals Has Doubled since 2000, Report Finds," Military, April 17, 2019, https://www.military.com/daily-news/2019/04/17/number-female-generals-admirals-has-doubled-2000-report-finds.html.

17. Pew Research Center, "Highlights of Women's Earnings in 2005," accessed June 22, 2019, http://download.militaryonesource.mil/12038/MOS/Reports/2005%20Demographics%20Report.pdf; Pew Research Center, "Women CEOs in Fortune 500 Companies, 1995–2018," accessed June 22, 2019, https://www.pewsocialtrends.org/chart/women-ceos-in-fortune-500-companies-1995-2014/.

18. Karu F. Daniels, "Even with Chinese-Hawaiian Roots, Keanu Reeves Says He's Not a Spokesperson for Asians in Hollywood," *Daily News*, May 16, 2019, https://www.nydailynews.com/entertainment/movies/ny-keanu-reeves-not-spokesperson-asian-diversity-20190516-rxpec7y775cexkbxvv6qbcljmq-story.html; *The Matrix*, directed by Lana and Lilly Wachowski (Hollywood, CA: Warner Brothers, 1999); *The Matrix Reloaded*, directed by Lana and Lilly Wachowski (Hollywood, CA: Warner Brothers, 2003); *The Matrix Revolutions*, directed by Lana and Lilly Wachowski (Hollywood, CA: Warner Brothers, 2003).

19. Biography, "Halle Berry," accessed July 20, 2019, https://www.biography.com/actor/halle-berry; *Monster's Ball*, directed by Marc Forster (Santa Monica, CA: Lions Gate Films, 2001).

20. Britannica, "Colin Powell," accessed July 20, 2019, https://www.britannica.com/biography/Colin-Powell; Britannica, "Tiger Woods," accessed July 20, 2019, https://www.britannica.com/biography/Tiger-Woods.

21. *Battlestar Galactica*, created by Glen A. Larson and Ronald D. Moore, aired 2004–2007; EFE, "Latinos in Hollywood," Al Dia Culture, June 29, 2017, https://aldianews.com/articles/culture/latinos-hollywood-edward-james-olmos-receive-platino-honor-award/48935; Gary Younge, "Latinos Become Main Minority Group in US," *Guardian*, January 22, 2003, https://www.theguardian.com/world/2003/jan/23/usa.garyyounge.

22. Britannica, "Yao Ming," accessed July 20, 2019, https://www.britannica.com/biography/Yao-Ming; Angela Perez Baraquio, accessed July 20, 2019, http://www.angelaperezbaraquio.com.

23. Yvette Smith, "Astronaut John Herrington Carried a Piece of Native American History to Space," NASA, last updated November 5, 2019, https://www.nasa.gov/image-feature/astronaut-john-herrington-carried-a-piece-of-native-american-history-to-space.

24. Secretary of Defense, *2005 Demographics Report*, accessed June 21, 2019, http://download.militaryonesource.mil/12038/MOS/Reports/2005%20Demographics%20Report.pdf.

25. C. N. Le, "Employment and Occupational Patterns," Asian-Nation, accessed June 28, 2019, http://www.asian-nation.org/employment.shtml#sthash.N0RUzvTN.dpbs.

26. Jesse D. McKinnon and Claudette E. Bennett, "We the People: Blacks in the United States: Census 2000 Special Report," Census, August 2005, https://www.census.gov/prod/2005pubs/censr-25.pdf.

27. *Star Trek: Enterprise*, season 2, episode 23, "Regeneration," directed by David Livingston, aired May 7, 2003, on UPN.

28. *Star Trek: Enterprise*, season 4, episode 6, "The Augments," directed by LaVar Burton, aired November 12, 2004, on UPN.

29. The following episodes were viewed to collect snapshots: "Unexpected" (Michael Vejar, S1e5); "Breaking the Ice" (Terry Windell, S1e8); "Sleeping Dogs" (Les Landau, S1e14); "Desert Crossing" (David Straiton, S1e24); "The Catwalk" (Michael Vejar, S2e12); "Cease Fire" (David Straiton, S2e15); "Judgment" (James L. Conway, S2e19); "Cogenitor" (LeVar Burton, S2e22); "Impulse" (David Livingston, S3e5); "Proving Ground" (David Livingston, S3e13); "Zero Hour" (Allan Kroeker, S3e24); "Home" (Allan Kroeker, S4e3); "Borderland" (David Livingston, S4e4); "Demons" (LeVar Burton, S4e20). See full citations in the filmography.

30. *Star Trek: Enterprise*, season 3, episode 21, "E²," directed by Roxann Dawson, aired May 5, 2004, on UPN.

31. Richard Fry, Ruth Igielnik, and Eileen Patten, "How Millennials Today Compare with Their Grandparents 50 Years Ago," Pew Research Center, March 16, 2018, https://www.pewresearch.org/fact-tank/2018/03/16/how-millennials-compare-with-their-grandparents/.

7. INTERLUDE II

1. Jason Silva is a TV personality and motivational speaker. See Brainy Quotes, "Jason Silva Quotes," accessed November 3, 2019, https://www.brainyquote.com/quotes/jason_silva_621971; Jason Silva, accessed April 3, 2020, https://www.thisisjasonsilva.com.

2. *Dr. Who*, created by Sydney Newman, C. E. Webber, and Donald Wilson, aired 2005– on BBC, https://www.doctorwho.tv.

3. Facebook, accessed April 3, 2020, https://www.Facebook.com; Twitter, accessed April 3, 2020, https://www.Twitter.com.

4. CBS, accessed April 3, 2020, https://www.cbs.com; Memory Alpha, accessed May 17, 2018, https://memory-alpha.fandom.com/wiki/Portal:Main; Star-Trek.com, accessed April 3, 2020, https://www.startrek.com; ViacomCBS, accessed December 18, 2019, https://www.viacbs.com.

5. ArcGames, *Star Trek* Online, accessed July 10, 2019, https://www.arcgames.com/en/splash/ads/startrekonline?gclid=Cj0KCQjw9fntBRCGARIsAGjFq5GtIUxuE3pMRaEF1lUkKnyrW3zJllkMZ0sST3-sNn-ROKWNdJ6zUngaAjnbEALw_wcB.

6. Ryan Rushing, interviewed by K. M. Heath, July 10, August 15, and October 16, 2019.

7. Danny Hakim, "'Star Trek' Fans, Deprived of a Show, Recreate the Franchise on Digital Video," *New York Times*, June 18, 2006, https://www.nytimes.com/2006/06/18/arts/television/18trek.html; Jonathan Lane, "A History of *Star Trek* Fan Films," January 2016, https://fanfilmfactor.com/wp-content/uploads/2016/12/The-History-of-STAR-TREK-fan-films-Jonathan-Lane.pdf.

8. David Hill, Hidden Frontiers Productions, accessed December 18, 2019, http://www.hiddenfrontier.net.

9. Peter Walker and Stephan Mittelstrass, *Star Trek New Voyages: Phase II, International*, accessed December 18, 2019, https://www.stnv.de/en/about_us.php.

10. Thomas Vinciguerra, "A 'Trek' Script Is Grounded in Cyberspace," *New York Times*, March 29, 2012, https://www.nytimes.com/2012/03/29/arts/television/cbs-blocks-use-of-unused-star-trek-script-by-spinrad.html.

11. Jack Trevino and Ethan H. Calk, *Star Trek of Gods and Men*, accessed December 18, 2019, http://startrekofgodsandmen.com/main/.

12. Steven Dengler, *Star Trek Continues*, accessed December 18, 2019, https://www.startrekcontinues.com.

13. *Axanar*, created by Alec Peters, accessed December 18, 2019, https://axanar.com.

14. StarTrek.com, "Fan Films," accessed July 31, 2019, https://www.startrek.com/fan-films.

15. Ethan Calk et al., *Renegades: The Series*, accessed December 18, 2019, http://renegades.show/home/.

16. Creation Entertainment, "The Official *Star Trek* Convention," last modified July 28, 2019, http://www.creationent.com/cal/st_lasvegas.html; Massive Events, "Destination *Star Trek*," accessed August 10, 2019, https://www.destinationstartrek.com.

17. Entertainment Cruise Productions, accessed August 10, 2019, https://www.ecpcruises.com.

18. This section is largely based on Rushing, July 10, August 15, and October 16, 2019. See also, Lucien King. *Game On: The History and Culture of Video Games* (New York: Universe, 2002).

19. Ubisoft Entertainment, *Star Trek: Bridge Crew*, accessed December 18, 2019, https://www.ubisoft.com/en-us/game/star-trek-bridge-crew/.

20. Jon Radoff et al., *Star Trek Timelines*, accessed December 18, 2019, https://www.disruptorbeam.com/games/star-trek-timelines.

21. IDW, *Star Trek Collections!* accessed December 18, 2019, https://www.idwpublishing.com/product-category/star-trek/.

22. IDW, *Star Trek: Best of Klingons*, accessed December 18, 2019, https://www.idwpublishing.com/product/star-trek-best-of-klingons/.

23. Modiphius Entertainment, *Star Trek* Adventures Tabletop RPG, accessed April 3, 2020, https://www.modiphius.net/collections/star-trek-adventures.

24. *The Big Bang Theory*, accessed April 3, 2020, https://the-big-bang-theory.com.

25. *The Big Bang Theory*, season 6, episode 13, "The Bakersfield Expedition," directed by Mark Cendrowski, aired January 10, 2013, on CBS.

26. *Star Trek: Enterprise*, season 3, episode 20, "The Forgotten," directed by LeVar Burton, aired April 28, 2004, on UPN; *Star Trek: Enterprise*, season 4, episode 15, "Affliction," directed by Michael Grossman, aired February 18, 2005, on UPN.

27. *The Orville*, created by Seth MacFarlane, aired 2017– on Fox, https://www.fox.com/the-orville/?cmpid=org=dcg::ag=merkle::mc=cpc::src=google::cmp=foxweb::add=the_orville&gclsrc=aw.ds&ds_rl=1264074&gclid=Cj0KCQjw9fntBRCGARIsAGjFq5F41WGW5xx5PKCqwL7oZ3f3alMnC7jdCngOFjm8EcxoThxYp11_zSEaAnApEALw_wcB.

28. *Black Mirror*, created by Charlie Brooker, aired 2011– on Netflix, https://www.netflix.com/title/70264888.

29. *Black Mirror*, season 4, episode 1, "USS *Callister*," directed by Toby Haynes, aired December 29, 2017, on Netflix.

30. *Star Trek*, directed by J. J. Abrams (Hollywood, CA: Paramount Pictures, 2009); *Star Trek Beyond*, directed by Justin Lin (Hollywood, CA: Paramount Pictures, 2016); *Star Trek into Darkness*, directed by J. J. Abrams (Hollywood, CA: Paramount Pictures, 2013).

31. IMDbPro, "Box Office Mojo," accessed April 3, 2020, https://www.boxofficemojo.com.

8. CONTEXT IS FOR KINGS

1. Michael Burnham shows Cadet Tilly the book *Alice in Wonderland* given to her by Amanda Grayson, her foster mother; *Star Trek: Discovery*, season 1, episode 3, "Context Is for Kings," directed by Akiva Goldsman, aired October 1, 2017, on CBS All Access.

2. *Black Mirror*, created by Charlie Brooker, aired 2011– on Netflix; *Gunsmoke*, created by Norman Macdonnell and John Meston, aired 1955–1975 on CBS; *Stranger Things*, created by Matt Duffer and Ross Duffer, aired 2016– on Netflix.

3. Bob Dylan, "The Times They Are a-Changin'" (New York: Columbia Records, 1963).

4. Anemona Hartocollis and Yamiche Alcindor, "Women's March Highlights as Huge Crowds Protest Trump: 'We're Not Going Away,'" *New York Times*, January 21, 2017, https://www.nytimes.com/2017/01/21/us/womens-march.html.

5. Jonathan Capehart, "June 26, 2015: America at Its Greatest," *Washington Post*, June 26, 2017, https://www.washingtonpost.com/blogs/post-partisan/wp/2017/06/26/june-26-2015-america-at-its-greatest/?noredirect=on.

6. Mary Shown, "Mayor Pete Buttigieg Marries Partner Chasten Glezman in Downtown South Bend," *South Bend Tribune*, June 17, 2018, https://www.southbendtribune.com/news/local/mayor-pete-buttigieg-marries-partner-chasten-glezman-in-downtown-south/article_b9bb722b-bbb0-5b55-a73d-e014ac7e4bf1.html.

7. Samantha Cooney, "Here Are Some of the Women Who Made History in the Midterm Elections," *Time*, November 19, 2017, https://time.com/5323592/2018-elections-women-history-records/.

8. *Captain Marvel*, directed by Anna Boden and Ryan Fleck (Burbank, CA: Walt Disney Studios, 2019); CNN, "It's Not the Year of the Woman. It's the 'Year of the Women,'" updated November 4, 2018, https://www.cnn.com/2018/11/03/opinions/midterm-elections-year-of-woman-roundup/index.html; W. Geiger and Kim Parker, "For Women's History Month, a Look at Gender Gains—and Gaps—in the U.S.," Pew Research Center, March 15, 2018, https://www.pewresearch.org/fact-tank/2018/03/15/for-womens-history-month-a-look-at-gender-gains-and-gaps-in-the-u-s/; Janet Napolitano, "Women Earn More College Degrees and Men Still Earn More Money," Forbes, September 4, 2018, https://www.forbes.com/sites/janetnapolitano/2018/09/04/women-earn-more-college-degrees-and-men-still-earn-more-money/#1a7cc96c39f1; NFHS, "High School Sports Participation Increases for 29th Consecutive Year," National Federation of State High School Associations, September 11, 2018,https://www.nfhs.org/articles/high-school-sports-participation-increases-for-29th-

consecutive-year/; Steidinger, Joan. *Stand Up and Shout Out: Women's Fight for Equal Pay, Equal Rights, and Equal Opportunities in Sports*. Lanham, MD: Rowman & Littlefield, 2020; *Wonder Woman*, directed by Patty Jenkins (Burbank, CA: Warner Brothers, 2017).

9. Meghann Myers, "Almost 800 Women Are Serving in Previously Closed Army Combat Jobs. This Is How They're Faring," *Army Times*, October 9, 2018, https://www.armytimes.com/news/your-army/2018/10/09/almost-800-women-are-serving-in-previously-closed-army-combat-jobs-this-is-how-theyre-faring/.

10. Bente Birkeland, "A First: Women Take the Majority in Nevada Legislature and Colorado House," NPR, February 4, 2019, https://www.npr.org/2019/02/04/691198416/a-first-women-take-the-majority-in-nevada-legislature-and-colorado-house; Samantha Cooney, "Here Are Some of the Women Who Made History in the Midterm Elections," *Time*, November 19, 2017, https://time.com/5323592/ 2018-elections-women-history-records/.

11. Dudley Postin and Rogelio Saenz, "The US White Majority Will Soon Disappear Forever," *Chicago Reporter*, May 16, 2019, https://www.chicagoreporter.com/the-us-white-majority-will-soon-disappear-forever/.

12. *Crazy Rich Asians*, directed by John M. Chu (Burbank, CA: Warner Brothers, 2018).

13. Aimee Lewis, "Chloe Kim: US teenager makes history at Winter Olympics, *CNN*, February 13, 2018. https://www.cnn.com/2018/02/13/sport/chloe-kim-snowboard-winter-olympics-intl/index.html; Edward Knowles, "Mirai Nagasu on 2018 routine and landing triple axel at Winter Olympics," *OlympicChannel*, February 13, 2018. https://www.olympicchannel.com/en/stories/news/detail/mirai-nagasu-triple-axel-2018-winter-olympics/

14. Agnes Constante, "For Second Congress in a Row, Elected Asian Americans and Pacific Islanders Hit New High," NBC News, December 26, 2018, https://www.nbcnews.com/news/asian-america/second-congress-row-elected-asian-americans-pacific-islanders-hit-new-n950371.

15. *Black Panther*, directed by Ryan Coogler (Burbank, CA; Walt Disney, 2018).

16. Lois M. Collins, "Most Black Males Reach the Middle Class or Higher," *Deseret News*, July 2, 2018, https://www.deseret.com/2018/7/2/20648205/most-black-males-reach-the-middle-class-or-higher-here-s-what-drives-their-success.

17. Molly Fosco, "The Most Successful Ethnic Group in the U.S. May Surprise You," Ozy, June 7, 2018, https://www.ozy.com/fast-forward/the-most-successful-ethnic-group-in-the-us-may-surprise-you/86885.

18. Aspen Institute, "Latino Success Is American Success," July 20, 2017, https://www.aspeninstitute.org/blog-posts/latino-success-americas-success/.

19. Rory Cellan-Jones, "Stephen Hawking Warns Artificial Intelligence Could End Mankind," BBC, December 2, 2014, https://www.bbc.com/news/

technology-30290540; Nicolas Vega, "Elon Musk: AI Will Soon Make Us Look Like Apes," *New York Post*, August 29, 2019, https://nypost.com/2019/08/29/elon-musk-ai-will-soon-make-us-look-like-monkeys/.

20. Bernard Marr, "Is Artificial Intelligence Dangerous? 6 AI Risks Everyone Should Know About," *Forbes*, November 19, 2018, https://www.forbes.com/sites/bernardmarr/2018/11/19/is-artificial-intelligence-dangerous-6-ai-risks-everyone-should-know-about/#290c0aa12404.

21. Dom Galeon, and Christianna Reedy, "Ray Kurtzweil Claims Singularity Will Happen by 2045," Kurzweilai, March 20, 2017, https://www.kurzweilai.net/futurism-ray-kurzweil-claims-singularity-will-happen-by-2045.

22. S. A. Bonn, "Fear-Based Anger Is the Primary Motive for Violence: Anger Induced Violence Is Rooted in Fear," *Psychology Today*, July 17, 2017, https://www.psychologytoday.com/us/blog/wicked-deeds/201707/fear-based-anger-is-the-primary-motive-violence.

23. US Department of Justice, "2017 Hate Crime Statistics," accessed September 29, 2019, https://www.justice.gov/hatecrimes/hate-crime-statistics.

24. Heidi Stevens, "It's Official: 2016 Is the Year of Xenophobia," *Chicago Tribune*, November 29, 2016, https://www.chicagotribune.com/columns/heidi-stevens/ct-xenophobia-word-of-the-year-balancing-1129-20161129-column.html.

25. Greg Lacour, "White Supremacist Found Guilty on All Counts in Charleston Church Massacre," Reuters, December 15, 2016, https://www.reuters.com/article/us-south-carolina-shooting-roof/white-supremacist-found-guilty-on-all-counts-in-charleston-church-massacre-idUSKBN14418R.

26. Mary Emily O'Hara, "Abortion Clinics Report Threats of Violence on the Rise," NBC News, February 13, 2017, https://www.nbcnews.com/news/us-news/abortion-clinics-report-threats-violence-rise-n719426.

27. Katayoun Kishi, "Assaults against Muslims in US Surpass 2001 Level," Pew Research Center, November 15, 2017, https://www.pewresearch.org/fact-tank/2017/11/15/assaults-against-muslims-in-u-s-surpass-2001-level/.

28. Lou Chibbaro Jr., "DC Sees Alarming Increase in Anti-LGBT Hate Crimes in 2018," *Washington Blade*, February 6, 2019, https://www.washingtonblade.com/2019/02/06/d-c-sees-alarming-increase-in-anti-lgbt-hate-crimes-in-2018/.

29. Mallory Simon and Sara Sidner, "A Gunman Slaughtered 11 Jewish Worshipers. Then People Hunted for Hate Online," CNN, updated May 15, 2019, https://www.cnn.com/2019/05/15/us/anti-semitic-searches-pittsburgh-poway-shootings-soh/index.html.

30. Suzanne Gamboa, "Anti-Hispanic Violence That Pierced El Paso Has Been Part of Texas' History," NBC News, August 16, 2019, https://www.

nbcnews.com/news/latino/anti-hispanic-violence-pierced-el-paso-has-been-part-texas-n1041921.

31. The following episodes were viewed to collect snapshots: "Battle at the Binary Stars" (Adam Kane, S1e2); "The Butcher's Knife Cares Not for the Lamb's Cry" (Olatunde Osunsanmi, S1e4); "Vaulting Ambitions" (Hanelle Culpepper, S1e12); "Saints of Imperfection" (David Barrett, S2e5); "Through the Valley of Shadows" (Douglas Aarniokoski, S2e12). See full citations in the filmography.

32. Center for American Women and Politics, "Women in the US House 2018," accessed October 19, 2019, https://cawp.rutgers.edu/women-us-house-representatives-2018.

33. Service Women's Active Network, "Women in the Military: Where They Stand," accessed October 19, 2019, 38, tab. 4, https://www.servicewomen.org/wp-content/uploads/2019/04/SWAN-Where-we-stand-2019-0416revised.pdf; Clair Zillman, "The Fortune 500 Has More Female CEOs than Ever Before," *Fortune*, May 16, 2019, https://fortune.com/2019/05/16/fortune-500-female-ceos/.

34. Congressional Research Service, "Membership of the 115th Congress: A Profile," accessed October 19, 2019, https://fas.org/sgp/crs/misc/R44762.pdf.

35. Diversity Defense, "Total Force Military Demographics," accessed October 19, 2019, https://diversity.defense.gov/LinkClick.aspx?fileticket=gxMVqhkaHh8%3D&portalid=51. See page 44, Table Race/Ethnicity for Officers; Leo Shane III, "White Nationalism Remains a Problem for the Military, Poll Suggests," *Military Times*, February 26, 2019, https://www.militarytimes.com/news/pentagon-congress/2019/02/28/white-nationalism-remains-a-problem-for-the-military-poll-shows/.

36. Deb DeHass et al., "Missing Pieces Report: The 2018 Board Diversity Census of Women and Minorities on Fortune 500 Boards," Harvard Law School Forum on Corporate Governance, February 5, 2019, https://corpgov.law.harvard.edu/2019/02/05/missing-pieces-report-the-2018-board-diversity-census-of-women-and-minorities-on-fortune-500-boards/.

37. Mick Joest, "William Shatner Defends *Star Trek*'s Unchanging Vision: It May Be Controversial to Some," Cinemablend, accessed October 18, 2019, https://www.cinemablend.com/television/2482170/william-shatner-defends-star-trek-unchanging-vision-it-may-be-controversial-to-some.

9. *STAR TREK* IN THE THEATERS

1. Spock, to Captain Kirk, in *Star Trek II: The Wrath of Kahn*, directed by Nicholas Meyer (Hollywood, CA: Paramount Pictures, 1982).

2. *Star Trek*, directed by J. J. Abrams (Hollywood, CA: Paramount Pictures, 2009); *Star Trek: First Contact*, directed by Jonathan Frakes (Hollywood, CA: Paramount Pictures, 1996); *Star Trek: Generations*, directed by David Carson (Hollywood, CA: Paramount Pictures, 1994); *Star Trek: Insurrection*, directed by Jonathan Frakes (Hollywood, CA: Paramount Pictures, 1998); *Star Trek: Nemesis*, direct by Stuart Baird (Hollywood, CA: Paramount Pictures, 2002); *Star Trek: The Motion Picture*, directed by Robert Wise (Hollywood, CA: Paramount Pictures, 1979); *Star Trek II: The Wrath of Khan*, directed by Nicholas Meyer (Hollywood, CA: Paramount Pictures, 1982; *Star Trek III: The Search for Spock*, directed by Leonard Nimoy (Hollywood, CA: Paramount Pictures, 1984); *Star Trek IV: The Voyage Home*, directed by Leonard Nimoy (Hollywood, CA: Paramount Pictures, 1986); *Star Trek V: The Final Frontier*, directed by William Shatner (Hollywood, CA: Paramount Pictures, 1989); *Star Trek VI: The Undiscovered Country*, directed by Nicholas Meyer (Hollywood, CA: Paramount Pictures, 1991); *Star Trek Beyond*, directed by Justin Lin (Hollywood, CA: Paramount Pictures, 2016); *Star Trek into Darkness*, directed by J. J. Abrams (Hollywood, CA: Paramount Pictures, 2013).

3. Mike Wall, "35 Years Ago: NASA Unveils First Space Shuttle, *Enterprise*," September 17, 2011, Space.com, https://www.space.com/12991-nasa-space-shuttle-enterprise-35-years.html.

4. *Star Wars: Episode IV—A New Hope*, directed by George Lucas (Los Angeles: Twentieth Century Fox, 1977).

5. ESPN, "History," accessed August 9, 2019, https://espncareers.com/working-here/history; *Star Wars: Episode IV*.

6. *Wrath of Kahn*, the most beloved of the *Star Trek* movies, saved the *Star Trek* franchise and was not designed to be a trilogy. See Juliette Harrisson, "*Star Trek II–IV*: An Overlooked Movie Trilogy," Den of Geek, June 9, 2015, https://www.denofgeek.com/us/movies/star-trek/246841/star-trek-ii-iv-an-overlooked-movie-trilogy.

7. *Star Trek: The Original Series*, season 1, episode 22, "Space Seed," directed by Marc Daniels, aired February 16, 1967, on NBC.

8. Carl E. Pickhardt, "Developmental Dislike of Parents during Early Adolescence," *Psychology Today*, April 20, 2015, https://www.psychologytoday.com/us/blog/surviving-your-childs-adolescence/201504/developmental-dislike-parents-during-early-adolescence.

9. Racebending, "*Star Trek*: Into Whiteness," May 9, 2013, http://www.racebending.com/v4/featured/star-trek-whiteness/.

10. Sam Ashurst, "All 13 *Star Trek* Movies, Ranked," Digital Spy, November 28, 2018, https://www.digitalspy.com/movies/a871507/star-trek-movies-ranked/.

11. Morgan Jeffery, "Here's Why *Star Trek* Should Quit Movies and Focus Just on TV Shows: It's Time for the Franchise to Boldly Go Back to Its Roots,"

Digital Spy, August 15, 2018, https://www.digitalspy.com/tv/ustv/a863985/star-trek-discovery-movies-tv-shows/.

12. Richard Newby, "The Stakes of *Star Trek 4*," *Hollywood Reporter*, November 21, 2019, https://www.hollywoodreporter.com/heat-vision/why-star-trek-4-is-a-high-stakes-game-paramount-1256970; Ryan Rushing, interviewed by K. M. Heath, July 10, August 15, and October 16, 2019.

10. MELDING FIFTY-PLUS YEARS

1. Polly W. Wiessner, "Embers of Society: Firelight Talk among the Ju/'hoansi Bushman." *Proceedings of the National Academy of Sciences* 111, no. 39 (2014): 14027–35.

2. *Star Trek: Short Treks*, season 2, episode 5, "The Girl Who Made the Stars," directed by Olatunde Osunsanmi, aired December 12, 2019, on CBS All Access.

BIBLIOGRAPHY

Academy of Motion Picture Arts and Sciences. "The 38th Academy Awards: 1966." Accessed July 20, 2017. https://www.oscars.org/oscars/ceremonies/1966.

Alexander, David. "The Roddenberry Interview." *Humanist* 51, no. 2 (1991): 5–30.

Allen, Steve, and Robert J. Thompson. "The 1990s: The Loss of Shared Experience." *Britannica*. July 1, 2019. https://www.britannica.com/art/television-in-the-United-States/The-1990s-the-loss-of-shared-experience.

American Disposal Services. "A Brief History of Recycling." Accessed November 30, 2019. https://americandisposal.com/blog/a-brief-history-of-recycling/.

Anderson, Kirk. "The Best Decade Ever? The 1990s, Obviously." *New York Times*, February 6, 2015. https://www.nytimes.com/2015/02/08/opinion/sunday/the-best-decade-ever-the-1990s-obviously.html.

ArcGames. "*Star Trek* Online." Accessed July 10, 2019. https://www.arcgames.com/en/games/star-trek-online/news.

Ashurst, Sam. "All 13 *Star Trek* Movies, Ranked." Digital Spy. November 28, 2018. https://www.digitalspy.com/movies/a871507/star-trek-movies-ranked/.

Aspen Institute. "Latino Success Is American Success." July 20, 2017. https://www.aspeninstitute.org/blog-posts/latino-success-americas-success/.

Baby Boomer Headquarters. "The Boomer Stats." Accessed August 1, 2017. https://www.bbhq.com/bomrstat.htm.

Baraquio, Angela Perez. Accessed July 20, 2019. http://www.angelaperezbaraquio.com.

Bastien, Angelica Jade. "*Deep Space Nine* Is TV's Most Revolutionary Depiction of Black Fatherhood." Vulture. January 19, 2018. https://www.vulture.com/2018/01/deep-space-nine-revolutionary-depiction-of-black-fatherhood.html.

Baugher, Eleanor, and Leatha Lamison-White. "Poverty in the United States: 1995." Bureau of the Census. September 1996. https://www2.census.gov/prod2/popscan/p60-194.pdf.

Bernard, Russell H. *Research Methods in Anthropology: Qualitative and Quantitative Approaches.* Lanham, MD: Rowman & Littlefield, 2017.

The Big Bang Theory. Accessed April 3, 2020. https://the-big-bang-theory.com.

Biography. "Clint Eastwood." April 27, 2017. https://www.biography.com/actor/clint-eastwood.

———. "Halle Berry." Accessed July 20, 2019. https://www.biography.com/actor/halle-berry.

Birkeland, Bente. "A First: Women Take the Majority in Nevada Legislature and Colorado House." *NPR*. February 4, 2019. https://www.npr.org/2019/02/04/691198416/a-first-women-take-the-majority-in-nevada-legislature-and-colorado-house.

Black Male Re-Imagined II. *Transforming Perception: Black Men and Boys: Executive Summary*. Los Angeles: University of California, Los Angeles, November 2016. https://equity.ucla.edu/wp-content/uploads/2016/11/Transforming-Perception.pdf.

Blackmore, Erin. "The Revolutionary War Hero Who Was Openly Gay." *History*. June 14, 2018. https://www.history.com/news/openly-gay-revolutionary-war-hero-friedrich-von-steuben.

Blow, Charles M. "Black Dads Are Doing Best of All." *New York Times*, June 8, 2015. https://www.nytimes.com/2015/06/08/opinion/charles-blow-black-dads-are-doing-the-best-of-all.html.

Bonn, S. A. "Fear-Based Anger Is the Primary Motive for Violence: Anger Induced Violence Is Rooted in Fear." *Psychology Today*, July 17, 2017. https://www.psychologytoday.com/us/blog/wicked-deeds/201707/fear-based-anger-is-the-primary-motive-violence.

Bono, Sonny. "I Got You Babe." New York: ATCO Records, 1966.

Booker, M. Keith. *Star Trek: A Cultural History*. Lanham, MD: Rowman & Littlefield, 2018.

Boston, Rob. "Inside the Christian Coalition." *Americans United*. November 2004. https://www.au.org/church-state/november-2004-church-state/featured/inside-the-christian-coalition.

Brainy Quotes. "Jason Silva Quotes." Accessed November 3, 2019. https://www.brainyquote.com/quotes/jason_silva_621971.

Britannica. "Colin Powell." Accessed July 20, 2019. https://www.britannica.com/biography/Colin-Powell.

———. "Collapse of the Soviet Union." Accessed March 4, 2018. https://www.britannica.com/event/the-collapse-of-the-Soviet-Union.

———. "Don't Ask, Don't Tell." Accessed February 14, 2018. https://www.britannica.com/event/Dont-Ask-Dont-Tell.

———. "Eileen Collins." Accessed March 20, 2018. https://www.britannica.com/biography/Eileen-Collins.

———. "Janet Reno." Accessed March 20, 2018. https://www.britannica.com/biography/Janet-Reno.

———. "Madeleine Albright." May 23, 2019. https://www.britannica.com/biography/Madeleine-Albright.

———. "Muriel Seibert." Accessed August 7, 2017. https://www.britannica.com/biography/Muriel-Siebert.

———. "The Riots of the Long, Hot Summers." Accessed February 20, 2017. https://www.britannica.com/story/the-riots-of-the-long-hot-summer.

———. "Tet Offensive." Accessed March 22, 2017. https://www.britannica.com/topic/Tet-Offensive.

———. "Tiger Woods." Accessed July 20, 2019. https://www.britannica.com/biography/Tiger-Woods.

———. "Yao Ming." Accessed July 20, 2019. https://www.britannica.com/biography/Yao-Ming.

Brown, Helen Gurley. *Sex and the Single Girl*. New York: Bernard Geis Associates, 1964.

Burrelli, David F. "Don't Ask, Don't Tell: The Law and Military Policy on Same-Sex Behavior." Congressional Research Service. October 14, 2010. https://fas.org/sgp/crs/misc/R40782.pdf.

Calk, Ethan, et al. *Renegades: The Series*. Accessed December 18, 2019. http://renegades.show/home/.

Capehart, Jonathan. "June 26, 2015: America at Its Greatest." *Washington Post*, June 26, 2017. https://www.washingtonpost.com/blogs/post-partisan/wp/2017/06/26/june-26-2015-america-at-its-greatest/?noredirect=on.

Carpenter, Julia. "Women in the Fortune 500: 64 CEOs in Half a Century." *CNN Money*. August 7, 2017. https://money.cnn.com/interactive/pf/female-ceos-timeline/.

Castleman, Harry, and Walter J. Podrazik. *Watching TV: Eight Decades of American Television*. Syracuse, NY: Syracuse University Press, 2016.

CBS. Accessed April 3, 2020. https://www.cbs.com.

Cellan-Jones, Rory. "Stephen Hawking Warns Artificial Intelligence Could End Mankind." *BBC*. December 2, 2014. https://www.bbc.com/news/technology-30290540.

Center for American Women and Politics. "History of Women in the US Congress." Accessed August 7, 2017. https://cawp.rutgers.edu/history-women-us-congress.

————. "Milestones for Women in American Politics." Accessed June 22, 2019. https://cawp.rutgers.edu/facts/milestones-for-women.

————. "Women in the US House 2018." Accessed October 19, 2019, https://cawp.rutgers.edu/women-us-house-representatives-2018.

Chagnon, Napoleon. *Adaptation and Human Behavior: An Anthropological Perspective.* Abingdon, UK: Routledge, 2017.

Chibbaro, Lou, Jr. "DC Sees Alarming Increase in Anti-LGBT Hate Crimes in 2018." *Washington Blade*, February 6, 2019. https://www.washingtonblade.com/2019/02/06/d-c-sees-alarming-increase-in-anti-lgbt-hate-crimes-in-2018/.

Chiles, Farrell J. "African American Warrant Officers and the Vietnam War." *Newsliner*, February 2014. https://warrantofficerhistory.org/PDF/AfricanAmericanWO-Vietnam-War.pdf.

The Citadel. "Women at the Citadel: A Decade of Change and Progress." Accessed January 27, 2020. http://www3.citadel.edu/pao/women/10_years.html.

Cloud, John. "*Star Trek* Inc." *Time*, December 11, 2002. http://content.time.com/time/magazine/article/0,9171,397512,00.html.

CNN. "It's Not the Year of the Woman. It's the 'Year of the Women.'" Last modified November 4, 2018. https://www.cnn.com/2018/11/03/opinions/midterm-elections-year-of-woman-roundup/index.html.

————. "Transcript of President Bush's Address." September 21, 2001. https://edition.cnn.com/2001/US/09/20/gen.bush.transcript/.

Cold War Museum. "The Strategic Defense Initiative SDI: Star Wars." Accessed February 25, 2018. http://www.coldwar.org/articles/80s/SDI-StarWars.asp.

Coles, Roberta L., and Charles Green. *The Myth of the Missing Black Father.* New York: Columbia University Press, 2010.

Collins, Lois M. "Most Black Males Reach the Middle Class or Higher." *Deseret News*, July 2, 2018. https://www.deseret.com/2018/7/2/20648205/most-black-males-reach-the-middle-class-or-higher-here-s-what-drives-their-success.

Compendio, Chris. "50 Longest-Running TV Series." *Stacker*. September 9, 2019, https://thestacker.com/stories/2372/50-longest-running-tv-series#5.

Congressional Research Service. "Membership of the 115th Congress: A Profile." Accessed October 19, 2019. https://fas.org/sgp/crs/misc/R44762.pdf.

Constante Agnes. "For Second Congress in a Row, Elected Asian Americans and Pacific Islanders Hit New High." *NBC News*. December 26, 2018. https://www.nbcnews.com/news/asian-america/second-congress-row-elected-asian-americans-pacific-islanders-hit-new-n950371.

Cooney, Samantha. "Here Are Some of the Women Who Made History in the Midterm Elections." *Time*, November 19, 2017. https://time.com/5323592/2018-elections-women-history-records/.

Coppa, Francesca. "A Brief History of Media Fandom." In *Fan Fiction and Fan Communities in the Age of the Internet*, edited by Karen Hellekson and Kristina Busse, 41–59. Jefferson, NC: McFarland, 2006).

Cornish, Audie. "Who Is an Evangelical? Looks at the History of Evangelical Christians and the GOP." *NPR*. November 14, 2019. https://www.npr.org/2019/11/14/779465137/who-is-an-evangelical-looks-at-history-of-evangelical-christians-and-the-gop.

Correll, John T. "The Emergence of Smart Bombs." *Air Force Magazine*, March 2010. https://www.airforcemag.com/PDF/MagazineArchive/Documents/2010/March%202010/0310bombs.pdf.

Coupland, Douglas. "1990s: The Good Decade." *History*. March 17, 2017.http://www.history.com/news/1990s-the-good-decade.

Creation Entertainment. "The Official *Star Trek* Convention." Last modified July 28, 2019. http://www.creationent.com/cal/st_lasvegas.html.

CSPAN. "A Look at the 1940 Census." April 2, 2012. https://www.census.gov/newsroom/cspan/1940census/CSPAN_1940slides.pdf.

Danhauser, Curt, "Curt Danhauser's Guide to the Animated Star Trek," *DanhauserTrek*, March 25, 1996. http://www.danhausertrek.com/AnimatedSeries/Main.html.

Daniels, Karu F. "Even with Chinese-Hawaiian Roots, Keanu Reeves Says He's Not a Spokesperson for Asians in Hollywood." *Daily News*, May 16, 2019. https://www.nydailynews.com/entertainment/movies/ny-keanu-reeves-not-spokesperson-asian-diversity-20190516-rxpec7y775cexkbxvv6qbcljmq-story.html.

Daunt, Tina, and Tina Nguyen. "Homeless Camp Weighed in L.A. Industrial Area." *Los Angeles Times*, October 14, 1994. https://www.latimes.com/archives/la-xpm-1994-10-14-mn-50276-story.html.

Davis, Nicola. "Dark Matter and Dinosaurs: Meet Lisa Randall, America's Superstar Scientist." *Guardian*, January 12, 2016. https://www.theguardian.com/science/2016/jan/12/dark-matter-physics-dinosaurs-extinction-lisa-randell.

Defense Advanced Research Projects Agency. "Where the Future Becomes Now." Accessed November 30, 2019. https://www.darpa.mil/about-us/darpa-history-and-timeline?PP=8.

DeHass, Deb, et al. "Missing Pieces Report: The 2018 Board Diversity Census of Women and Minorities on Fortune 500 Boards." Harvard Law School Forum on Corporate Governance, February 5, 2019. https://corpgov.law.harvard.edu/2019/02/05/missing-pieces-report-the-2018-board-diversity-census-of-women-and-minorities-on-fortune-500-boards/.

Dengler, Steven. *Star Trek Continues*. Accessed December 18, 2019. https://www.startrekcontinues.com.

Department of Justice. "The USA PATRIOT Act: Preserving Life and Liberty." Accessed June 20, 2019. https://www.justice.gov/archive/ll/highlights.htm.

Dickey, Beth. "Women in the News—Eileen Marie Collins; Women's Work: Space Commander." *New York Times*, July 24, 1999. https://www.nytimes.com/1999/07/24/us/woman-in-the-news-eileen-marie-collins-womans-work-space-commander.html.

Diversity Defense. "Total Force Military Demographics." Accessed October 19, 2019. https://diversity.defense.gov/LinkClick.aspx?fileticket=gxMVqhkaHh8%3D&portalid=51.

"Don't Trust Anyone over 30, unless It's Jack Weinberg." *Berkeley Daily Planet*, April 6, 2000. http://www.berkeleydailyplanet.com/issue/2000-04-06/article/759.

Dvorak, Petula. "Nancy Pelosi Is Showing Women How to Age Fearlessly and Ferociously." *Washington Post*, December 19, 2019. https://www.washingtonpost.com/local/2019/12/19.

Dylan, Bob. "The Times They Are a-Changin.'" New York: Columbia Records, 1963.

EFE. "Latinos in Hollywood." Al Dia Culture. June 29, 2017. https://aldianews.com/articles/culture/latinos-hollywood-edward-james-olmos-receive-platino-honor-award/48935.

Entertainment Cruise Productions. Accessed August 10, 2019. https://www.ecpcruises.com.

Environmental History Timeline. "Nineties 1990–99." Accessed November 30, 2019. http://environmentalhistory.org/20th-century/nineties/.

Epstein, Helen C. "America's Secret Role in the Rwandan Genocide." *Guardian*, September 12, 2017. https://www.theguardian.com/news/2017/sep/12/americas-secret-role-in-the-rwandan-genocide.

ESPN. "History." Accessed August 9, 2019. https://espncareers.com/working-here/history.

Facebook. Accessed April 3, 2020. https://www.facebook.com.

Famous Scientists. "Mae Carol Jemison." Accessed March 15, 2018. https://www.famousscientists.org/mae-carol-jemison/.

Feagin, Joe R., and Melvin P. Sikes. *Living with Racism: The Black Middle-Class Experience*. Boston: Beacon Press, 1994.

"Female Pilots Dropped Bombs in Iraq Mission." *Los Angeles Times*, December 23, 1998. https://www.latimes.com/archives/la-xpm-1998-dec-23-mn-56925-story.html.

Fern, Yvonne, and Gene Roddenberry. *Gene Roddenberry: The Last Conversation: A Dialogue with the Creator of* Star Trek. Berkeley: University of California Press, 1994.

Fisher, Anne. "How Executive Women Avoid Being Called the B-Word." *Fortune*, September 16, 2015. https://fortune.com/2015/09/16/how-executive-women-avoid-being-called-the-b-word/.

Forbes, Bruce David, and Jeffrey H. Mahan, eds. *Religion and Popular Culture in America*. Berkeley: University of California Press, 2017.

Forrest, Conner. "Tech Nostalgia: The Top 15 Innovations of the 1990s." *Tech Republic*, May 8, 2015. https://www.techrepublic.com/pictures/tech-nostalgia-the-top-15-innovations-of-the-1990s/.

Fosco Molly. "The Most Successful Ethnic Group in the US May Surprise You." Ozy. June 7, 2018. https://www.ozy.com/fast-forward/the-most-successful-ethnic-group-in-the-us-may-surprise-you/86885.

Friedan, Betty. *The Feminine Mystique*. New York: W. W. Norton, 2013.

Fry, Richard, Ruth Igielnik, and Eileen Patten. "How Millennials Today Compare with Their Grandparents 50 Years Ago." Pew Research Center. March 16, 2018. https://www.pewresearch.org/fact-tank/2018/03/16/how-millennials-compare-with-their-grandparents/.

Galeon, Dom, and Christianna Reedy. "Ray Kurtzweil Claims Singularity Will Happen by 2045." Kurzweilai. March 20, 2017. https://www.kurzweilai.net/futurism-ray-kurzweil-claims-singularity-will-happen-by-2045.

Gallagher, John, and Chris Bull. *Perfect Enemies: The Religious Right, the Gay Movement, and the Politics of the 1990s*. New York: Crown, 1996.

Gamboa, Suzanne. "Anti-Hispanic Violence That Pierced El Paso Has Been Part of Texas' History." *NBC News*. August 16, 2019. https://www.nbcnews.com/news/latino/anti-hispanic-violence-pierced-el-paso-has-been-part-texas-n1041921.

Gander, Kashmira. "The Terror and Prejudice of the 1980s AIDS Crisis Remembered by a Gay Man Who Lived through It." *Independent*, January 6, 2017. https://www.independent.co.uk/life-style/love-sex/aids-crisis-1980-eighties-remember-gay-man-hiv-positive-funerals-partners-disease-michael-penn-a7511671.html.

Geiger, W., and Kim Parker. "For Women's History Month, a Look at Gender Gains—and Gaps—in the US." Pew Research Center. March 15, 2018. https://www.pewresearch.org/fact-tank/2018/03/15/for-womens-history-month-a-look-at-gender-gains-and-gaps-in-the-u-s/

George, Alice. "The 1969 Kerner Commission Got It Right, but Nobody Listened." *Smithsonian*. March 1, 2008. https://www.smithsonianmag.com/smithsonian-institution/1968-kerner-commission-got-it-right-nobody-listened-180968318/.

Gerrold, David. *The World of Star Trek*. Dallas, TX: BenBella Books, 2014.

Goldin, Claudia. "The Quiet Revolution That Transformed Women's Employment, Education, and the Family." *American Economic Review*, 2006. https://scholar.harvard.edu/files/goldin/files/the_quiet_revolution_that_transformed_womens_employment_education_and_family.pdf.

Gowdy, Kristen. "Five Biggest Victories for Women in Sports 2018." Women's Sports Foundation. Accessed October 2, 2019. https://www.womenssportsfoundation.org/sports/five-biggest-victories-women-sports-2018/.

Gross, Terry. "Congressman, Civil Rights Icon John Lewis." *Fresh Air*, January 19, 2009. https://www.npr.org/templates/story/story.php?storyId=99560979.

Guerrier, Jacqueline. "Where No Fandom Has Gone Before: Exploring the Development of Fandom through *Star Trek* Fanzines." Master's thesis, James Madison University, Fall 2018.

Guo, Jeff. "The Real Reasons the US Became Less Racist toward Asian Americans." *Washington Post*, November 29, 2016. https://www.washingtonpost.com/news/wonk/wp/2016/11/29/the-real-reason-americans-stopped-spitting-on-asian-americans-and-started-praising-them/.

Hakim, Danny. "'*Star Trek*' Fans, Deprived of a Show, Recreate the Franchise on Digital Video." *New York Times*, June 18, 2006. https://www.nytimes.com/2006/06/18/arts/television/18trek.html.

Harrisson, Juliette. "*Star Trek II–IV*: An Overlooked Movie Trilogy." Den of Geek. June 9, 2015. https://www.denofgeek.com/us/movies/star-trek/246841/star-trek-ii-iv-an-overlooked-movie-trilogy.

Hartlaub, Peter. "Let's Time-Travel to 1976 Bay Area Sci-Fi Convention." *San Francisco Chronicle*, March 18, 2016. https://www.sfchronicle.com/oursf/article/Let-s-time-travel-back-to-1976-Bay-Area-science-6922053.php.

Hartocollis, Anemona, and Yamiche Alcindor. "Women's March Highlights as Huge Crowds Protest Trump: 'We're Not Going Away.'" *New York Times*, January 21, 2017. https://www.nytimes.com/2017/01/21/us/womens-march.html.

Healey, Melissa. "Colin Powell to Be Named Head of Joint Chiefs." *Los Angeles Times*, August 10, 1989. https://www.latimes.com/archives/la-xpm-1989-08-10-mn-413-story.html.

Higgins, Bill. "Hollywood Flashback: *Star Trek* Showed TV's First Interracial Kiss in 1969." *Hollywood Reporter*, May 26, 2016. https://www.hollywoodreporter.com/news/tvs-first-interracial-kiss-star-896843.

Hilburn, Robert. "Bonnie Raitt, Midler Win Top Grammys." *Los Angeles Times*, February 22, 1990. https://www.latimes.com/archives/la-xpm-1990-02-22-mn-1696-story.html.

Hill, David. Hidden Frontiers Productions. Accessed December 18, 2019. http://www.hiddenfrontier.net.

History. "Civil Rights Movement Timeline." December 4, 2017. https://www.history.com/topics/civil-rights-movement/civil-rights-movement-timeline.

Hodge, Karl. "*Star Trek*: Gene Roddenberry—An Appreciation." Den of Geek. May 6, 2009. https://www.denofgeek.com/us/movies/star-trek/21181/star-trek-gene-roddenberry-an-appreciation.

Howard, Todd, designer. *The Elder Scrolls III: Morrowwind*. Bethesda Game Studios. April 22, 2002. https://store.steampowered.com/app/22320/The_Elder_Scrolls_III_Morrowwind_Game_of_the_Year_Edition/.

Ibarra, Herminia, and Morton T. Hansen. "Women CEOs: Why So Few?" *Harvard Business Review*, December 21, 2009. https://hbr.org/2009/12/women-ceo-why-so-few.

IDW. *Star Trek: Best of Klingons*. Accessed December 18, 2019. https://www.idwpublishing.com/product/star-trek-best-of-klingons/.

———. *Star Trek Collections!* Accessed December 18, 2019. https://www.idwpublishing.com/product-category/star-trek/.

IMDb. "Christopher Plummer, Biography." Accessed August 15, 2017. https://www.imdb.com/name/nm0001626/bio.

———. "Julie Andrews, Biography." Accessed August 15, 2017. https://www.imdb.com/name/nm0000267/.

IMDbPRO. "Box Office Mojo." Accessed December 18, 2019. https://www.boxofficemojo.com.

Isikoff, Michael. "Christian Coalition Steps Boldly into Politics." *Washington Post*, September 10, 1992. https://www.washingtonpost.com/archive/politics/1992/09/10/christian-coalition-steps-boldly-into-politics/90c8bf0b-3268-4088-ba12-b49c93537bba/.

Jason Silva. Accessed April 3, 2020. https://www.thisisjasonsilva.com.

Jeffery, Morgan. "Here's Why *Star Trek* Should Quit Movies and Focus Just on TV Shows: It's Time for the Franchise to Boldly Go Back to Its Roots." Digital Spy. August 15, 2018. https://www.digitalspy.com/tv/ustv/a863985/star-trek-discovery-movies-tv-shows/.

Jeffrey, Terence P. "7,231,000 Lost Jobs: Manufacturing Employment Down 37% from 1979 Peak." *CNS News*. May 12, 2015. https://www.cnsnews.com/news/article/terence-p-jeffrey/7231000-lost-jobs-manufacturing-employment-down-37-1979-peak.

Jindra, Michael. "Star Trek Fandom as a Religious Phenomenon." *Sociology of Religion* 55, no. 1 (1994): 27–51.

Joest, Mick. "William Shatner Defends *Star Trek*'s Unchanging Vision: It May Be Controversial to Some." Cinemablend. Accessed October 18, 2019. https://www.cinemablend.com/television/2482170/william-shatner-defends-star-trek-unchanging-vision-it-may-be-controversial-to-some.

Jones, Bomani. "Oh Pleez GAWD I Can't Handle the Success." Salon. October 24, 2002. https://www.salon.com/2002/10/23/cobain_2/.

Kane, Gregory P. "Reginald Lewis Climbed into the Moneyed Class." *Baltimore Sun*, December 18, 1994. https://www.baltimoresun.com/news/bs-xpm-1994-12-18-1994352029-story.html.

"Kathleen McGrath, 50; 1st Woman to Command a US Navy Warship." *Los Angeles Times*, October 3, 2002, https://www.latimes.com/archives/la-xpm-2002-oct-03-me-mcgrath3-story.html.

Kealoha, Samantha. "Sharon Pratt Dixon Kelly." *Black Past*. April 18, 2007. https://www.blackpast.org/african-american-history/kelly-sharon-pratt-dixon-1944/.

Kelly, Kimberly Carter. "Defense of Marriage Act." *Britannica*. April 28, 2016. https://www.britannica.com/topic/Defense-of-Marriage-Act.

King, Lucien. *Game On: The History and Culture of Video Games*. New York: Universe, 2002.

Kishi, Katayoun. "Assaults against Muslims in US Surpass 2001 Level." *Pew Research Center*. November 15, 2017. https://www.pewresearch.org/fact-tank/2017/11/15/assaults-against-muslims-in-u-s-surpass-2001-level/.

Kleiman, Carol. "Women's Work in the 90s Has Few Boundaries." *Chicago Tribune*, January 30, 1996. https://www.chicagotribune.com/news/ct-xpm-1996-01-30-9601300266-story.html.

Kohler, Chris. "July 29, 1994: Videogame Makers Propose Ratings Board to Congress." *Wired*, July 29, 2009. https://www.wired.com/2009/07/dayintech-0729/.

Kohut, Andrew. "Berlin Wall's Fall Marked the End of the Cold War for the American Public." Pew Research Center. November 3, 2014. https://www.pewresearch.org/fact-tank/2014/11/03/berlin-walls-fall-marked-the-end-of-the-cold-war-for-the-american-public/.

Kreitner, Richard. "Setting up the European Union." *Nation*, November 1, 2015. https://www.thenation.com/article/november-1-1993-the-maastricht-treaty-is-ratified-setting-up-the-european-union/.

Lacour, Greg. "White Supremacist Found Guilty on All Counts in Charleston Church Massacre." *Reuters*. December 15, 2016. https://www.reuters.com/article/us-south-carolina-shooting-roof/white-supremacist-found-guilty-on-all-counts-in-charleston-church-massacre-idUSKBN14418R.

Lane, Jonathan. "A History of *Star Trek* Fan Films." *Fan Film Factor*, January 2016. https://fanfilmfactor.com/wp-content/uploads/2016/12/The-History-of-STAR-TREK-fan-films-Jonathan-Lane.pdf.

Le, C. N. "Employment and Occupational Patterns." Asian-Nation. Accessed June 28, 2019. http://www.asian-nation.org/employment.shtml#sthash.N0RUzvTN.dpbs.

Leakey, Louise. "Louise Leakey: Where Did Human Beings Originate?" Interview by Raz Guy. *TED Radio Hour*. NPR. October 24, 2014. https://www.npr.org/templates/transcript/transcript.php?storyId=358148127.

Lee, Richard M. "The Transracial Adoption Paradox: History, Research, and Counseling Implications of Cultural Socialization." *Counseling Psychologist* 31, no. 6 (2003): 711–44.

Leight, Elias. "How Michael Jackson's 'Bad' Scored a Staggering Five Number Ones." *Rolling Stone*, August 31, 2007. https://www.rollingstone.com/music/music-features/how-michael-jacksons-bad-scored-a-staggering-five-number-ones-117653/.

Lichtenberg, Jacqueline, Sondra Marshak, and Joan Winston. *Star Trek Lives!* London: Corgi, 1975.

Lowood, Henry E. "*The Legend of Zelda*." *Britannica*. May 7, 2004. https://www.britannica.com/topic/The-Legend-of-Zelda-1688275.

Maloney, Thomas N. "African Americans in the Twentieth Century." EH.Net. January 14, 2002. http://eh.net/encyclopedia/african-americans-in-the-twentieth-century/.

Marr, Bernard. "Is Artificial Intelligence Dangerous? 6 AI Risks Everyone Should Know About." *Forbes*, November 19, 2018. https://www.forbes.com/sites/bernardmarr/2018/11/19/is-artificial-intelligence-dangerous-6-ai-risks-everyone-should-know-about/#290c0aa12404.

Martin, Paul, and Patrick Bateson. *Measuring Behaviour: An Introductory Guide* . Cambridge, UK: Cambridge University Press, 1993.

Massive Events. "Destination *Star Trek*." Accessed August 10, 2019. https://www.destinationstartrek.com.

May, Elaine Tyler. *America and the Pill: A History of Promise, Peril, and Liberation*. New York: Basic Books, 2010.

McKinnon, Jesse D., and Claudette E. Bennett. "We the People: Blacks in the United States: Census 2000 Special Report." Census. August 2005. https://www.census.gov/prod/2005pubs/censr-25.pdf.

McNally, Victoria. "Women Who Love *Star Trek* Are the Reason That Modern Fandom Exists." Revelist. September 8, 2016. http://www.revelist.com/tv/star-trek-fandom-50th/4643.

Memory Alpha. Accessed May 17, 2018. https://memoryalpha.fandom.com/wiki/Portal:Main.

———. "CBS Consumer Products." Accessed May 23, 2019. https://memory-alpha.fandom.com/wiki/CBS_Consumer_Products.

Milligan, Peter. *Hellblazer*. New York: DC Comics, 1988–2013; 2019–. Accessed December 18, 2019. https://www.dccomics.com/search?keyword=Hellblazer.

Modiphius Entertainment. *Star Trek* Adventures Tabletop RPG. Accessed December 18, 2019. https://www.modiphius.net/collections/star-trek-adventures.

Muir, John Kenneth. *A Critical History of* Doctor Who *on Television*. Jefferson, NC: McFarland, 2007.

Myers, Meghann. "Almost 800 Women Are Serving in Previously Closed Army Combat Jobs. This Is How They're Faring." *Army Times*, October 9, 2018. https://www.armytimes.com/news/your-army/2018/10/09/almost-800-women-are-serving-in-previously-closed-army-combat-jobs-this-is-how-theyre-faring/.

Napolitano, Janet. "Women Earn More College Degrees and Men Still Earn More Money." Forbes. September 4, 2018. https://www.forbes.com/sites/janetnapolitano/2018/09/04/women-earn-more-college-degrees-and-men-still-earn-more-money/#1a7cc96c39f1.

The National Committee on Pay Equity. "The Wage Gap over Time." Accessed February 20, 2018. https://www.pay-equity.org/info-time.html.

NCC Staff. "On This Day, All Indians Made United States Citizens." Constitution Daily. June 2, 2019. https://constitutioncenter.org/blog/on-this-day-in-1924-all-indians-made-united-states-citizens.

Nellan, Terence. "Bush Pulls Out of ABM Treaty; Putin Calls Move a Mistake." *New York Times*, December 13, 2001. https://www.nytimes.com/2001/12/13/international/bush-pulls-out-of-abm-treaty-putin-calls-move-a-mistake.html.

Newbeck, Phyl. *Virginia Hasn't Always Been for Lovers: Interracial Marriage Bans and the Case of Richard and Mildred Loving*. Carbondale: Southern Illinois University Press, 2008.

Newby, Richard. "The Stakes of *Star Trek 4*." *Hollywood Reporter*, November 21, 2019. https://www.hollywoodreporter.com/heat-vision/why-star-trek-4-is-a-high-stakes-game-paramount-1256970.

NFHS. "High School Sports Participation Increases for 29th Consecutive Year." National Federation of State High School Associations. September 11, 2018. https://www.nfhs.org/articles/high-school-sports-participation-increases-for-29th-consecutive-year/.

Nikolchev, Alexandra. "A Brief History of the Birth Control Pill." PBS. May 7, 2010. http://www.pbs.org/wnet/need-to-know/health/a-brief-history-of-the-birth-control-pill/480/.

The Nobel Prize. "Marie Curie Biographical." Accessed December 4, 2019. https://www.nobelprize.org/prizes/physics/1903/marie-curie/biographical/.

Oberlander, Jonathan. "Learning from Failure in Health Care Reform." *New England Journal of Medicine* 357, no. 17 (2007): 1677–79.

O'Hara, Mary Emily. "Abortion Clinics Report Threats of Violence on the Rise." NBC News. February 13, 2017. https://www.nbcnews.com/news/us-news/abortion-clinics-report-threats-violence-rise-n719426.

The Old Robots Website. "The Armatron—2346." Accessed April 1, 2020, http://www.theoldrobots.com/armatron1.html.

———. "Dustbot—SO-G—5409 by Tomy." Accessed April 1, 2020, http://www.theoldrobots.com/dustbot.html.

Oliphant, J. Baxter. "The Iraq War Continues to Divide the US Public, 15 Years after It Began." Pew Research Center. March 19, 2018. https://www.pewresearch.org/fact-tank/2018/03/19/iraq-war-continues-to-divide-u-s-public-15-years-after-it-began/.

Pascale, Anthony. "D. C. Fontana on *TAS* Canon (and Sybok)." TrekMovie. July 22, 2007. https://trekmovie.com/2007/07/22/dc-fontana-on-tas-canon-and-sybok/.

Patten, Eileen, and Kim Parker. "Women in the US Military: Growing Share, Distinctive Profile." Pew Research Center. Accessed June 21, 2019. https://www.pewresearch.org/wp-content/uploads/sites/3/2011/12/women-in-the-military.pdf.

Peters, Alec. *Axanar*. Accessed December 18, 2019. https://axanar.com.

Pew Research Center. "The Data on Women Leaders." September 13, 2018. https://www.pewsocialtrends.org/fact-sheet/the-data-on-women-leaders/.

———. "Highlights of Women's Earnings in 2005." Accessed June 22, 2019. http://download.militaryonesource.mil/12038/MOS/Reports/2005%20Demographics%20Report.pdf.

———. "Women CEOs in Fortune 500 Companies, 1995–2018." Accessed June 22, 2019. https://www.pewsocialtrends.org/chart/women-ceos-in-fortune-500-companies-1995-2014/.

Pickhardt, Carl E. "Developmental Dislike of Parents during Early Adolescence." *Psychology Today*, April 20, 2015. https://www.psychologytoday.com/us/blog/surviving-your-childs-adolescence/201504/developmental-dislike-parents-during-early-adolescence.

Plaut, Thomas, and Bernard S. Arons. "President Clinton's Proposal for Health Care Reform: Key Provisions and Issues." *Psychiatric Services* 45, no. 9 (1994): 871–76.

Population Reference Bureau. "Why Concentrated Poverty Fell in the United States in the 1990s." August 1, 2005. https://www.prb.org/whyconcentratedpoverty fellinthe unitedstatesinthe1990s/.

Porter, Alan J. Star Trek: *A Comics History*. New Castle, PA: Hermes Press, 2009.

Postin, Dudley, and Rogelio Saenz. "The US White Majority Will Soon Disappear Forever." *Chicago Reporter*, May 16, 2019. https://www.chicagoreporter.com/the-us-white-majority-will-soon-disappear-forever/.

Pruitt, Sarah. "8 Ways the Original 'Star Trek' Made History." History. September 8, 2016. https://www.history.com/news/8-ways-the-original-star-trek-made-history.

Queer Nation. "Queer Nation NY History." Accessed February 14, 2018. https://queernationny.org/history.

Racebending. "*Star Trek*: Into Whiteness." May 9, 2013. http://www.racebending.com/v4/featured/star-trek-whiteness/.

Radoff, Jon, et al. "*Star Trek* Timelines." Disrupter Beam. Accessed December 18, 2019. https://www.disruptorbeam.com/games/star-trek-timelines.

Ray, Michael. "Executive Order 9981." *Britannica*. May 11, 2010. https://www.britannica.com/topic/Executive-Order-9981.

Reagan Foundation. "Her Causes." Accessed February 10, 2018. https://www.reaganfoundation.org/ronald-reagan/nancy-reagan/her-causes/.

The Reagan Vision. "The Reykjavik Summit." Accessed March 3, 2018. https://www.thereaganvision.org/the-reykjavik-summit-the-story/.

Reference for Business. "Minority-Owned Businesses." Accessed November 14, 2019. http://www.referenceforbusiness.com/encyclopedia/Man-Mix/Minority-Owned-Businesses.html.

Robinson, Peter. "Tear Down This Wall." *Prologue Magazine* 39, no. 2 (Summer 2007). https://www.archives.gov/publications/prologue/2007/summer/berlin.html.

Rosenthal, Jack. "US Birth Rate Drops to a Record Low." *New York Times*, March 2, 1973. https://www.nytimes.com/1973/03/02/archives/us-birth-rate-drops-to-a-record-low-birth-rate-drops-to-record-low.html.

Rosenwald, Michael S. "No Woman Served on the Senate Judiciary Committee in 1991. The Ugly Anita Hill Hearings Changed That." *Washington Post*, September 18, 2018. https://www.washingtonpost.com/history/2018/09/18/no-women-served-senate-judiciary-committee-ugly-anita-hill-hearings-changed-that/.

Rovner, Julie. "Why Do People Hate Obamacare, Anyway?" Kaiser Health News. December 13, 2017. https://khn.org/news/why-do-people-hate-obamacare-anyway/.

Rubin, Phillip M. "Obama Named New Law Review President." *Harvard Crimson*, February 6, 1990. https://www.thecrimson.com/article/1990/2/6/obama-named-new-law-review-president.

Sagoff, Mark. "The Great Environmental Awakening." *American Prospect*, December 5, 2000. https://prospect.org/environment/great-environmental-awakening/.

Schifferes, Steve. "US Names Coalition of the Willing." BBC. March 18, 2003. http://news.bbc.co.uk/2/hi/americas/2862343.stm.

Schlozman, Daniel. "How the Christian Right Ended Up Transforming American Politics." Talking Points Memo. August 25, 2015. https://talkingpointsmemo.com/cafe/brief-history-of-the-christian-right.

ScienceDirect. "Nanoprobes." Accessed February 25, 2018. https://www.sciencedirect.com/topics/chemical-engineering/nanoprobes

Secretary of Defense. *2005 Demographics Report*. Accessed June 21, 2019. http://download.militaryonesource.mil/12038/MOS/Reports/2005%20Demographics%20Report.pdf.

Serafino, Nina M. "CRS Report for Congress." Congressional Research Service. January 24, 2007. https://fas.org/sgp/crs/natsec/RL33557.pdf.

Service Women's Active Network. "Women in the Military: Where They Stand." October 19, 2019. https://www.servicewomen.org/wp-content/uploads/2019/04/SWAN-Where-we-stand-2019-0416revised.pdf.

Shane, Leo, III. "White Nationalism Remains a Problem for the Military, Poll Suggests." *Military Times*, February 26, 2019. https://www.militarytimes.com/news/pentagon-congress/2019/02/28/white-nationalism-remains-a-problem-for-the-military-poll-shows/.

Shown, Mary. "Mayor Pete Buttigieg Marries Partner Chasten Glezman in Downtown South Bend." *South Bend Tribune*, June 17, 2018. https://www.southbendtribune.com/news/local/mayor-pete-buttigieg-marries-partner-chasten-glezman-in-downtown-south/article_b9bb722b-bbb0-5b55-a73d-e014ac7e4bf1.html.

Simon, Joe, and Jack Kirby. *Sandman*. New York: DC Comics, 1974–1976. Accessed December 18, 2019. https://www.dccomics.com/search?keyword=Sandman.

Simon, Mallory, and Sara Sidner, "A Gunman Slaughtered 11 Jewish Worshipers. Then People Hunted for Hate Online." CNN. Last modified May 15, 2019. https://www.cnn.com/2019/05/15/us/anti-semitic-searches-pittsburgh-poway-shootings-soh/index.html.

Sisk, Richard. "Number of Female Generals, Admirals Has Doubled since 2000, Report Finds." Military. April 17, 2019. https://www.military.com/dailynews/2019/04/17/number-female-generals-admirals-has-doubled-2000-report-finds.html.

Smith, Caroline, and James M. Lindsay. "Rally 'round the Flag: Opinion in the United States before and after the Iraq War." Brookings. June 1, 2003. https://www.brookings.edu/articles/rally-round-the-flag-opinion-in-the-united-states-before-and-after-the-iraq-war/.

Smith, Yvette. "Astronaut John Herrington Carried a Piece of Native American History to Space." NASA. Last modified November 5, 2019. https://www.nasa.gov/image-feature/astronaut-john-herrington-carried-a-piece-of-native-american-history-to-space.

Socarides, Richard. "Why Bill Clinton Signed the Defense of Marriage Act." *New Yorker*, June 18, 2017. https://www.newyorker.com/news/news-desk/why-bill-clinton-signed-the-defense-of-marriage-act.

Spain, Sarah. "Serena Williams Focusing on Business, Charity, and Family while Away from Tennis." ESPN. June 23, 2017. https://www.espn.com/espnw/voices/espnw-columnists/story/_/id/19719611/serena-williams-focusing-business-charity-family-away-tennis.

Starr, Paul. "What Happened to Health Care Reform?" *American Prospect*, November 19, 2001. https://prospect.org/health/happened-health-care-reform/.

StarTrek.com. Accessed April 3, 2020. https://www.startrek.com.

———. "Fan Films." Accessed July 31, 2019. https://www.startrek.com/fan-films.

StarTrek.com Staff. "Bjo Trimble: The Woman Who Saved *Star Trek*—Part I." StarTrek.com. Accessed August 20, 2017. https://www.startrek.com/article/bjo-trimble-the-woman-who-saved-star-trek-part-1.

Steidinger, Joan. *Stand Up and Shout Out: Women's Fight for Equal Pay, Equal Rights, and Equal Opportunities in Sports*. Lanham, MD: Rowman & Littlefield, 2020.

Stevens, Heidi. "It's Official: 2016 Is the Year of Xenophobia." *Chicago Tribune*, November 29, 2016. https://www.chicagotribune.com/columns/heidi-stevens/ct-xenophobia-word-of-the-year-balancing-1129-20161129-column.html.

Stiglitz, Joseph. "The Roaring Nineties." *Atlantic*, October 2002. https://www.theatlantic.com/magazine/archive/2002/10/the-roaring-nineties/302604/.

Streitfeld, David. "Author Toni Morrison Wins Nobel Prize." *Washington Post*, October 8, 1993. https://www.washingtonpost.com/archive/politics/1993/10/08/author-toni-morrison-wins-nobel-prize/6077f17d-d7b7-49a3-ad90-8111cf8478d1/.

Thernstrom, Abigail, and Stephen Thernstrom. "Black Progress: How Far We've Come, and How Far We Have to Go." Brookings. March 1, 1998. https://www.brookings.edu/articles/black-progress-how-far-weve-come-and-how-far-we-have-to-go/.

Trevino, Jack, and Ethan H. Calk. *Star Trek of Gods and Men*. Accessed December 18, 2019. http://startrekofgodsandmen.com/main/.

Twitter. Accessed April 3, 2020. https://www.twitter.com.

Ubisoft Entertainment. *Star Trek: Bridge Crew*. Accessed December 18, 2019. https://www.ubisoft.com/en-us/game/star-trek-bridge-crew/.

United States Environmental Protection Agency. "Milestones in EPA and Environmental History." Accessed November 30, 2019. https://www.epa.gov/history.

US Department of Homeland Security. "About DHS." Accessed June 20, 2019. https://www.dhs.gov.

US Department of Housing and Urban Development. "History of Fair Housing." Accessed February 20, 2018. https://www.hud.gov/program_offices/fair_housing_equal_opp/aboutfheo/history.

US Department of Justice. "2017 Hate Crime Statistics." Accessed September 29, 2019. https://www.justice.gov/hatecrimes/hate-crime-statistics.

Vandelli, Vittorio. "Genoa G8 Summit in 2001: The Days Berlusconi's Italy Went Back to Fascism." September 15, 2015. http://www.vittorio-vandelli.com/genoa-g8-summit-police-torture/.

Vega, Nicolas. "Elon Musk: AI Will Soon Make Us Look Like Apes." *New York Post*, August 29, 2019. https://nypost.com/2019/08/29/elon-musk-ai-will-soon-make-us-look-like-monkeys/.

ViacomCBS. Accessed December 18, 2019. https://www.viacbs.com.

Vinciguerra, Thomas. "A 'Trek' Script Is Grounded in Cyberspace." *New York Times*, March 29, 2012. https://www.nytimes.com/2012/03/29/arts/television/cbs-blocks-use-of-unused-star-trek-script-by-spinrad.html.

Walker, Juliet. *The History of Black Business in America: Capitalism, Race, Entrepreneurship*. Chapel Hill: University of North Carolina Press Books, 2009.

Walker, Peter, and Stephan Mittelstrass. *Star Trek New Voyagers: Phase II, International*. Accessed December 18, 2019. https://www.stnv.de/en/about_us.php.

Wall, Mike. "35 Years Ago: NASA Unveils First Space Shuttle, *Enterprise*." Space.com, September 17, 2011. https://www.space.com/12991-nasa-space-shuttle-enterprise-35-years.html.

Wallenfeldt, Jeff. "Los Angeles Riots of 1992." *Britannica*. April 27, 2012. https://www.britannica.com/event/Los-Angeles-Riots-of-1992.

Walsh, Kenneth T. "The 1960s: A Decade of Change for Women." *US News and World Report*, March 12, 2010. https://www.usnews.com/news/articles/2010/03/12/the-1960s-a-decade-of-change-for-women.

Wetzel, James R. "American Families: 70 Years of Change." *Monthly Labor Review*, March 1990. https://www.bls.gov/mlr/1990/03/art1full.pdf.

The White House: President George W. Bush. "President Signs National Defense Authorization Act." Accessed February 20, 2018. https://georgewbush-whitehouse.archives.gov/news/releases/2002/12/images/20021202-8_defense-12022002-d—515h.html.

Whitfield, Stephen E., and Gene Roddenberry. *The Making of* Star Trek. New York: Ballantine Books, 1968.

Wiessner, Polly W. "Embers of Society: Firelight Talk among the Ju/'hoansi Bushmen." *Proceedings of the National Academy of Sciences* 111, no. 39 (2014): 14027–35.

Williams, Joseph P. "Old Enough to Fight, Old Enough to Vote: The 26th Amendment's Mixed Legacy." *US News and World Report*, July 7, 2016. https://www.usnews.com/news/articles/2016-07-01/old-enough-to-fight-old-enough-to-vote-the-26th-amendments-mixed-legacy.

Williamson, Kevin. "9/11 Ended a Golden Age." *National Review*, September 11, 2017. https://www.nationalreview.com/2017/09/911-sixteen-years-later/.

Winfrey, Lee. "Cosby Tightens Grip on the Nielsen Ratings." *Chicago Tribune*, December 10, 1986. https://www.chicagotribune.com/news/ct-xpm-1986-12-10-8604020309-story.html.

The Women's Memorial. "1960s: The Decade." May 7, 2017. https://www.womensmemorial.
org/history/detail/?s=1960s-the-decade.
———. "1990s." Accessed November 20, 2019. https://www.womensmemorial.org/history/
detail/?s=1990s.
———. "Highlights in the History of Military Women." Accessed November 2, 2019. https://
www.womensmemorial.org/content/resources/highlights.pdf.
Yockel, Michael. "100 Years: The Riots of 1968." *Baltimore Magazine*, May 2007. https://
www.baltimoremagazine.com/2007/5/1/100-years-the-riots-of-1968.
Younge, Gary. "Latinos Become Main Minority Group in US." *Guardian*, January 22, 2003.
https://www.theguardian.com/world/2003/jan/23/usa.garyyounge.
Zillman, Clair. "The Fortune 500 Has More Female CEOs than Ever Before." *Fortune*, May
16, 2019. https://fortune.com/2019/05/16/fortune-500-female-ceos/.

FURTHER READINGS

Ayers, Jeff. *Voyages of Imagination: The Star Trek Fiction Companion*. New York: Simon and
Schuster, 2006.
Barad, Judith A., and Ed Robertson. *The Ethics of Star Trek*. New York: HarperCollins, 2000.
Barton, Matt. *Dungeons and Desktops: The History of Computer Role-Playing Games*. Boca
Raton, FL: CRC Press, 2008.
Brode, Douglas, and Shea T. Brode. *The Star Trek Universe: Franchising the Final Frontier*.
Lanham, MD: Rowman & Littlefield, 2015.
Califano, Joseph A. *The Triumph and Tragedy of Lyndon Johnson: The White House Years*.
New York: Simon and Schuster, 2015.
DeBenedetti, Charles, and Charles Chatfield. *An American Ordeal: The Antiwar Movement of
the Vietnam Era*. Syracuse, NY: Syracuse University Press, 1990.
Grainge, Paul. *Brand Hollywood: Selling Entertainment in a Global Media Age*. Abingdon,
UK: Routledge, 2007.
Harrison, Colin. *American Culture in the 1990s*. Edinburgh, UK: Edinburgh University Press,
2010.
Ichbiah, Daniel. *Robots: From Science Fiction to Technological Revolution*. New York: Harry
N. Abrams, 2005.
Kapell, Matthew W., and Ace G. Pilkington. *The Kelvin Timeline of* Star Trek*: Essays on J. J.
Abrams' Final Frontier*. Jefferson, NC: McFarland, 2019.
Maney, Patrick J. *Bill Clinton: New Gilded Age President*. Lawrence: University Press of
Kansas, 2016.
McWhorter, John H. *Losing the Race: Self-Sabotage in Black America*. New York: Simon and
Schuster, 2000.
Meehan, Eileen R. *Why TV Is Not Our Fault: Television Programming, Viewers, and Who's
Really in Control*. Lanham, MD: Rowman & Littlefield, 2005.
Okuda, Michael, Denise Okuda, and Debbie Mirek. *The* Star Trek *Encyclopedia*. New York:
Simon and Schuster, 2011.
Poe, Stephen Edward. *A Vision of the Future*. New York: Simon and Schuster, 1998.
Tapscott, Don. *Grown Up Digital*. Boston: McGraw-Hill Education, 2008.
Thompson, Graham. *American Culture in the 1980s*. Edinburgh, UK: Edinburgh University
Press, 2007.
Van Dijck, José. *The Culture of Connectivity: A Critical History of Social Media*. Oxford, UK:
Oxford University Press, 2013.

FILMOGRAPHY

STAR TREK FILMS CITED

Abrams, J. J., dir. *Star Trek*. Hollywood, CA: Paramount Pictures, 2009.

———, dir. *Star Trek into Darkness*. Hollywood, CA: Paramount Pictures, 2013.

Baird, Stuart, dir. *Star Trek: Nemesis*. Hollywood, CA: Paramount Pictures, 2002.

Carson, David, dir. *Star Trek: Generations*. Hollywood, CA: Paramount Pictures, 1994.

Frakes, Jonathan, dir. *Star Trek: First Contact*. Hollywood, CA: Paramount Pictures, 1996.

———, dir. *Star Trek: Insurrection*. Hollywood, CA: Paramount Pictures, 1998.

Lin, Justin, dir. *Star Trek Beyond*. Hollywood, CA: Paramount Pictures, 2016.

Meyer, Nicholas, dir. *Star Trek II: The Wrath of Khan*. Hollywood, CA: Paramount Pictures, 1982.

———, dir. *Star Trek VI: The Undiscovered Country*. Hollywood, CA: Paramount Pictures, 1991.

Nimoy, Leonard, dir. *Star Trek III: The Search for Spock*. Hollywood, CA: Paramount Pictures, 1984.

———, dir. *Star Trek IV: The Voyage Home*. Hollywood, CA: Paramount Pictures, 1986.

Shatner, William, dir. *Star Trek V: The Final Frontier*. Hollywood, CA: Paramount Pictures, 1989.

Wise, Robert, dir. *Star Trek: The Motion Picture*. Hollywood, CA: Paramount Pictures, 1979.

STAR TREK SERIES CITED

In chronological order

Star Trek: The Original Series (*TOS*). Created by Gene Roddenberry. 3 seasons. Los Angeles: Desilu Productions. Aired 1966–1969 on NBC.

Star Trek: The Animated Series (*TAS*). Created by Gene Roddenberry. 2 seasons. Hollywood, CA: Paramount Television. Aired 1973–1974 on NBC.

Star Trek: The Next Generation (*TNG*). Created by Gene Roddenberry. 7 seasons. Hollywood, CA: Paramount Television. Aired 1987–1994 on CBS.

Star Trek: Deep Space Nine (*DS9*). Created by Rick Berman and Michael Piller. 7 seasons. Hollywood, CA: Paramount Television. Aired 1993–1999 on CBS.

Star Trek: Voyager (*VOY*). Created by Rick Berman, Michael Piller, and Jeri Taylor. 7 seasons. Hollywood, CA: Paramount Television. Aired 1995–2001 on UPN.

Star Trek: Enterprise (*ENT*). Created by Rick Berman and Brannon Braga. 7 seasons. Hollywood, CA: Braga Productions, Paramount Television. Aired 2001–2005 on UPN.

Star Trek: Discovery (*DSC*). Created by Brian Fuller and Alex Kurtzman. 3 seasons. Hollywood, CA: CBS Television Studios. Aired 2017–present on CBS All Access.

Star Trek: Short Treks (*ST*). Created by Alex Kurtzman and Brian Fuller. 2 seasons. Hollywood, CA: CBS Television Studios. Aired 2018–present on CBS All Access.

Star Trek: Picard (*STP*). Created by Alex Kurtzman. 1 season. Hollywood, CA: CBS Television Studios. Aired 2020–present on CBS All Access.

Star Trek: Lower Decks. Created by Mike McMahan. 1 season. Hollywood, CA: CBS Television Studios. Aired 2020–present on CBS All Access.

STAR TREK EPISODES CITED

In chapter order

Chapter 1, "Mirror, Mirror: *Star Trek*: The Original Series, 1966–1969"

Alexander, David, dir. *Star Trek*. Season 3, episode 10, "Plato's Stepchildren." Aired November 22, 1968, on NBC.

Butler, Robert, dir. *Star Trek*. Season 1, episode 0, "The Cage." Aired November 27, 1988, in syndication, CBS.

Chomsky, Marvin J., dir. *Star Trek*. Season 3, episode 23, "All Our Yesterdays." Aired March 14, 1969, on NBC.

Daniels, Marc, dir. *Star Trek*. Season 1, episode 1, "The Man Trap." Aired September 8, 1966, on NBC.

———, dir. *Star Trek*. Season 1, episode 4, "The Naked Time." Aired September 29, 1966, on NBC.

———, dir. *Star Trek*. Season 1, episode 22, "Space Seed." Aired February 15, 1967, on NBC.

———, dir. *Star Trek*. Season 2, episode 2, "Who Mourns for Adonais?" Aired September 22, 1967, on NBC.

———, dir. *Star Trek*. Season 2, episode 4, "Mirror, Mirror." Aired October 6, 1967, on NBC.

———, dir. *Star Trek*. Season 2, episode 6, "The Doomsday Machine." Aired October 20, 1967, on NBC.

———, dir. *Star Trek*. Season 2, episode 8, "I, Mudd." Aired November 3, 1967, on NBC.

———, dir. *Star Trek*. Season 2, episode 19, "A Private Little War." Aired February 2, 1968, on NBC.

Daugherty, Herschel, dir. *Star Trek*. Season 3, episode 22, "The Savage Curtain." Aired March 7, 1969, on NBC.

Dobkin, Lawrence, dir. *Star Trek*. Season 1, episode 2, "Charlie X." Aired September 15, 1966, on NBC.

Gist, Robert, dir. *Star Trek*. Season 1, episode 16, "The Galileo Seven." Aired January 5, 1967, on NBC.

Goldstone, James, dir. *Star Trek*. Season 1, episode 7, "What Are Little Girls Made Of?" Aired October 20, 1966.

Hart, Harvey, dir. *Star Trek*. Season 1, episode 6, "Mudd's Women." Aired October 13, 1966, on NBC.

McEveety, Vincent, dir. *Star Trek*. Season 1, episode 8, "Miri." Aired October 27, 1966, on NBC.

———, dir. *Star Trek*. Season 1, episode 14, "Balance of Terror." Aired December 15, 1966, on NBC.

Newland, John, dir. *Star Trek*. Season 1, episode 26, "Errand of Mercy." Aired March 22, 1967, on NBC.

Penn, Leo, dir. *Star Trek*. Season 1, episode 5, "The Enemy Within." Aired October 6, 1966, on NBC.

Pevney, Joseph, dir. *Star Trek*. Season 1, episode 28, "The City on the Edge of Forever." Aired April 5, 1967, on NBC.

———, dir. *Star Trek*. Season 2, episode 5, "The Apple." Aired October 13, 1967, on NBC.

———, dir. *Star Trek*. Season 2, episode 12, "The Deadly Years." Aired December 8, 1967, on NBC.

Senensky, Ralph, dir. *Star Trek*. Season 1, episode 24, "This Side of Paradise." Aired March 1, 1967, on NBC.

———, dir. *Star Trek*. Season 2, episode 13, "Obsession." Aired December 15, 1967, on NBC.

———, dir. *Star Trek*. Season 3, episode 5, "Is There in Truth No Beauty?" Aired October 18, 1968, on NBC.

Taylor, Jud, dir. *Star Trek*. Season 3, episode 15, "Let That Be Your Last Battlefield." Aired January 10, 1969, on NBC.

Wallerstein, Herb, dir. *Star Trek*. Season 3, episode 9, "The Tholian Web." Aired November 15, 1968, on NBC.

———, dir. *Star Trek*. Season 3, episode 24, "Turnabout Intruder." Aired June 3, 1969, on NBC.

Chapter 2, "Interlude I: *Star Trek* Fandom: 1969–1987"

Butler, Robert, dir. *Star Trek*. Season 1, episode 0, "The Cage." Aired November 27, 1988, on CBS.

Reed, Bill, and Hal Sutherland, dirs. *Star Trek: The Animated Series*. Season 2, episode 5, "How Sharper than a Serpent's Tooth." Aired October 5, 1974, on NBC.

Sutherland, Hal, dir. *Star Trek: The Animated Series*. Season 1, episode 2, "Yesteryear." Aired September 15, 1973, on NBC.

———, dir. *Star Trek: The Animated Series*. Season 1, episode 4, "The Lorelei Signal." Aired September 29, 1973, on NBC.

———, dir. *Star Trek: The Animated Series*. Season 1, episode 7, "The Infinite Vulcan." Aired October 20, 1973, on NBC.

Chapter 3, "Encounter at Farpoint: *The Next Generation*: 1987–1994"

Allen, Corey, dir. *Star Trek: The Next Generation*. Season 1, episode 1, "Encounter at Farpoint." Aired September 28, 1987, on CBS.

———, dir. *Star Trek: The Next Generation*. Season 5, episode 6, "The Game." Aired October 28, 1991, on CBS.

Beaumont, Gabrielle, dir. *Star Trek: The Next Generation*. Season 3, episode 6, "Booby Trap." Aired October 30, 1989, on CBS.

———, dir. *Star Trek: The Next Generation*. Season 4, episode 4, "Suddenly Human." Aired October 15, 1990, on CBS.

Bole, Cliff, dir. *Star Trek: The Next Generation*. Season 3, episode 21, "Hollow Pursuits." Aired May 1, 1990, on CBS.

———, dir. *Star Trek: The Next Generation*. Season 3, episode 26, "The Best of Both Worlds, Part 1." Aired June 18, 1990, on CBS.

————, dir. *Star Trek: The Next Generation*. Season 4, episode 1, "The Best of Both Worlds, Part 2." Aired September 24, 1990, on CBS.

————, dir. *Star Trek: The Next Generation*. Season 5, episode 8, "Unification, Part 2." Aired November 11, 1991, on CBS.

————, dir. *Star Trek: The Next Generation*. Season 6, episode 2, "Realm of Fear." Aired September 28, 1992, on CBS.

————, dir. *Star Trek: The Next Generation*. Season 6, episode 13, "Aquiel." Aired February 1, 1993, on CBS.

————, dir. *Star Trek: The Next Generation*. Season 6, episode 22, "Suspicions." Aired May 10, 1993, on CBS.

————, dir. *Star Trek: The Next Generation*. Season 7, episode 2, "Liaisons." Aired September 27, 1992, on CBS.

————, dir. *Star Trek: The Next Generation*. Season 7, episode 23, "Emergence." Aired May 9, 1994, on CBS.

Bowman, Rob, dir. *Star Trek: The Next Generation*. Season 1, episode 13, "Datalore." Aired January 18, 1988, on CBS.

————, dir. *Star Trek: The Next Generation*. Season 2, episode 1, "The Child." Aired November 21, 1988, on CBS.

————, dir. *Star Trek: The Next Generation*. Season 2, episode 10, "The Dauphin." Aired February 20, 1989, on CBS.

————, dir. *Star Trek: The Next Generation*. Season 2, episode 16, "Q Who?" Aired May 8, 1989, on CBS.

————, dir. *Star Trek: The Next Generation*. Season 2, episode 19, "Manhunt." Aired June 19, 1989, on CBS.

————, dir. *Star Trek: The Next Generation*. Season 4, episode 10, "The Loss." Aired January 1, 1991, on CBS.

Burton, LeVar, dir. *Star Trek: The Next Generation*. Season 6, episode 24, "Second Chances." Aired May 24, 1993, on CBS.

Carson, David, dir. *Star Trek: The Next Generation*. Season 5, episode 24, "The Next Phase." Aired May 18, 1988, on CBS.

Chalmers, Chip, dir. *Star Trek: The Next Generation*. Season 4, episode 12, "The Wounded." Aired January 29, 1991, on CBS.

Compton, Richard, dir. *Star Trek: The Next Generation*. Season 1, episode 11, "Haven." Aired November 30, 1987, on CBS.

Conway, James, dir. *Star Trek: The Next Generation*. Season 1, episode 26, "The Neutral Zone." Aired May 16, 1988, on CBS.

Curry, Dan, dir. *Star Trek: The Next Generation*. Season 6, episode 17, "Birthright, Part 2." Aired March 1, 1993, on CBS.

Frakes, Jonathan, dir. *Star Trek: The Next Generation*. Season 4, episode 7, "Reunion." Aired November 6, 1990, on CBS.

————, dir. *Star Trek: The Next Generation*. Season 7, episode 14, "Sub-Rosa." Aired January 31, 1994, on CBS.

Iscove, Robert, dir. *Star Trek: The Next Generation*. Season 2, episode 14, "The Icarus Factor." Aired April 22, 1989, on CBS.

Kolbe, Winrich, dir. *Star Trek: The Next Generation*. Season 3, episode 1, "Evolution." Aired September 25, 1989, on CBS.

————, dir. *Star Trek: The Next Generation*. Season 4, episode 16, "Galaxy's Child." Aired March 12, 1991, on CBS.

————, dir. *Star Trek: The Next Generation*. Season 5, episode 13, "The Masterpiece Society." Aired February 10, 1992, on CBS.

Landau, Les, dir. *Star Trek: The Next Generation*. Season 3, episode 17, "Sins of the Fathers." Aired March 20, 1990, on CBS.

————, dir. *Star Trek: The Next Generation*. Season 3, episode 23, "Sarek." Aired May 15, 1990, on CBS.

————, dir. *Star Trek: The Next Generation*. Season 4, episode 2, "Family." Aired October 1, 1990, on CBS.

————, dir. *Star Trek: The Next Generation*. Season 4, episode 17, "Night Terrors." Aired March 19, 1991, on CBS.

————, dir. *Star Trek: The Next Generation*. Season 5, episode 7, "Unification, Part 1." Aired November 4, 1991, on CBS.

————, dir. *Star Trek: The Next Generation*. Season 6, episode 11, "Chain of Command, Part 2." Aired December 21, 1992, on CBS.

Legato, Robert, dir. *Star Trek: The Next Generation*. Season 3, episode 24, "Ménage à Troi." Aired May 28, 1990, on CBS.

Lynch, Paul, dir. *Star Trek: The Next Generation*. Season 2, episode 7, "Unnatural Selection." Aired January 30, 1989, on CBS.

Mayberry, Russ, dir. *Star Trek: The Next Generation*. Season 1, episode 4, "Code of Honor." Aired October 12, 1987, on CBS.

Rush, Marvin V., dir. *Star Trek: The Next Generation*. Season 4, episode 23, "The Host." Aired May 13, 1991, on CBS.

Scanlan, Joseph L., dir. *Star Trek: The Next Generation*. Season 1, episode 12, "The Big Goodbye." Aired January 11, 1988, on CBS.

Scheerer, Robert, dir. *Star Trek: The Next Generation*. Season 2, episode 9, "The Measure of a Man." Aired February 13, 1989, on CBS.

————, dir. *Star Trek: The Next Generation*. Season 5, episode 10, "New Ground." Aired January 6, 1992, on CBS.

————, dir. *Star Trek: The Next Generation*. Season 5, episode 17, "The Outcast." Aired March 16, 1992, on CBS.

————, dir. *Star Trek: The Next Generation*. Season 6, episode 10, "Chain of Command, Part 1." Aired December 14, 1992, on CBS.

————, dir. *Star Trek: The Next Generation*. Season 7, episode 10, "Inheritance." Aired November 22, 1993, on CBS.

Singer, Alexander, dir. *Star Trek: The Next Generation*. Season 2, episode 3, "Elementary, Dear Data." Aired December 5, 1988, on CBS.

————, dir. *Star Trek: The Next Generation*. Season 6, episode 4, "Relics." Aired October 12, 1992, on CBS.

————, dir. *Star Trek: The Next Generation*. Season 6, episode 12, "Ship in a Bottle." Aired January 25, 1993, on CBS.

Stewart, Patrick, dir. *Star Trek: The Next Generation*. Season 4, episode 25, "In Theory." Aired June 3, 1991, on CBS.

————, dir. *Star Trek: The Next Generation*. Season 5, episode 11, "Hero Worship." Aired January 25, 1992, on CBS.

————, dir. *Star Trek: The Next Generation*. Season 6, episode 8, "A Fistful of Datas." Aired November 9, 1992, on CBS.

West, Jonathan, dir. *Star Trek: The Next Generation*. Season 7, episode 21, "Firstborn." Aired April 25, 1994, on CBS.

Chapter 4, "Q-Less: *Deep Space Nine*: 1993–1999"

Allen, Corey, dir. *Star Trek: Deep Space Nine*. Season 1, episode 6, "Captive Pursuit." Aired January 31, 1992, on UPN.

————, dir. *Star Trek: Deep Space Nine*. Season 2, episode 2, "The Circle." Aired October 3, 1993, on UPN.

————, dir. *Star Trek: Deep Space Nine*. Season 2, episode 15, "Paradise." Aired February 13, 1994, on UPN.

Auberjonois, Rene, dir. *Star Trek: Deep Space Nine*. Season 3, episode 16, "Profit Motives." Aired February 20, 1995, on UPN.

Badiyi, Reza, dir. *Star Trek: Deep Space Nine*. Season 3, episode 11, "Past Tense, Part 1." Aired January 2, 1995, on UPN.

————, dir. *Star Trek: Deep Space Nine*. Season 4, episode 12, "Paradise Lost." Aired January 8, 1996, on UPN.

Bole, Cliff, dir. *Star Trek: Deep Space Nine.* Season 3, episode 22, "Explorers." Aired May 8, 1995, on UPN.

Brooks, Avery, dir. *Star Trek: Deep Space Nine.* Season 3, episode 20, "Improbable Cause." Aired April 24, 1995, on UPN.

———, dir. *Star Trek: Deep Space Nine.* Season 4, episode 6, "Rejoined." Aired October 30, 1995, on UPN.

———, dir. *Star Trek: Deep Space Nine.* Season 5, episode 19, "Ties of Blood and Water." Aired April 14, 1997, on UPN.

———, dir. *Star Trek: Deep Space Nine.* Season 7, episode 24, "The Dogs of War." Aired May 26, 1999, on UPN.

Burton, LeVar, dir. *Star Trek: Deep Space Nine.* Season 6, episode 4, "Behind the Lines." Aired October 20, 1997, on UPN.

———, dir. *Star Trek: Deep Space Nine.* Season 6, episode 8, "Resurrection." Aired November 17, 1997, on UPN.

Carson, David, dir. *Star Trek: Deep Space Nine.* Season 1, episode 1, "Emissary, Parts 1 and 2." Aired January 3, 1993, on UPN.

Chalmers, Chip, dir. *Star Trek: Deep Space Nine.* Season 6, episode 10, "The Magnificent Ferengi." Aired January 1, 1998, on UPN.

Conway, James, L., dir. *Star Trek: Deep Space Nine.* Season 4, episode 1, "The Way of the Warrior, Part 1." Aired October 2, 1995, on UPN.

———, dir. *Star Trek: Deep Space Nine.* Season 4, episode 2, "The Way of the Warrior, Part 2." Aired October 2, 1995, on UPN.

Frakes, Jonathan, dir. *Star Trek: Deep Space Nine.* Season 3, episode 8, "Meridian." Aired November 14, 1994, on UPN.

———, dir. *Star Trek: Deep Space Nine.* Season 3, episode 12, "Past Tense, Part 2." Aired January 9, 1995, on UPN.

Friedman, Kim, dir. *Star Trek: Deep Space Nine.* Season 2, episode 22, "The Wire." Aired May 8, 1994, on UPN.

———, dir. *Star Trek: Deep Space Nine.* Season 5, episode 22, "Children of Time." Aired May 5, 1997, on UPN.

Kolbe, Winrich, dir. *Star Trek: Deep Space Nine.* Season 1, episode 2, "Past Prologue." Aired January 10, 1993, on UPN.

———, dir. *Star Trek: Deep Space Nine.* Season 2, episode 1, "The Homecoming." Aired September 26, 1993, on UPN.

Kroeker, Allan, dir. *Star Trek Deep Space Nine.* Season 5, episode 9, "The Ascent." Aired November 25, 1996, on UPN.

———, dir. *Star Trek: Deep Space Nine.* Season 7, episode 7, "Once More unto the Breach." Aired November 11, 1998, on UPN.

Landau, Les, dir. *Star Trek: Deep Space Nine.* Season 1, episode 15, "Progress." Aired May 9, 1993, on UPN.

———, dir. *Star Trek: Deep Space Nine.* Season 2, episode 10, "Sanctuary." Aired November 28, 1993, on UPN.

———, dir. *Star Trek: Deep Space Nine.* Season 3, episode 3, "The House of Quark." Aired October 10, 1994, on UPN.

Livingston, David, dir. *Star Trek: Deep Space Nine.* Season 1, episode 11, "The Nagus." Aired March 21, 1993, on UPN.

———, dir. *Star Trek: Deep Space Nine.* Season 1, episode 20, "In the Hands of the Prophets." Aired June 20, 1993, on UPN.

———, dir. *Star Trek: Deep Space Nine.* Season 4, episode 3, "The Visitor." Aired October 9, 1995, on UPN.

———, dir. *Star Trek: Deep Space Nine.* Season 5, episode 16, "Doctor Bashir, I Presume." Aired February 24, 1997, on UPN.

———, dir. *Star Trek Deep Space Nine.* Season 6, episode 16, "Change of Heart." Aired March 4, 1998, on UPN.

Lynch, Paul, dir. *Star Trek: Deep Space Nine.* Season 1, episode 4, "A Man Alone." Aired January 17, 1993, on UPN.

———, dir. *Star Trek: Deep Space Nine.* Season 1, episode 7, "Q-Less." Aired February 7, 1993, on UPN.

———, dir. *Star Trek: Deep Space Nine.* Season 1, episode 9, "The Passenger." Aired February 21, 1993, on UPN.

Posey, Stephen L., dir. *Star Trek: Deep Space Nine.* Season 7, episode 6, "Treachery, Faith, and the Great River." Aired November 4, 1998, on UPN.

———, dir. *Star Trek: Deep Space Nine.* Season 7, episode 14, "Chimera." Aired February 17, 1999, on UPN.

Singer, Alexander, dir. *Star Trek: Deep Space Nine.* Season 4, episode 7, "Starships Down." Aired November 6, 1995, on UPN.

Trevino, Jesus Salvador, dir. *Star Trek: Deep Space Nine.* Season 6, episode 21, "The Reckoning." Aired April 29, 1998, on UPN.

West, Jonathan, dir. *Star Trek: Deep Space Nine.* Season 4, episode 14, "Return to Grace." Aired February 5, 1996, on UPN.

Wiemer, Robert, dir. *Star Trek: Deep Space Nine.* Season 2, episode 18, "Profit and Loss." Aired March 20, 1994, on UPN.

Chapter 5, "Living Witness: *Voyager*: 1995–2001"

Biller, Kenneth, dir. *Star Trek: Voyager.* Season 4, episode 25, "One." Aired May 13, 1998, on UPN.

Bole, Cliff, dir. *Star Trek: Voyager.* Season 2, episode 19, "Lifesigns." Aired February 26, 1996, on UPN.

———, dir. *Star Trek: Voyager.* Season 5, episode 3, "Extreme Risk." Aired October 28, 1998, on UPN.

———, dir. *Star Trek: Voyager.* Season 5, episode 15, "Dark Frontier, Part 1." Aired February 17, 1999, on UPN.

Burton, LeVar, dir. *Star Trek: Voyager.* Season 2, episode 17, "Dreadnought." Aired February 12, 1996, on UPN.

———, dir. *Star Trek: Voyager.* Season 4, episode 6, "The Raven." Aired October 8, 1997, on UPN.

———, dir. *Star Trek: Voyager.* Season 7, episode 23, "Homestead." Aired May 9, 2001, on UPN.

Eastman, Allan, dir. *Star Trek: Voyager.* Season 4, episode 16, "Prey." Aired February 18, 1998, on UPN.

Friedman, Kim, dir. *Star Trek: Voyager.* Season 1, episode 3, "Parallax." Aired January 23, 1995, on UPN.

———, dir. *Star Trek: Voyager.* Season 2, episode 6, "Twisted." Aired October 2, 1995, on UPN.

Kolbe, Winrich, dir. *Star Trek: Voyager.* Season 1, episode 1, "Caretaker, Parts 1 and 2." Aired January 16, 1995, on UPN.

———, dir. *Star Trek: Voyager.* Season 1, episode 5, "Phage." Aired February 6, 1995, on UPN.

———, dir. *Star Trek: Voyager.* Season 4, episode 1, "Scorpion, Part 2." Aired September 3, 1997, on UPN.

———, dir. *Star Trek: Voyager.* Season 5, episode 9, "30 Days." Aired December 9, 1998, on UPN.

———, dir. *Star Trek: Voyager.* Season 7, episode 4, "Repression." Aired October 25, 2000, on UPN.

Kretchmer, John T., dir. *Star Trek: Voyager.* Season 5, episode 25, "Warhead." Aired May 19, 1999, on UPN.

Kroeker, Allan, dir. *Star Trek: Voyager.* Season 4, episode 8, "Year of Hell, Part 1." Aired November 5, 1997, on UPN.

———, dir. *Star Trek: Voyager.* Season 4, episode 12, "Mortal Coil." Aired December 17, 1997, on UPN.

————, dir. *Star Trek: Voyager*. Season 5, episode 12, "Bride of Chaotica." Aired January 27, 1999, on UPN.

————, dir. *Star Trek: Voyager*. Season 5, episode 21, "Juggernaut." Aired April 26, 1999, on UPN.

————, dir. *Star Trek: Voyager*. Season 6, episode 11, "Fair Haven." Aired January 12, 2000, on UPN.

————, dir. *Star Trek: Voyager*. Season 6, episode 26, "Unimatrix Zero, Part 1." Aired May 24, 2000, on UPN.

————, dir. *Star Trek: Voyager*. Season 7, episode 25, "Endgame, Parts 1 and 2." Aired May 23, 2001, on UPN.

Landau, Les, dir. *Star Trek: Voyager*. Season 1, episode 10, "Prime Factors." Aired March 20, 1995, on UPN.

————, dir. *Star Trek: Voyager*. Season 2, episode 14, "Alliances." Aired January 22, 1996, on UPN.

————, dir. *Star Trek: Voyager*. Season 3, episode 3, "The Chute." Aired September 18, 1996, on UPN.

Lauritson, Peter, dir. *Star Trek: Voyager*. Season 7, episode 12, "Lineage." Aired January 24, 2001, on UPN.

————, dir. *Star Trek: Voyager*. Season 2, episode 21, "Deadlock." Aired March 18, 1996, on UPN.

————, dir. *Star Trek: Voyager*. Season 3, episode 26, "Scorpion, Part 1." Aired May 21, 1997, on UPN.

————, dir. *Star Trek: Voyager*. Season 5, episode 1, "Night." Aired October 14, 1998, on UPN.

————, dir. *Star Trek: Voyager*. Season 5, episode 23, "11:59." Aired May 5, 1999, on UPN.

————, dir. *Star Trek: Voyager*. Season 6, episode 1, "Equinox, Part 2." Aired September 22, 1999, on UPN.

————, dir. *Star Trek: Voyager*. Season 6, episode 17, "Spirit Folk." Aired February 23, 2000, on UPN.

————, dir. *Star Trek: Voyager*. Season 7, episode 2, "Imperfection." Aired October 11, 2000, on UPN.

McNeill, Robert Duncan, dir. *Star Trek: Voyager*. Season 3, episode 7, "Sacred Ground." Aired October 30, 1996, on UPN.

————, dir. *Star Trek: Voyager*. Season 3, episode 17, "Unity." Aired February 12, 1997, on UPN.

Picardo, Robert, dir. *Star Trek: Voyager*. Season 6, episode 8, "One Small Step." Aired November 17, 1999, on UPN.

Russ, Tim, dir. *Star Trek: Voyager*. Season 4, episode 23, "Living Witness." Aired April 29, 1998, on UPN.

Singer, Alexander, dir. *Star Trek: Voyager*. Season 2, episode 25, "Resolutions." Aired May 13, 1996, on UPN.

————, dir. *Star Trek: Voyager*. Season 3, episode 12, "Macrocosm." Aired December 11, 1996, on UPN.

————, dir. *Star Trek: Voyager*. Season 3, episode 25, "Worst Case Scenario." Aired May 14, 1997, on UPN.

Trevino, Jesus Salvador, dir. *Star Trek: Voyager*. Season 3, episode 13, "Fair Trade." Aired January 8, 1997, on UPN.

————, dir. *Star Trek: Voyager*. Season 4, episode 3, "Day of Honor." Aired September 17, 1997, on UPN.

————, dir. *Star Trek: Voyager*. Season 4, episode 11, "Concerning Flight." Aired November 26, 1997, on UPN.

Vejar, Michael, dir. *Star Trek: Voyager*. Season 4, episode 9, "Year of Hell, Part 2." Aired November 12, 1997, on UPN.

————, dir. *Star Trek: Voyager*. Season 7, episode 1, "Unimatrix Zero, Part 2." Aired October 4, 2000, on UPN.

Williams, Anson, dir. *Star Trek: Voyager*. Season 4, episode 2, "The Gift." Aired September 10, 1997, on UPN.

Windell, Terry, dir. *Star Trek: Voyager*. Season 5, episode 16, "Dark Frontier, Part 2." Aired February 17, 1999, on UPN.

———, dir. *Star Trek: Voyager*. Season 6, episode 24, "Life Line." Aired May 10, 2000, on UPN.

———, dir. *Star Trek: Voyager*. Season 6, episode 9, "The Voyager Conspiracy." Aired November 24, 1999, on UPN.

———, dir. *Star Trek: Voyager*. Season 7, episode 5, "Critical Care." Aired November 1, 2000, on UPN.

Chapter 6, "Terra Prime: *Enterprise*: 2001–2005"

Barrett, David, dir. *Star Trek: Enterprise*. Season 4, episode 16, "Divergence." Aired February 25, 2005, on UPN.

Burton, LeVar, dir. *Star Trek: Enterprise*. Season 2, episode 22, "Cogenitor." Aired April 30, 2003, on UPN.

———, dir. *Star Trek: Enterprise*. Season 4, episode 6, "The Augments." Aired November 12, 2004, on UPN.

———, dir. *Star Trek: Enterprise*. Season 4, episode 20, "Demons." Aired May 6, 2005, on UPN.

Charleston, Jim, dir. *Star Trek: Enterprise*. Season 1, episode 20, "Oasis." Aired April 3, 2002, on UPN.

Contner, James A., dir. *Star Trek: Enterprise*. Season 2, episode 20, "Horizon." Aired April 16, 2003, on UPN.

Conway, James L., dir. *Star Trek: Enterprise*. Season 1, episode 1, "Broken Arrow, Parts 1 and 2." Aired September 26, 2001, on UPN.

———, dir. *Star Trek: Enterprise*. Season 2, episode 19, "Judgment." Aired April 9, 2003, on UPN.

———, dir. *Star Trek: Enterprise*. Season 4, episode 18, "In a Mirror, Darkly, Part 1." Aired April 22, 2005, on UPN.

Dawson, Roxann, dir. *Star Trek: Enterprise*. Season 1, episode 7, "The Andorian Incident." Aired October 31, 2001, on UPN.

———, dir. *Star Trek: Enterprise*. Season 3, episode 21, "E^2." Aired May 6, 2004, on UPN.

———, dir. *Star Trek: Enterprise*. Season 4, episode 8, "Awakening." Aired November 26, 2004, on UPN.

Grossman, Michael, dir. *Star Trek: Enterprise*. Season 4, episode 7, "The Forge." Aired November 19, 2004, on UPN.

———, dir. *Star Trek: Enterprise*. Season 4, episode 15, "Affliction." Aired February 18, 2005, on UPN.

Kroeker, Allan, dir. *Star Trek: Enterprise*. Season 2, episode 26, "The Expanse." Aired May 21, 2003, on UPN.

———, dir. *Star Trek: Enterprise*. Season 3, episode 1, "The Xindi." Aired September 10, 2003, on UPN.

———, dir. *Star Trek: Enterprise*. Season 3, episode 24, "Zero Hour." Aired May 26, 2004, on UPN.

———, dir. *Star Trek: Enterprise*. Season 4, episode 3, "Home." Aired October 22, 2004, on UPN.

———, dir. *Star Trek: Enterprise*. Season 4, episode 17, "Bound." Aired April 15, 2005, on UPN.

———, dir. *Star Trek: Enterprise*. Season 4, episode 22, "These Are the Voyages" Aired May 13, 2005, on UPN.

Landau, Les, dir. *Star Trek: Enterprise*. Season 1, episode 14, "Sleeping Dogs." Aired January 30, 2002, on UPN.

Livingston, David, dir. *Star Trek: Enterprise.* Season 2, episode 23, "Regeneration." Aired May 7, 2003, on UPN.

———, dir. *Star Trek: Enterprise.* Season 3, episode 5, "Impulse." Aired October 8, 2003, on UPN.

———, dir. *Star Trek: Enterprise.* Season 3, episode 13, "Proving Ground." Aired January 21, 2004, on UPN.

———, dir. *Star Trek: Enterprise.* Season 4, episode 4, "Borderland." Aired October 29, 2004, on UPN.

———, dir. *Star Trek: Enterprise.* Season 4, episode 9, "Kir'Shara." Aired December 3, 2004, on UPN.

McNeill, Robert Duncan, dir. *Star Trek: Enterprise.* Season 3, episode 23, "Countdown." Aired May 19, 2004, on UPN.

Rush, Marvin V., dir. *Star Trek: Enterprise.* Season 4, episode 19, "In a Mirror, Darkly, Part 2." Aired April 29, 2005, on UPN.

———, dir. *Star Trek: Enterprise.* Season 4, episode 21, "Terra Prime." Aired May 13, 2005, on UPN.

Straiton, David, dir. *Star Trek: Enterprise.* Season 1, episode 24, "Desert Crossing." Aired May 8, 2002, on UPN.

———, dir. *Star Trek: Enterprise.* Season 2, episode 15, "Cease Fire." Aired February 12, 2003, on UPN.

———, dir. *Star Trek: Enterprise.* Season 4, episode 12, "Babel One." Aired January 28, 2005, on UPN.

Vejar, Michael, dir. *Star Trek: Enterprise.* Season 1, episode 5, "Unexpected." Aired October 17, 2001, on UPN.

———, dir. *Star Trek: Enterprise.* Season 2, episode 12, "The Catwalk." Aired December 18, 2002, on UPN.

———, dir. *Star Trek: Enterprise.* Season 4, episode 5, "Cold Station 12." Aired November 5, 2004, on UPN.

Whitmore, James, Jr., dir. *Star Trek: Enterprise.* Season 1, episode 19, "Acquisition." Aired March 27, 2002, on UPN.

Windell, Terry, dir. *Star Trek: Enterprise.* Season 1, episode 8, "Breaking the Ice." Aired November 7, 2001, on UPN.

Chapter 7, "Interlude II: *Star Trek* Fandom: 2005–2017"

Burton, LeVar, dir. *Star Trek: Enterprise.* Season 3, episode 20, "The Forgotten." Aired April 28, 2004, on UPN.

Grossman, Michael, dir. *Star Trek: Enterprise.* Season 4, episode 15, "Affliction." Aired February 18, 2005, on UPN.

Chapter 8, "Context Is for Kings: *Discovery*: 2017

Aarniokoski, Douglas, dir. *Star Trek: Discovery.* Season 1, episode 6, "Lethe." Aired October 22, 2017, on CBS All Access.

———, dir. *Star Trek: Discovery.* Season 2, episode 12, "Through the Valley of Shadows." Aired April 4, 2019, on CBS All Access.

———, dir. *Star Trek: Short Treks.* "The Brightest Star." Aired December 6, 2018, on CBS All Access.

Barrett, David, dir. *Star Trek: Discovery.* Season 2, episode 5, "Saints of Imperfection." Aired February 14, 2019, on CBS All Access.

Byrne, Christopher J., dir. *Star Trek: Discovery.* Season 1, episode 9, "Into the Forest I Go." Aired November 12, 2017, on CBS All Access.

Culpepper, Hanelle, M., dir. *Star Trek: Discovery*. Season 1, episode 12, "Vaulting Ambitions." Aired January 21, 2018, on CBS All Access.

———, dir. *Star Trek: Discovery*. Season 2, episode 10, "The Red Angel." Aired March 21, 2017, on CBS All Access.

Frakes, Jonathan, dir. *Star Trek: Discovery*. Season 2, episode 9, "Project Daedalus." Aired March 14, 2019, on CBS All Access.

———, dir. *Star Trek: Discovery*. Season 1, episode 10, "Despite Yourself." Aired January 7, 2018, on CBS All Access.

Goldsman, Akiva, dir. *Star Trek: Discovery*. Season 1, episode 3, "Context Is for Kings." Aired October 1, 2017, on CBS All Access.

———, dir. *Star Trek: Discovery*. Season 1, episode 15, "Will You Take My Hand?" Aired February 11, 2018, on CBS All Access.

Kane, Adam, dir. *Star Trek: Discovery*. Season 1, episode 2, "Battle at the Binary Stars." Aired September 24, 2017, on CBS All Access.

Kurtzman, Alex, dir. *Star Trek: Discovery*. Season 2, episode 1, "Brother." Aired January 17, 2019, on CBS All Access.

Lucas, John Meredyth, dir. *Star Trek*. Season 2, episode 24, "The Ultimate Computer." Aired March 8, 1968, on NBC.

Osunsanmi, Olatunde, dir. *Star Trek: Discovery*. Season 1, episode 4, "The Butcher's Knife Cares Not for the Lamb's Cry." Aired October 8, 2017, on CBS All Access.

———, dir. *Star Trek: Discovery*. Season 1, episode 13, "What's Past Is Prologue." Aired January 28, 2018, on CBS All Access.

———, dir. *Star Trek: Discovery*. Season 2, episode 3, "Point of Light." Aired January 31, 2019, on CBS All Access.

———, dir. *Star Trek: Discovery*. Season 2, episode 13, "Such Sweet Sorrow." Aired April 11, 2019, on CBS All Access.

———, dir. *Star Trek: Discovery*. Season 2, episode 14, "Such Sweet Sorrow, Part 2." Aired April 18, 2019, on CBS All Access.

Rose, Lee, dir. *Star Trek: Discovery*. Season 2, episode 4, "An Obol for Charon." Aired February 7, 2019, on CBS All Access.

———, dir. *Star Trek: Discovery*. Season 1, episode 5, "Choose Your Pain." Aired October 15, 2017, on CBS All Access.

Semel, David, dir. *Star Trek: Discovery*. Season 1, episode 1, "The Vulcan Hello." Aired September 24, 2017, on CBS All Access.

Vrvilo, Maja, dir. *Star Trek: Discovery*. Season 2, episode 11, "Perpetual Infinity." Aired March 28, 2019, on CBS All Access.

Chapter 9, "*Star Trek* in the Theaters"

Daniels, Marc, dir. *Star Trek*. Season 1, episode 22, "Space Seed." Aired February 15, 1967, on NBC.

Chapter 10, "Melding Fifty-Plus Years"

Osunsanmi, Olatunde, dir., *Star Trek: Short Treks*. Season 2, episode 4, "The Girl Who Made the Stars." Aired December 12, 2019, on CBS All Access.

NON–*STAR TREK* FILMS CITED

Anderson, Michael, dir. *Logan's Run*. Beverly Hills, CA: Metro-Goldwyn-Mayer, 1976.

Beresford, Bruce, dir. *Driving Miss Daisy*. Hollywood, CA: Warner Bros., 1990.

Boden, Anna, and Ryan Fleck, dirs. *Captain Marvel*. Burbank, CA: Walt Disney Studios Motion Pictures, 2019.

Cameron, James, dir. *The Terminator*. Los Angeles: Orion Pictures, 1984.

———, dir. *Terminator 2: Judgment Day*. Culver City, CA: TriStar Pictures, 1991.

Chu, John M., dir. *Crazy Rich Asians*. Burbank, CA: Warner Bros., 2018.

Columbus, Chris, dir. *Harry Potter and the Sorcerer's Stone*. Hollywood, CA: Warner Bros., 2001.

———, dir. *Home Alone*. Los Angeles: Twentieth Century Fox, 1990.

Coogler, Ryan, dir. *Black Panther*. Burbank, CA: Walt Disney Studios Motion Pictures, 2018.

Crichton, Michael, dir. *Westworld*. Beverly Hills, CA: Metro-Goldwyn-Mayer, 1973.

Docter, Pete, David Silverman, and Lee Unkrich, dirs. *Monsters, Inc*. Burbank, CA: Walt Disney Pictures Studios, 2001.

Eastwood, Clint, dir. *Million Dollar Baby*. Hollywood, CA: Warner Bros., 2004.

———, dir. *Unforgiven*. Hollywood, CA: Warner Bros., 1992.

Erman, John, dir. *An Early Frost*. NBC Productions, 1985.

Fleischer, Richard, dir. *Soylent Green*. Beverly Hills, CA: Metro-Goldwyn-Mayer, 1973.

Forster, Marc, dir. *Monster's Ball*. Santa Monica, CA: Lions Gate Films, 2001.

Huston, John, dir. *The Bible: In the Beginning*. Los Angeles: Twentieth Century Fox, 1966.

Jackson, Peter, dir. *Lord of the Rings: The Fellowship of the Rings*. Burbank, CA: New Line Cinema, 2001.

Jenkins, Patty, dir. *Wonder Woman*. Burbank, CA: Warner Bros., 2017.

Kubrick, Stanley, dir. *2001: A Space Odyssey*. Beverly Hills, CA: Metro-Goldwyn-Mayer, 1968.

Leone, Sergio, dir. *The Good, the Bad and the Ugly*. Hollywood, CA: United Artists, 1967.

Lucas, George, dir. *Star Wars: Episode IV—A New Hope*. Los Angeles: LucasFilm, Twentieth Century Fox, 1977.

Marshall, Garry, dir. *Pretty Woman*. Burbank, CA: Touchstone Pictures, 1990.

Marshall, Rob, dir. *Chicago*. Burbank, CA: Miramax, 2002.

McTiernan, John, dir. *Die Hard*. Los Angeles: Twentieth Century Fox, 1988.

Shin, Nelson, dir. *The Transformers: The Movie*. New York: Sunbow Productions, 1986.

Spielberg, Steven, dir. *Close Encounters of the Third Kind*. Culver City, CA: Columbia Pictures, 1977.

Stone, Oliver, dir. *Platoon*. Beverly Hills, CA: Metro-Goldwyn-Mayer, 1986.

Trumbull, Douglas, dir. *Silent Running*. Universal City, CA: Universal Pictures, 1972.

Verhoeven, Paul, dir. *RoboCop*. Los Angeles: Orion Pictures, 1987.

Wachowski, Lana, and Lilly Wachowski, dirs. *The Matrix*. Hollywood, CA: Warner Bros., 1999.

———, dirs. *The Matrix Reloaded*. Hollywood, CA: Warner Bros., 2003.

———, dirs. *The Matrix Revolutions*. Hollywood, CA: Warner Bros., 2003.

Wise, Robert, dir. *The Sound of Music*. Los Angeles: Twentieth Century Fox, 1965.

Zemeckis, Robert, dir. *Forrest Gump*. Hollywood, CA: Paramount Pictures, 1994.

Zucker, Jerry, dir. *Ghost*. 2009; Hollywood, CA: Paramount Pictures, 1990.

NON–*STAR TREK* SERIES CITED

Benny, Jack, creator. *The Jack Benny Program*. 15 seasons. Los Angeles: CBS. Aired 1950–1965 on CBS.

Brooker, Charlie, creator. *Black Mirror*. 5 seasons. Los Angeles: Netflix. Aired 2011–present on Netflix.

Brooks, James L., Matt Groening, and Sam Simons, creators. *The Simpsons*. 31 seasons. Los Angeles: Twentieth Century Fox Television. Aired 1989–present on FOX.

Cosby, Bill, creator. *A Different World*. 6 seasons. Los Angeles: Bill Cosby. Aired 1987–1993 on NBC.

Daniels, Greg, and Mike Judge, creators. *King of the Hill*. 13 seasons. Los Angeles: Twentieth Century Fox Television. Aired 1997–2010 on FOX.

David, Larry, and Jerry Seinfeld, creators. *Seinfeld*. 9 seasons. Sherman Oaks, CA: West-Shapiro. Aired 1989–1998 on NBC.

Dortort, David, creator. *Bonanza*. 14 seasons. Los Angeles: NBC. Aired 1959–1973 on NBC.

Duffer, Matt, and Ross Duffer, creators. *Stranger Things*. 4 seasons. Los Angeles: Netflix. Aired 2016–present on Netflix.

Garrison, Michael, creator. *The Wild Wild West*. 4 seasons. Los Angeles: CBS. Aired 1965–1969 on CBS.

Larsen, Glen A., and Ronald D. Moore, creators. *Battlestar Galactica*. 4 seasons. Universal City, CA: Universal Television. Aired 2004–2007 on NBC.

Leeson, Michael, creator. *The Cosby Show*. 8 seasons. Los Angeles: Bill Cosby. Aired 1984–1992 on NBC.

Lorre, Chuck, and Bill Prady, creators. *The Big Bang Theory*. 12 seasons. Burbank, CA: Chuck Lorre Productions. Aired 2007–2019 on CBS.

MacFarlane, Seth, creator. *The Orville*. 3 seasons. Los Angeles: Twentieth Century Fox Television. Aired 2017–present on FOX.

Martin, Dean, creator. *The Dean Martin Show*. 9 seasons. Burbank, CA: National Broadcasting Company. Aired 1965–1974 on NBC.

McGrath, Frank, Terry Wilson, and Robert Horton, creators. *Wagon Train*. 8 seasons. Los Angeles: NBC. Aired 1957–1962 on NBC; 1962–1965 on ABC.

Meadow, Herb, and Sam Rolfe, creators. *Have Gun Will Travel*. 6 seasons. Los Angeles: CBS. Aired 1957–1963 on CBS.

Monash, Paul, creator. *Judd, for the Defense*. 2 seasons. Los Angeles: Twentieth Century Fox Television. Aired 1967–1969. on ABC.

Nelson, Ozzie, creator. *The Adventures of Ozzie and Harriet*. 14 seasons. Los Angeles: ABC. Aired 1952–1966 on ABC.

Newman, Sydney, C. E. Webber, and Donald Wilson, creators. *Dr. Who*. 12 seasons. London: BBC One. Aired 2005–present on BBC.

Parker, Trey, Matt Stone, and Brian Graden, creators. *South Park*. 23 seasons. New York: Comedy Central. Aired 1997–present on Comedy Central.

Rubin, Aaron, creator. *Gomer Pyle, U.S.M.C.* 5 seasons. Andy Griffith Enterprises. Aired 1964–1979, on CBS.

Saks, Sol, creator. *Bewitched*. 8 seasons. Los Angeles: Ashmont Productions. Aired 1964–1972 on ABC.

Tibbles, George, creator. *My Three Sons*. 12 seasons. Los Angeles: CBS Television Network. Aired 1960–1972 on CBS.

Warren, Charles Marquis, Norman Macdonnell, and John Meston, creators. *Gunsmoke*. 20 seasons. Los Angeles: CBS Television Network. Aired 1955–1976 on CBS.

NON–*STAR TREK* EPISODES CITED

Benioff, David, and D. B. Weiss, dirs. *Game of Thrones*. Season 8, episode 6, "The Iron Throne." Aired May 19, 2019, on HBO.

Cendrowski, Mark, dir. *The Big Bang Theory*. Season 6, episode 13, "The Bakersfield Expedition." Aired January 10, 2013, on CBS.

Haynes, Toby, dir. *Black Mirror*. Season 4, episode 1. "USS *Callister*." Aired December 29, 2017, on Netflix.

Hughes, Terry, dir. *Golden Girls*. Season 4, episode 9, "Scared Straight." Aired December 10, 1988, on NBC.

INDEX

ABOUT THE AUTHORS

Kathleen M. Heath is an associate professor of anthropology at Indiana State University and the author of numerous peer-reviewed articles on topics in archaeology, evolution, behavioral ecology, culture, and genetics. She earned her PhD in anthropology from the University of Utah in 2001 and chose anthropology as a career because it combines a broad scope of topics, from humanities to the sciences. She now merges her academic training in anthropology with her lifelong interest in science fiction and fantasy to explore how imaginary worlds can capture the hearts of millions of people, from mainstream cultures to countercultures to subcultures.

Ann Sackrider Carlisle graduated from Saint Mary-of-the-Woods College with a BA in paralegal studies in 1993. After working for several years, she enrolled at Indiana State University, where she earned a BS in anthropology in 2012. While a student at ISU, she began integrating her academic concentration in cultural diversity with her keen interest in science/speculative fiction and found her passion in researching *Star Trek* as a phenomenon of American culture. She currently resides on her family farm in Indiana.